Pocket PC
Clear & Simple

Pocket PC
Clear & Simple

Craig Peacock

Digital Press
An imprint of Butterworth-Heinemann

BOSTON • OXFORD • AUCKLAND • JOHANNESBURG • MELBOURNE • NEW DELHI

⊄ Butterworth–Heinemann is a member of the Reed Elsevier group

Library of Congress Cataloging-in-Publication Data
Peacock, Craig, 1969–
        Pocket PC clear & simple / Craig Peacock.
                p.   cm.
        Includes index.
        ISBN 0-7506-7354-0 (alk. paper)
        1. Pocket computers. I. Title.
    QA76.5 .P368 2001
    004.16—dc21

                                00-065627

British Library Cataloging-in-Publication Data
A catalogue record for this book is available from the British Library

The publisher offers discounts on bulk orders of this book. For information, please write:
Manager of Special Sales
Butterworth–Heinemann
225 Wildwood Avenue
Woburn, MA 01801-2041
Tel: 781/904-2500
Fax: 781/904-2620

For information on all Digital Press publications available, contact our World Wide Web home page at: http://www.bh.com/digitalpress

10 9 8 7 6 5 4 3 2 1

Printed in the United States of America

Typeset by Elle & P.K. McBride, Southampton
Icons designed by Sarah Ward © 1994

Contents

Preface

As its title suggests, this book covers the Microsoft Pocket PC range of devices. Throughout the book you will see step-by-step instructions covering all the main Pocket PC applications. In addition, tips and notes are provided to help you get the most out of whichever model Pocket PC you own.

The Microsoft team has put together an incredibly feature-rich application set in the Pocket PC, and some of the applications, such as Notes, are really three applications in one. Notes allows you to record voice notes, and create text and handwritten notes, and in this book I'll show you how to utilize it and other functions.

Some of my favorite applications are covered near the back of the book in the Multimedia section. Whether you wish to use your Pocket PC to listen to music or read e-books when you are travelling, I hope this book helps make those tasks easier.

This book would not have been possible without the support of the folks at Digital Press, especially Peter McBride and Catherine Fear. Various people at Microsoft have also been extremely helpful despite their exceptionally busy schedules, notably Phil Holden, Andy Haon, Derek Brown, and John Kennedy.

Lily, my love for you is more than can be adequately said with words alone, and your support as always, has been fabulous throughout this project.

If you are thinking of buying a Pocket PC or are an existing user, then I hope you will find this book helpful in making your use of a Pocket PC easier, more efficient, and more fun.

Craig Peacock, 2001

1 Start here

Introducing Pocket PC

The Pocket PC is the latest generation of devices that run the Microsoft Windows CE operating system version 3.0. These have the processing power that PCs had only a few years ago. They are loaded with the latest state of the art applications that make it easy for users to keep track of all their personal information and also provide the facilities to perform e-mail tasks, listen to music and browse the Internet.

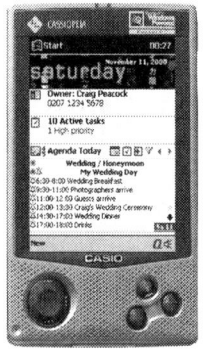

This is in addition to applications that help you manage your finances, contacts, diary, calendar, edit documents, and spreadsheets, connect up to the Internet via a modem or wirelessly via a cellular phone – and all this is included out-of-the-box. Pocket PC users can now get so much more done than simply storing some contact details.

It is more than just a piece of software. Changes to hardware and software combined make this platform the most feature-rich of any portable computing device that fits in your pocket.

In *Pocket PC Made Simple*, I will show you how to get the most out of these exciting new devices.

Since its launch in April 2000, the Windows-powered Pocket PC has created a great deal of interest all over the world.

Among the topics covered in this book are how to connect up to the Internet to browse the Web or collect e-mail, play music files, download the latest news stories, as well as keep track of all your contacts, appointments and tasks.

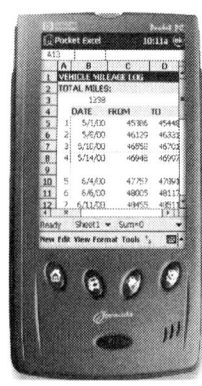

Pocket PCs are third-generation Windows CE devices in this small form. Over the years the functionality has been enhanced and the devices keep getting better and better.

While the first-generation devices allowed you to store contacts, calendar and other personal information, it is only very recently that it has been possible to play arcade quality games, watch movie clips in thousands of colors and listen to stereo quality sound on a device small enough to fit into your pocket.

Pocket PC built-in applications

These are the standard Microsoft applications. Some hardware manufacturers include other applications on their devices.

Notes	Pocket Word
Calendar	Pocket Excel
Contacts	Pocket Internet Explorer
Tasks	Inbox
File Explorer	AvantGo
ActiveSync	Pocket Money
Media Player	Voice Recorder
Reader	Calculator
Solitaire	

The user interface

The user interface on the Pocket PC has been designed to give you a clear view of all your important data and to facilitate single-handed operation where possible. Screens present as much information as possible to save scrolling.

Navigating is done with a stylus and applications respond to the single-tap method. This can be a little strange at first because it is unlike a desktop PC, where you typically double-click to launch an application. The single-tap saves you time and launches applications much quicker.

The Start button

With no icon / button on the screen labelled 'Start' one of the most common questions a person asks when they first pick up a device is 'Where's the Windows Start menu?' Answer: it's the Windows flag in the top left-hand corner of the screen.

As you use the Start menu to launch applications you will also see the name of the current application displayed at the top of the screen.

❏ Starting applications

1 Tap ⓐStart .

2 Tap the name of the application you want to run. The name of the application will change.

3 Tap ⓐStart again to run another application.

Tip

Using the Task switcher can save valuable key taps when launching applications. It remembers the last six ones you've used.

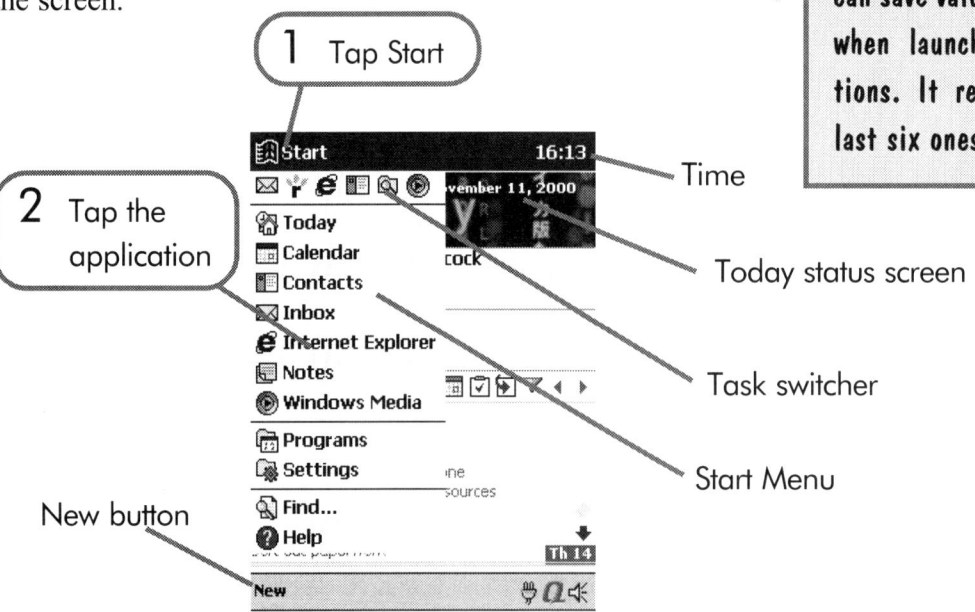

1 Tap Start

2 Tap the application

New button

Time

Today status screen

Task switcher

Start Menu

4

Basic steps

1 Tap Start .

2 Launch Calendar.

3 Tap Start .

4 Launch Tasks.

5 Tap Start .

6 Select an application from the Recently used list to switch to it.

Take note

Be careful not to put your Pocket PC into a bag or somewhere that the buttons could be easily pressed, as it could reduce battery life.

Tip

Tap and hold works in most applications. The menu options will, of course, differ.

Task switcher

The Pocket PC has a convenient and handy task-switching application. When you launch an application, its icon appears at the top of Start menu. Use icons to switch between your most recently run applications.

Hardware buttons

Another way to launch applications is to use the hardware buttons. These are in different places on different vendors' devices, but they all work in the same way.

Even if your Pocket PC is switched off, pressing one of the hardware icons will switch it on and open up the application for the button your pressed.

Other hardware buttons such as the rocker switch, menu, voice recorder and the action and exit buttons enable you to switch on the device and navigate to a particular application without needing to use the stylus.

In some applications the hardware buttons also perform special tasks when they are tapped, but I'll cover those in the Calendar and Contacts sections later in the book (Chapters 5 and 6).

Tap and hold menus

Tap and hold is another way that screen clutter is reduced. You can tap and hold on any piece of data or document to open a context-sensitive menu. This will display options that are relevant to the item of data that is highlighted. In our Contacts example, one of the options is the ability to send an e-mail to the selected contact.

You'll see the tap and hold menu used a lot as we go through *Pocket PC Made Simple.*

The Today screen

The Today screen shows you all the most relevant information at a glance. It comes in very handy when you want to see quickly what your next appointment is or to check if you remembered to login and send all those e-mails you composed earlier.

The Today screen can be customized and I'll show you how to change some of the options in the next chapter.

As well as showing you the key data, the Today screen shows status icons which indicate, for example, whether a backlight is on. The speaker icon is particularly handy as it lets you mute the entire device just by tapping on it.

1 Start up – the Today screen will appear.

❑ To mute the device

2 Tap the Speaker icon.

❑ To re-enable sounds

3 Tap the icon again.

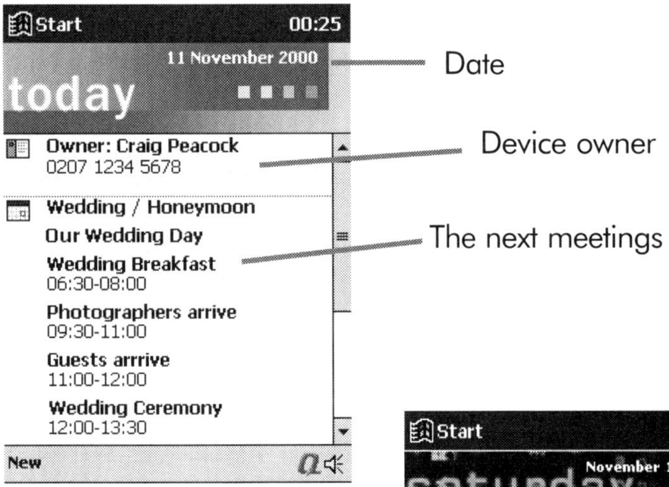

Start   00:25

11 November 2000

today ■ ■ ■ ■

Owner: Craig Peacock
0207 1234 5678

Wedding / Honeymoon
Our Wedding Day
Wedding Breakfast
06:30-08:00
Photographers arrive
09:30-11:00
Guests arrrive
11:00-12:00
Wedding Ceremony
12:00-13:30

New

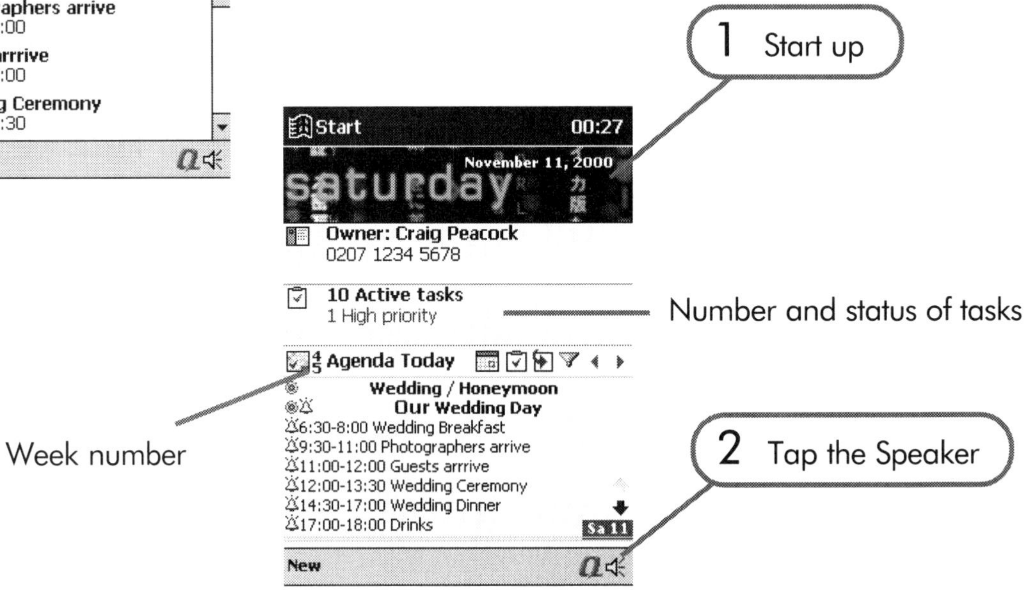

——— Date

——— Device owner

——— The next meetings

1 Start up

Start   00:27

November 11, 2000

saturday

Owner: Craig Peacock
0207 1234 5678

10 Active tasks
1 High priority ——— Number and status of tasks

4/5 Agenda Today
Wedding / Honeymoon
Our Wedding Day
6:30-8:00 Wedding Breakfast
9:30-11:00 Photographers arrive
11:00-12:00 Guests arrrive
12:00-13:30 Wedding Ceremony
14:30-17:00 Wedding Dinner
17:00-18:00 Drinks   Sa 11

New

Week number

2 Tap the Speaker

Connection icons

Certain icons may appear in the status area on the Today screen. They indicate the connection status with your desktop computer, and display warning signs such as low-battery conditions. Other applications may also add icons to this screen.

Icon	Meaning
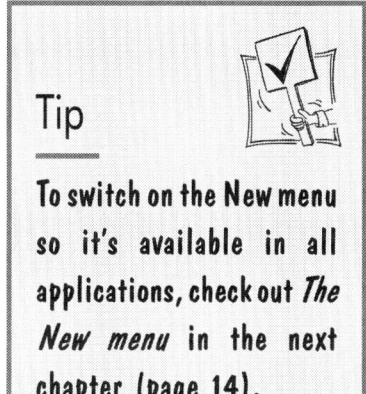	Dial-up connection
	Direct cable or infrared connection
	Backup battery is low
	Backup battery is very low
	Main batteries are charging
	Main batteries are low
	Main batteries are very low
	External power is connected

New menu

At the bottom left of the Today screen is the New menu, which lets you perform commonly-used tasks easily. Creating a new appointment, contact and e-mail can all be done directly from this menu, saving you from launching the application first.

Tip

To switch on the New menu so it's available in all applications, check out *The New menu* in the next chapter (page 14).

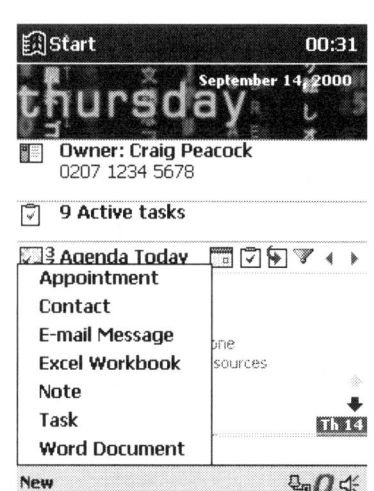

New Menu showing from the Today screen

7

Software keyboard input

A Pocket PC has no physical keyboard on it – instead, you enter information using a software keyboard, called the Software Input Panel or SIP. There are several versions available as standard, and third-party software vendors have also written other input panels for the Pocket PC. The most commonly used one is the keyboard version, which looks like a regular keyboard. Another is the handwriting recognition screen which enables you to write directly on the screen with the stylus. A third method, Transcriber, is on the ActiveSync CD-ROM.

On-screen keyboard

The SIP keyboard should look very much like a PC keyboard, but with the small screen you can't see all the characters at once. Shown here are the lower case, alternative character and numerical views. There are lots of characters available in the various views.

1 Tap 🞅Start , then Pocket Word.

2 Tap the arrow beside the keyboard icon.

3 Select Keyboard.

4 Tap [123], [Ctrl], [CAP] or [áü] to switch between the character sets.

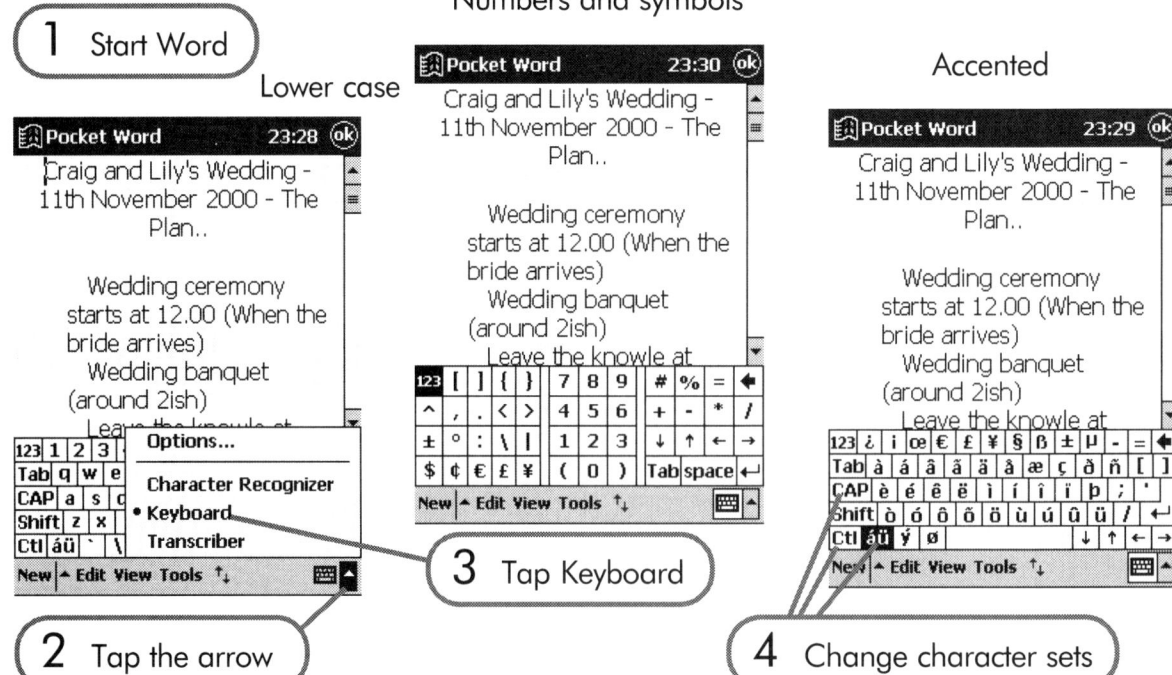

1 Start Word

Lower case

Numbers and symbols

Accented

3 Tap Keyboard

2 Tap the arrow

4 Change character sets

8

Basic steps

1 Tap the arrow beside the keyboard icon.

2 Select Character Recognizer.

Or

3 Select Transcriber.

Tip

You need to install Transcriber from the CD-ROM

Character recognition

One of the features included in Pocket PC is the ability to recognize handwritten characters and convert them to typed text. You can see it in action in the Pocket Word section.

Transcriber

This application is in the Extras directory on the ActiveSync CD-ROM included with your Pocket PC. It allows you to write anywhere on the screen.

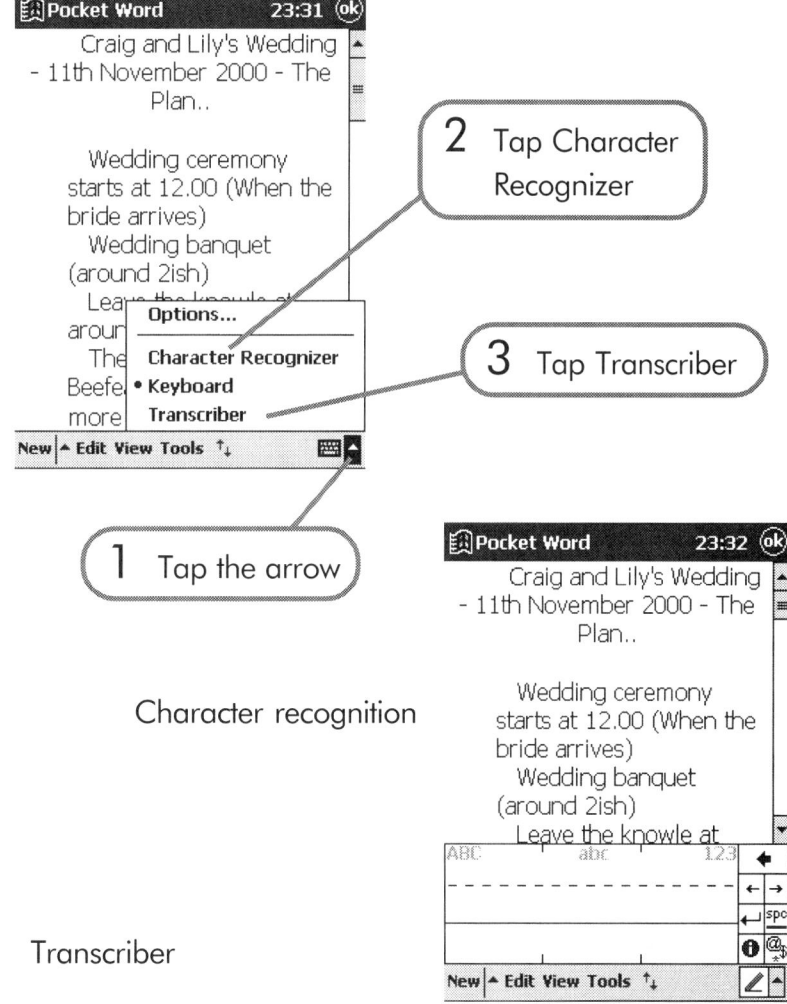

2 Tap Character Recognizer

3 Tap Transcriber

1 Tap the arrow

Character recognition

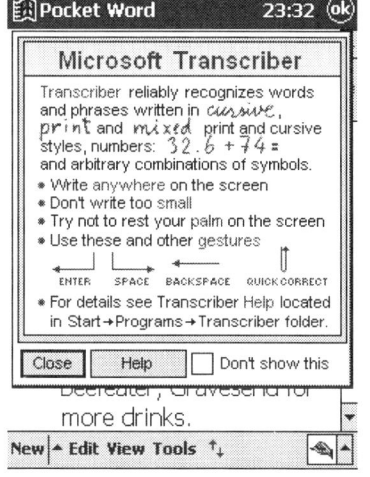

Transcriber

Summary

- ❑ Pocket PC devices are the latest generation of hand-held computers, running Windows CE 3.0.

- ❑ You can use your Pocket PC to produce documents and spreadsheets, browse the Web, and manage your e-mail, as well as to handle your personal information needs.

- ❑ Applications can be launched from the Start menu, via the New menu or from hardware buttons.

- ❑ The Task switcher, at the top of the Start menu, lets you switch between recently-used applications.

- ❑ If you tap and hold on an object, a menu will open, offering options relevant to the object.

- ❑ The Today screen gives a summary of your current appointments and tasks, and of the status of the device. Warnings such as 'low battery' are displayed here.

- ❑ Data can be entered through the software input panel, or by handwriting on the screen.

2 Setting up

The Settings

There are some settings on your Pocket PC that you will want to alter to fit the way that you work. There are a couple that I think should have been set as a default by Microsoft on all Pocket PCs and I'll cover those first, then I'll show you the rest of the settings that you can change.

There are three Settings screens – Personal, System, and Connections settings. Each has a different set of icons for features that you can customize. Not all of the features listed here will be present on every Pocket PC.

Personal settings

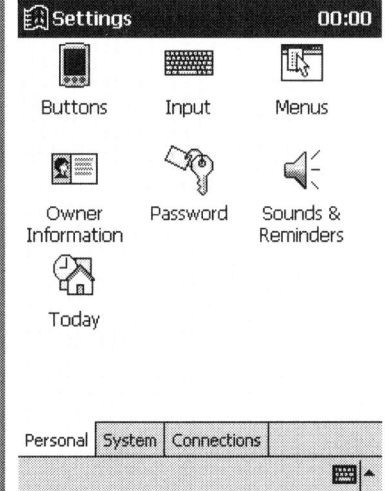

- **Buttons** changes the hardware buttons and what applications they run;

- **Input** changes software keyboard settings;

- **Menus** allows you to customize the icons that appear on the Start menu;

- **Owner Information** sets your details here;

- **Password** secures your device;

- **Sounds & Reminders** customizes the beep and alarm sounds;

- **Today** sets what information appears on the Today screen.

System settings

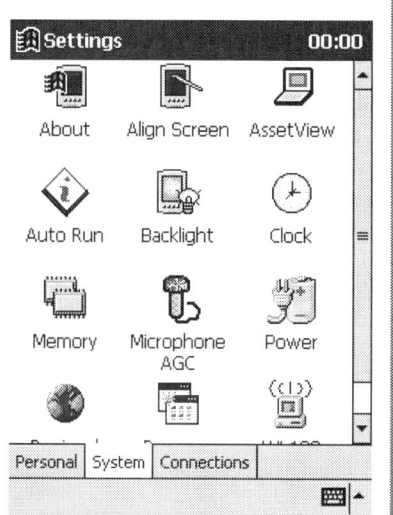

- **About** displays information about your Pocket PC;

- **Align Screen** adjusts the display within the device's screen;

- **Asset View** (Compaq devices only) shows serial number, etc.;

- **AutoRun** starts applications automatically when an external card is plugged in;

- **Backlight** customizes how bright your display is;

- **Clock** changes the time/date;

- **Memory** shows how much space your applications and data are taking up;

- **Microphone** allows you to alter the recording settings;

- **Power** monitors your device's battery status;

- **Regional Settings** lets you localize your device;

- **Remove Programs** allows you to delete applications;

- **WL100** – Compaq wireless LAN settings.

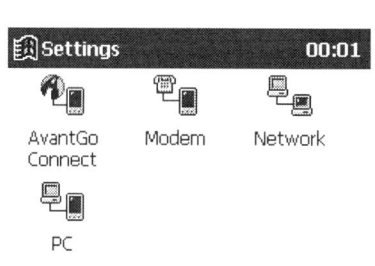

Connections settings

- **AvantGo Connect** – settings for AvantGo (page 71);

- **Modem** – generic modem settings;

- **Network** configures your device to your LAN;

- **PC** – settings for connection to your PC.

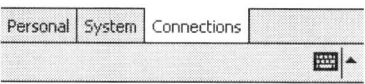

The New menu

Switching on the New menu gives you the ability to create appointments, contacts, e-mails, and other documents without having to launch the corresponding application first.

Once enabled, the New menu is really simple to use and is shown as an arrow on the toolbar.

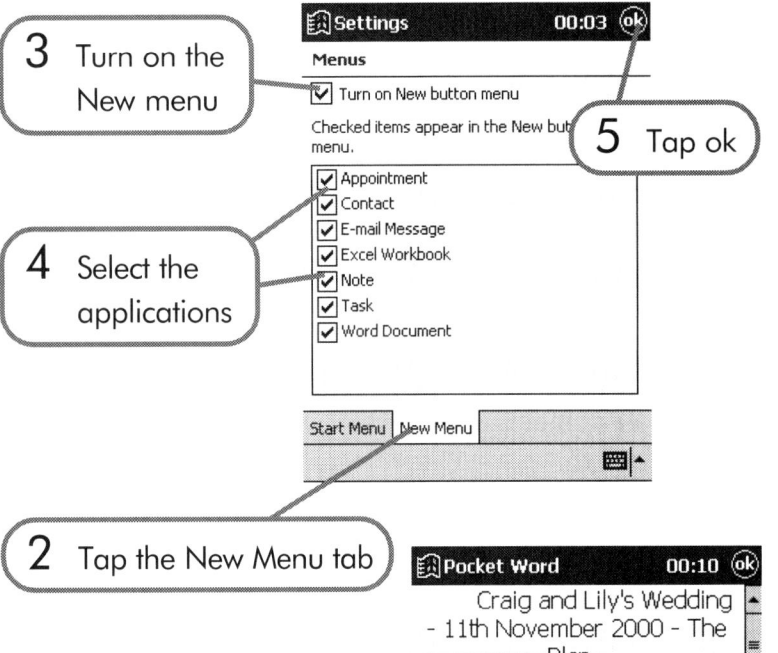

3 Turn on the New menu

4 Select the applications

5 Tap ok

2 Tap the New Menu tab

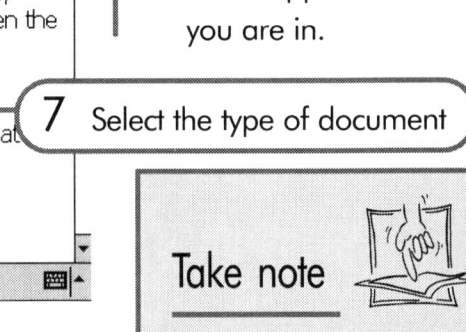

7 Select the type of document

6 Tap the up arrow

Basic steps

❏ Turning on the menu

1 Tap Start, Settings then Menus.

2 Tap the New Menu tab.

3 Tap Turn on New button menu to enable this feature.

4 Select the applications you want on the New menu.

5 Tap ok.

❏ Using the New menu

6 Tap the New menu up arrow.

7 Select the type of document to create.

❏ The templates at the top of the list are local to the application that you are in.

Tip

With the New menu enabled, you can create documents based on templates in applications such as Notes, Word, and Excel.

Take note

The New menu doesn't appear in all applications.

Basic steps

- ❏ To customize the Today screen

1 Tap Start, Settings, Today.

2 Uncheck the items you don't want to display.

- ❏ Calendar options

3 Tap Calendar.

4 Tap Options.

5 Tap Upcoming appointments, and All day events.

6 Tap ok.

Take note

The Tasks option only displays the number of tasks. DeveloperOne has written an application that will display the actual tasks on the Today screen.

The Today screen

The Today screen gives you at-a-glance information that is relevant and about to occur. How useful you find the default settings will depend on how you work. I changed my Calendar options almost immediately because they didn't display enough information.

I used a couple of the many third-party applications that are available to display extra information on the Today screen. Here's how I activated them after installation.

(See page 45, for more on installing third party software.)

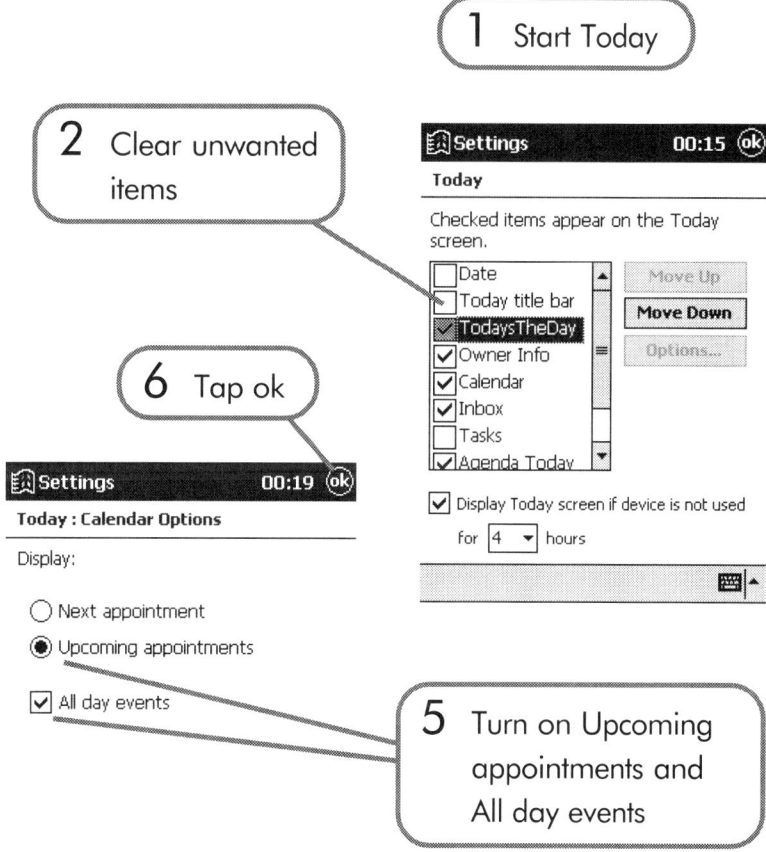

1 Start Today

2 Clear unwanted items

6 Tap ok

5 Turn on Upcoming appointments and All day events

Localize and calibrate

When you first set up your Pocket PC, a wizard would have taken you through the steps to pick the country you live in. During this process you also calibrated your stylus. It is sometimes necessary to make changes to some of these settings, for instance, if your taps on the screen are no longer accurate. These changes are made in the Settings menu.

Calibrating your screen

The calibration of your screen only needs to be done very occasionally and only if your device is not responding accurately to screen taps.

1 Tap Start and Settings.

2 Switch to the System tab.

3 Tap Align screen.

4 Tap the Align Screen button.

5 Tap the centre of the target in each location as it appears on the screen.

6 Tap ok.

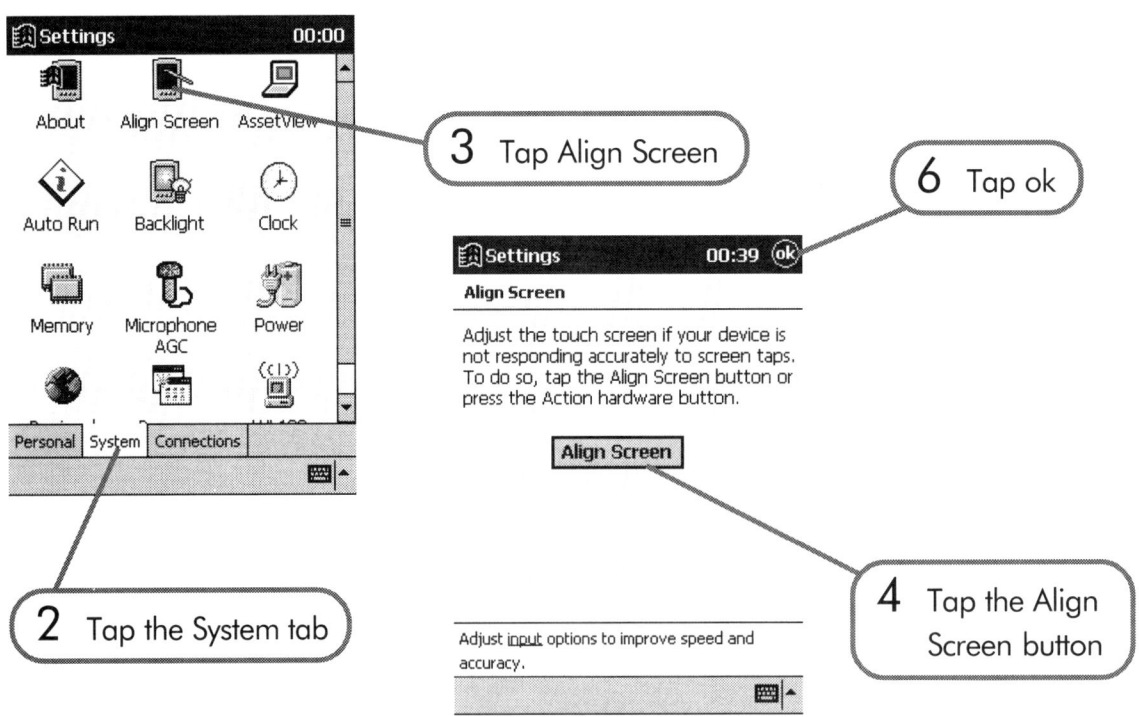

1 Start the Settings

3 Tap Align Screen

6 Tap ok

2 Tap the System tab

4 Tap the Align Screen button

16

Localizing

1   Tap Start, Settings and System.

2   Tap Regional Settings.

3   Tap your country in the drop-down Region box.

4   Switch to Number and define how you want them to appear.

continued...

In the Regional Settings section you will see five screens of options, Region, Number, Currency, Time and Date. You may well find you only wish to change one or two of the defaults.

The **Country** setting is key as it affects other applications such as Backup/Restore and how the date is displayed.

If you like to have the **Numbers** represented in a certain way, such as displaying negative numbers in brackets, e.g., (20) rather than –20, make the changes on the Numbers tab.

Currency settings are very similar to Numbers.

Use the **Time** settings to format the time display that appears at the top of the screen.

You can also customize how the **Date** is displayed.

2   Open Regional Settings

3   Select your country

Settings 00:40 (ok)

Regional Settings

Region:

English (United Kingdom)

Appearance samples

Time:	00:40:10
Short date:	14/09/00
Long date:	14 September 2000

Positive numbers:	123,456,789.00
Negative numbers:	-123,456,789.00
Positive currency:	£123,456,789.00
Negative currency:	-£123,456,789.00

Region	Number	Currency	Time	Date

Settings 00:40 (ok)

Regional Settings

Decimal symbol:	l
No. of decimal places:	2
Digit grouping symbol:	,
No. of digits in group:	3
List separators:	,
Negative sign symbol:	-
Negative number format:	-1.1
Display leading zero:	0.7
Measurement system:	Metric

Region	Number	Currency	Time	Date

4   Define the display of numbers

Tip

If the currency symbol you wish to use isn't displayed — e.g., for the Euro — bring up the Keyboard and select it from there.

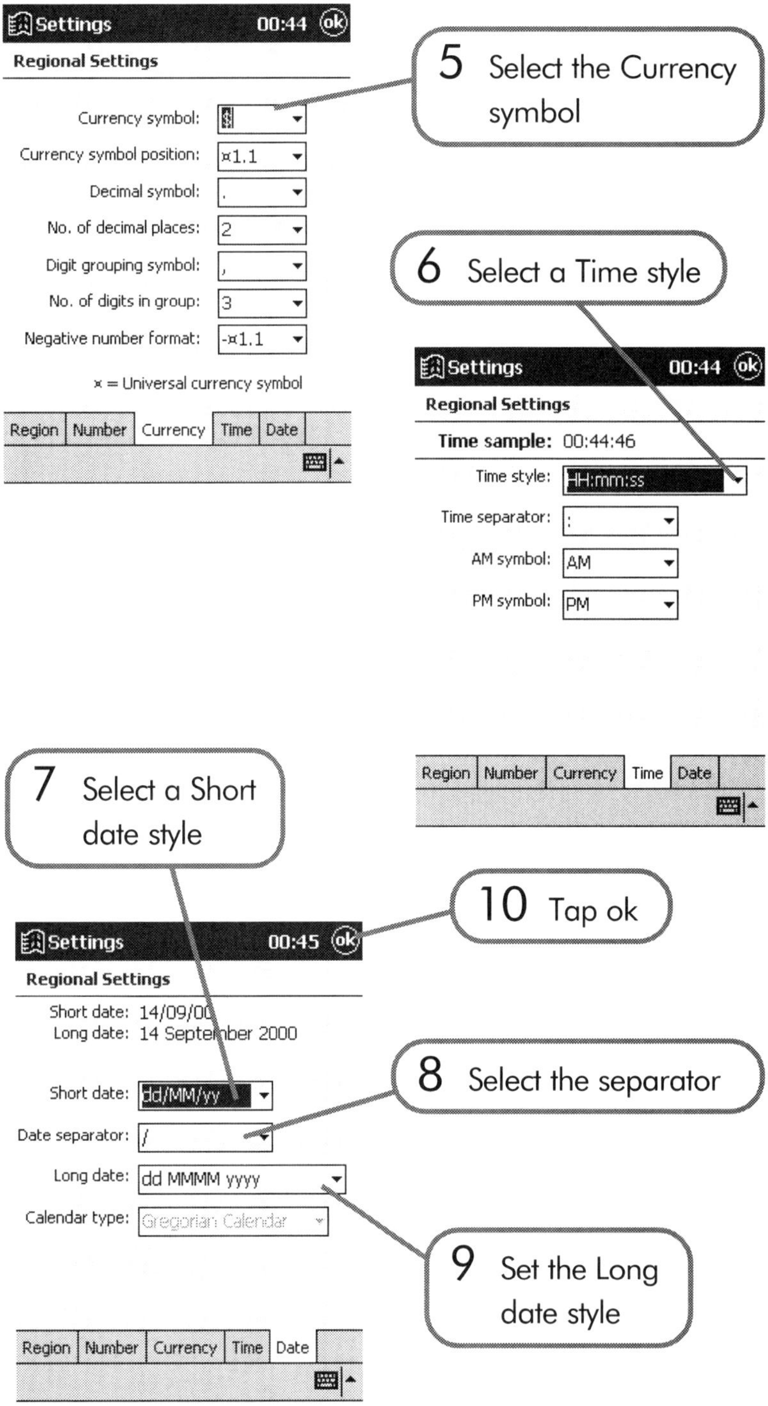

continued...

5 Switch to Currency and select the symbol.

6 On the Time tab, select a Time style: from the drop-down list.

7 Switch to the Date tab and select a Short date style from the drop-down list.

8 Tap the Separator field and enter the character you wish to use or select one from the list.

9 Select a Long date style.

10 Tap ok to save your settings and exit.

---

5 Select the Currency symbol

Settings 00:44 (ok)
Regional Settings

Currency symbol:	¤ ▾
Currency symbol position:	¤1.1 ▾
Decimal symbol:	. ▾
No. of decimal places:	2 ▾
Digit grouping symbol:	, ▾
No. of digits in group:	3 ▾
Negative number format:	-¤1.1 ▾

¤ = Universal currency symbol

| Region | Number | Currency | Time | Date |

---

6 Select a Time style

Settings 00:44 (ok)
Regional Settings

Time sample: 00:44:46

Time style:	HH:mm:ss ▾
Time separator:	: ▾
AM symbol:	AM ▾
PM symbol:	PM ▾

| Region | Number | Currency | Time | Date |

---

7 Select a Short date style

10 Tap ok

Settings 00:45 (ok)
Regional Settings

Short date: 14/09/00
Long date: 14 September 2000

Short date:	dd/MM/yy ▾
Date separator:	/ ▾
Long date:	dd MMMM yyyy ▾
Calendar type:	Gregorian Calendar ▾

8 Select the separator

9 Set the Long date style

| Region | Number | Currency | Time | Date |

Tip

Don't click ok until you have worked through all the screens. When you click ok the Regional Settings screen will close.

Password protecting

With so much valuable information stored on your Pocket PC, protecting it by using a password – actually, it's a number code – is a good idea. Here is how to set one up.

You can change your password at any time and as often as you feel is necessary.

Some manufacturers' devices have extra security options. These screenshots are from the HP Jornada Pocket PCs.

❏ Logging in with HP Password Protection

1 Tap Start, then Settings and select Password – if you have a HP Jornada then select HP Security.

2 Enter a 4-digit password.

3 On the HP device, you can select how long before the password is activated when the device is not used.

4 When you next switch on you will be asked for the password.

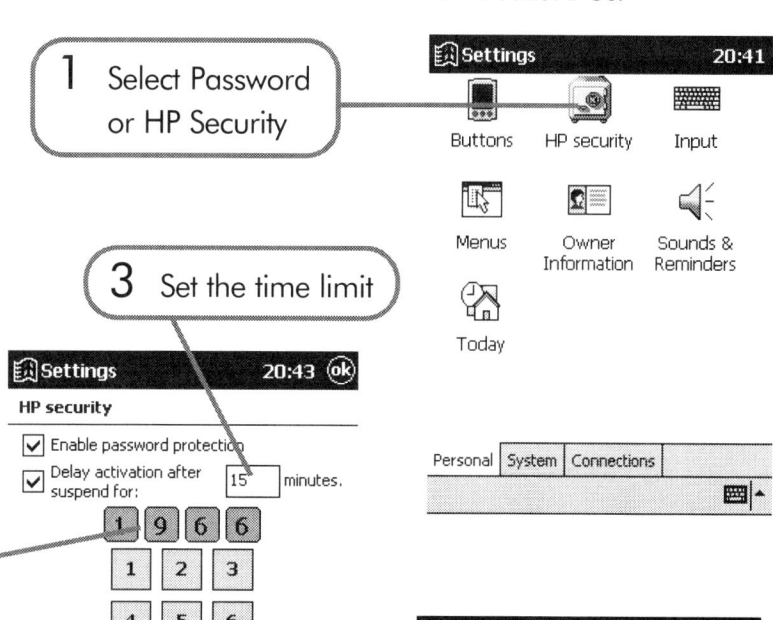

1 Select Password or HP Security

3 Set the time limit

2 Set a password

4 Enter the password to get started

Tip

On devices without the HP Security, if you get the password wrong after about 15 times, the system grinds to a virtual standstill.

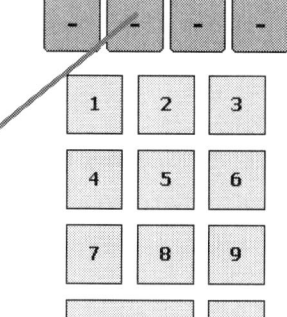

Password reminders

On the HP devices you can also set a password reminder and log the successful and failed login attempts. If you get your password wrong three times you will get a prompt screen displayed. When you successfully login you can carry on using your machine as normal.

Don't make the reminder as obvious as it is in my example or people could easily login to your device!

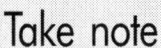

Take note

The only way to recover from a lost password is through a full hardware reset. This means that you will lose all your data and need to restore from a backup.

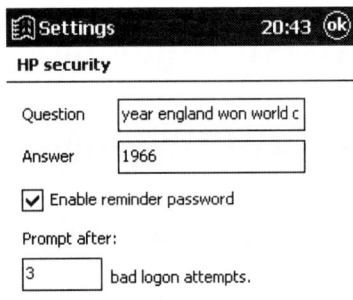

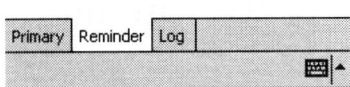

Go to the Reminder tab of the HP security screen to set up your password reminder

The Log tracks the usage of the password system

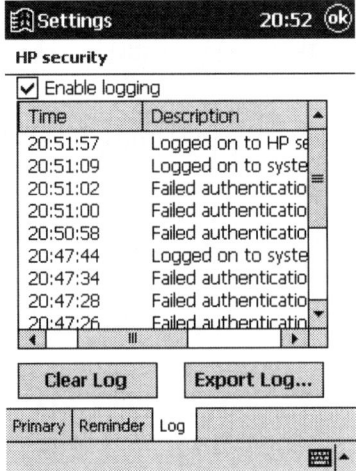

Tip

It's best to use a stylus to enter your password.

Basic steps

1 Tap Start, Contacts.
2 Tap Tools.
3 Tap Options…
4 Select the Country.
5 Enter or delete the Area code as applicable.
6 Tap ok.

In the Contacts application there are a couple of fields that are country/area specific; this is where you can change the defaults which are entered for you when you create a new contact on your Pocket PC. These can, of course, be overwritten, but if you have a lot of contacts in the same country or area code, setting these as the defaults will save time later.

Tip

If you will be entering a lot of contacts from different areas of your country or other countries then you may wish to leave these Options fields blank.

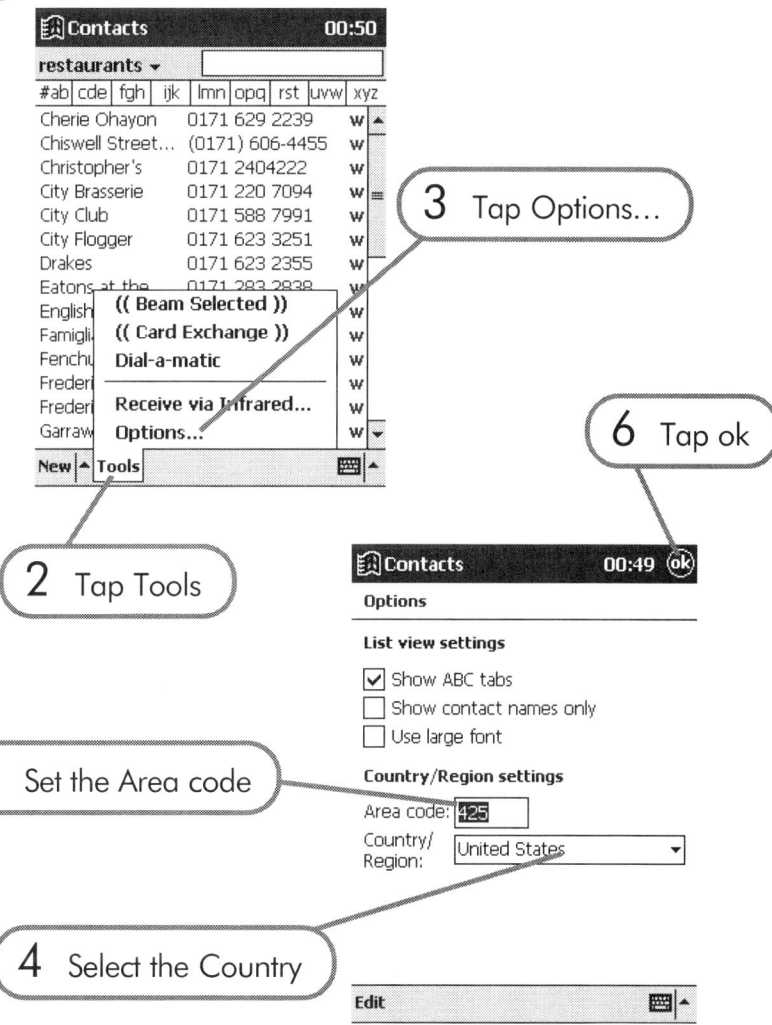

1 Start Contacts

3 Tap Options…

6 Tap ok

2 Tap Tools

5 Set the Area code

4 Select the Country

21

Dialing

If you are using your Pocket PC to dial up to the Internet (see Chapter 4) you can set your area code and dialing prefixes in the **Dialing** section of **Connections settings**.

If you are traveling a lot with your Pocket PC you can setup the dialing defaults. In this example you will see how to enter your own defaults and change the dialing patterns used. As standard, your Pocket PC has two dialing locations: Home and Work.

To change the local area code, tap in the box and the software keyboard should automatically appear, use the delete or backspace keys to remove the existing content, then enter the new details. Enter the country code in the same way.

1 Tap Start, Settings then Connections.

2 Tap Modem.

3 Tap the Dialing tab and select a Dialing Location – Home or Work – (or create a new one).

4 Change the Area code and Country code.

5 Tap Dialing Patterns.

6 Change as necessary (see opposite).

7 Tap ok twice.

5 Go to Dialing Patterns

7 Tap ok

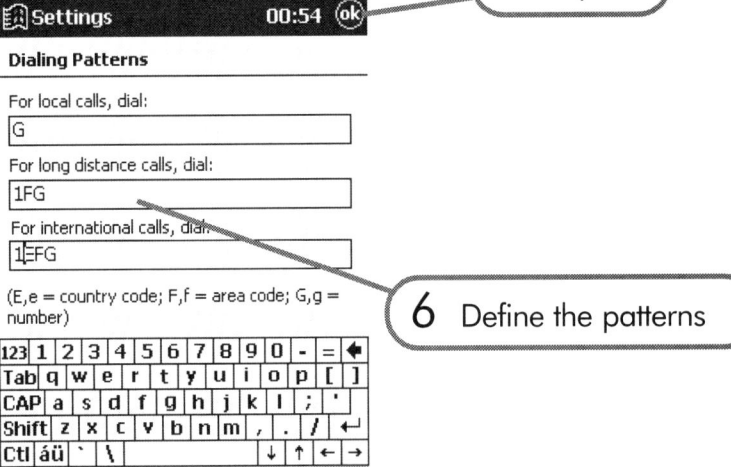

6 Define the patterns

Take note

You will have to change the country code, local area code and the dialing patterns for both home and work locations when you first localize them.

Dialing Patterns

As the way that you dial numbers is different all over the world, these settings will need to be changed depending on where you are. In the USA you dial 1 before the area code and number for a long distance call, whereas in the UK you dial just the area code and number.

This is the section to enter any special dialing needs, e.g,. if you have to enter a 9 for an outside line, or do not have to enter a 1 for long distance. Here are the most commonly used patterns.

, (comma)	creates a pause of two seconds
E	the country code
F	the area code
G	the (local) phone number
0-9	digits to be dialled

For example, in my Work location, I have these patterns.

Local: 9G   9 for an outside line, but no pause, then the number

Long Distance: 9FG   same as above but with the area code before the number

International: 900EFG   specifies 9 for an outside line, 00 for international access, then the country code, area code, and phone number.

With hotels around the world having different phone systems, getting a connection from a modem can be a challenge. You will probably have to experiment with pauses and possibly tone and pulse dialing (pulse dialing is much slower). For example:

Local: 1,,G   Two commas creates two pauses, each of 2 seconds, the 1 could be needed to get an outside line.

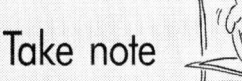

Take note

The default settings on the device are set for USA dialing patterns.

Summary

❏ The Settings screens carry icons for those features of the device that can be customized.

❏ If the New menu is enabled, you can create new documents without having to start the relevant application first.

❏ You can control the display of information on the Today screen – there are third party utilities that will allow you to show more.

❏ If your screen doesn't respond properly to taps, it may need aligning.

❏ The Regional Settings let you localize the display of numbers, currency, time and dates on your device.

❏ A password can be set to protect the information on your device.

❏ You can set the default country and area codes for new Contacts.

❏ If you use your device for dialing out, you should make sure that the dialing patterns are right for your locality.

3 Documents and Notes

Notes

One of the main functions of your Pocket PC is to allow you to store Notes and information. There are several ways to record them and several different types.

The three main types of Notes are: typed, handwritten, and voice recorded. Notes handles all three seamlessly.

Typed Notes are the default.

Basic steps

❑ Typing a Note

1 Tap Start, Programs, Notes.

2 Tap the Keyboard Input Panel Selector.

3 When the keyboard appears, type the Note. The text appears in the main Notes screen.

4 Tap the ok button to save the Note.

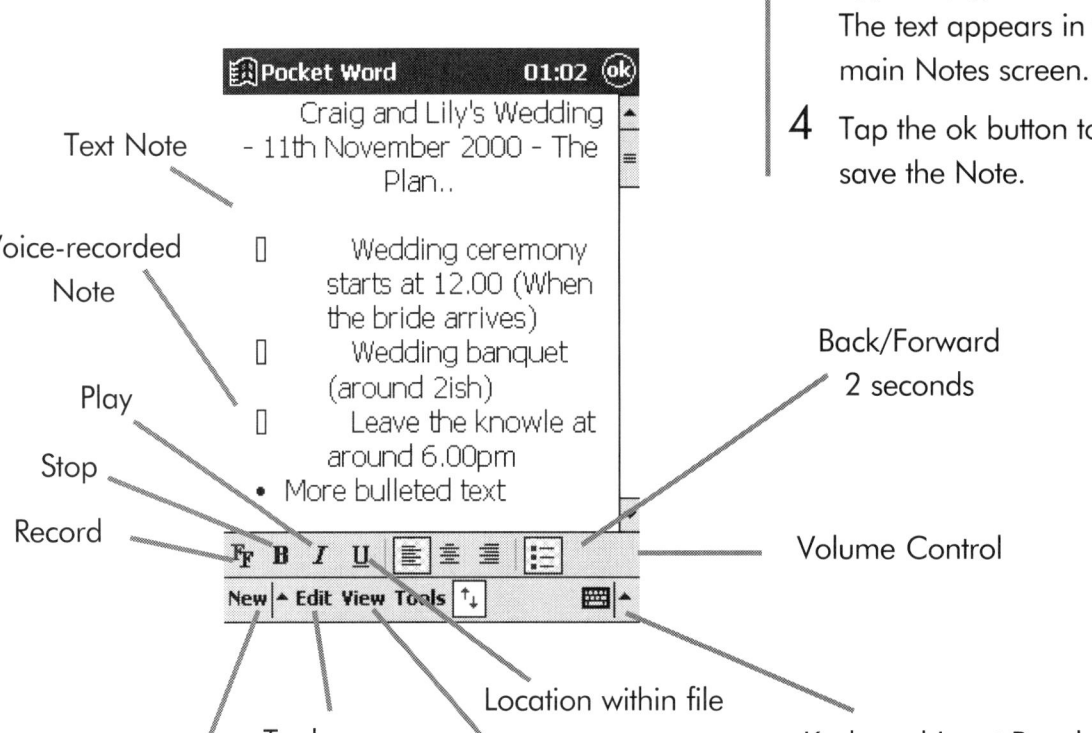

Text Note

Voice-recorded Note

Play

Stop

Record

New menu

Tools menu

Show/Hide Voice Recording toolbar

Location within file

Back/Forward 2 seconds

Volume Control

Keyboard Input Panel Selector

Basic steps

1 Tap Start, Programs, Notes.

2 Tap ok to return to the List view.

3 Tap Options.

4 Tap the drop-down box on the Save to field.

5 Select *Storage card 1* (if available).

6 Tap ok. The Note will be saved to the storage card.

Saving Notes

When you have typed your first Note, you don't actually need to worry about giving it a name; tapping the **ok** button will save it using the first few letters of the text as the filename.

When you want to rename your Note or give it a more meaning-ful name check out '*Renaming and moving Notes*' on the next page.

Saving a Note to a storage card

If you want to move a Note to a storage card only occasionally then see the next section, on renaming/moving Notes.

If you wish to alter your preferences so *all* your Notes are stored on a removable storage card, then read on.

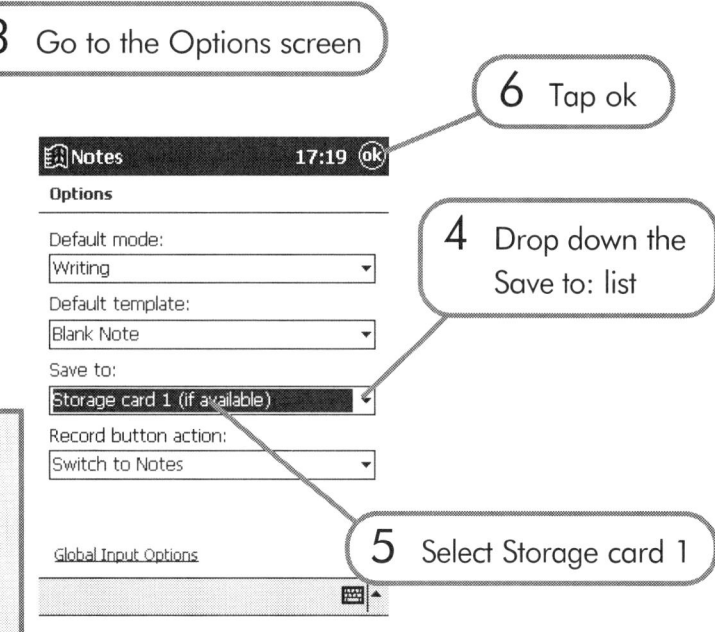

3 Go to the Options screen

6 Tap ok

4 Drop down the Save to: list

5 Select Storage card 1

Tap and hold in Notes

With any Note, handwritten, typed or voice-recorded, a tap and hold on the filename will give you options such as the ability to e-mail or send the file via infrared.

Renaming and moving Notes

When you've typed up a few Notes and hit the ok button you'll see them in the List view. This view lets you to see all the Notes you've recorded, and you can sort your Notes and perform file management tasks such as renaming, copying, and moving from this view.

When it comes to sorting your Notes or storing them in particular folders you need to first create the folders.

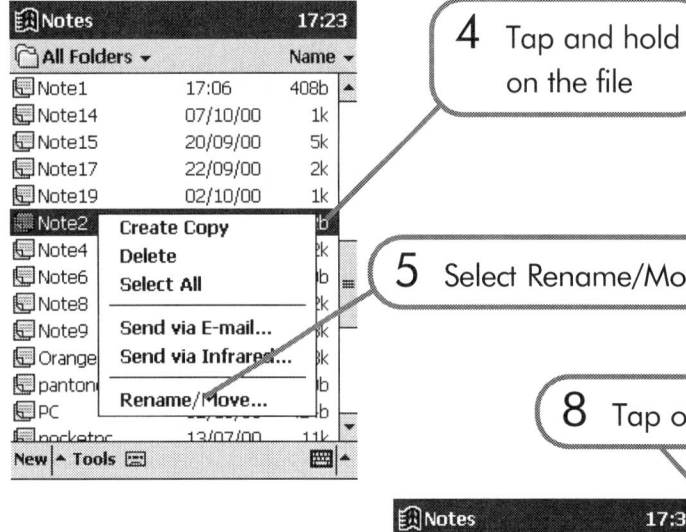

3 Go to List view

4 Tap and hold on the file

5 Select Rename/Move...

8 Tap ok

7 Enter the new name

6 Select the folder

Basic steps

❑ Creating a folder

1 Tap All Folders, then Add/Delete.

2 Tap New, name the folder and tap ok.

❑ Moving a Note

3 Navigate to the List view.

4 Tap and hold the stylus on the Note you want to move.

5 Select Rename/Move... from the pop-up menu.

6 To move, select the Folder you wish to move the Note to.

7 To rename, type in the new name in the slot.

8 Tap ok.

Basic steps

1 Tap Start, Programs, Notes.

2 Write your Note directly on the screen. When you get near the bottom it will scroll up to make room for the next part of your Note.

❑ Converting text

3 Tap to the left of the word and drag across it to the right (highlighting the word)

4 Tap and hold.

5 Select Convert Handwriting to Text.

Handwritten Notes

If you just need to quickly scribble down a phone number/contact name or anything else in a hurry, then using the handwriting option of Notes is the quickest way. All you do is write on the screen just as you would a piece of paper.

When you've handwritten a note, sometimes it's really handy to be able to convert that into text and be able to e-mail it to someone as text and not in your own handwriting. Here's how to get the handwriting converted to text.

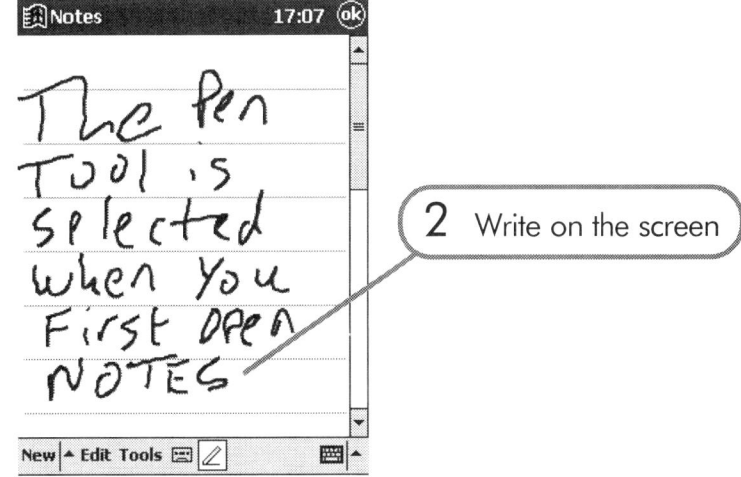

2 Write on the screen

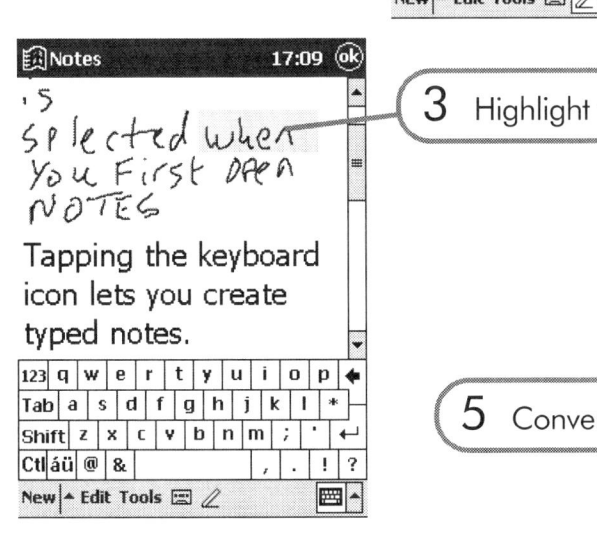

3 Highlight the word

5 Convert it to text

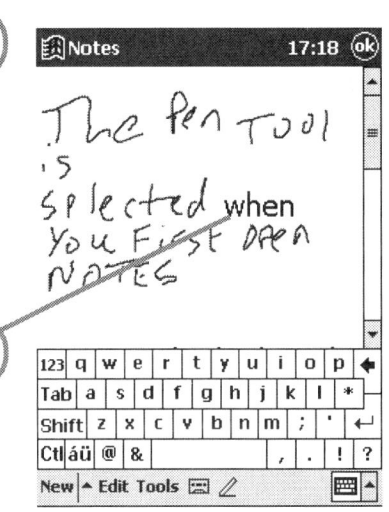

Recognizing handwritten Notes

While it's possible to convert a word one at a time this would be quite time-consuming, so here's how to convert the whole of a handwritten Note to typed text.

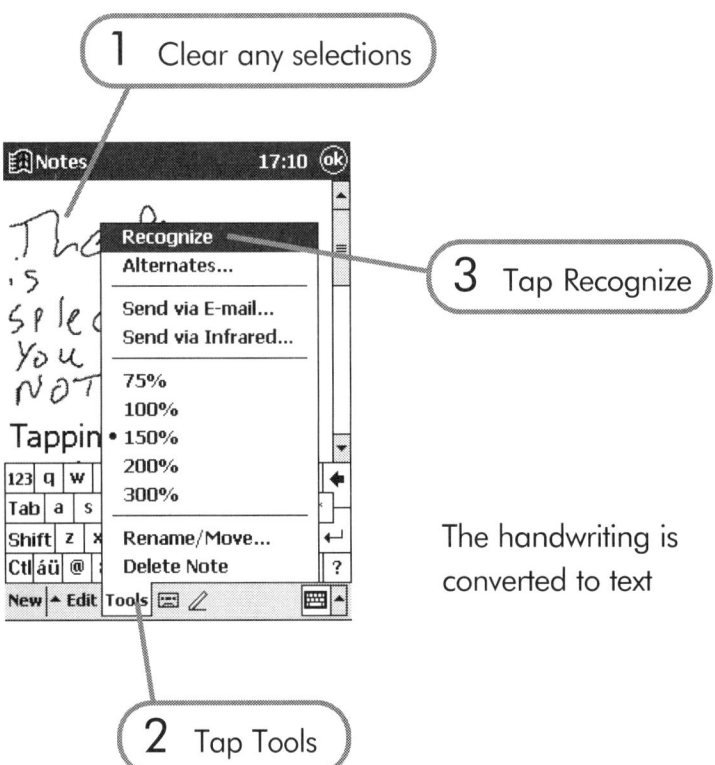

1 Clear any selections

3 Tap Recognize

The handwriting is converted to text

2 Tap Tools

Basic steps

1 Make sure that no text is selected.

2 Tap Tools.

3 Tap Recognize.

❑ The handwriting will be converted to typed text.

Take note

During synchronization with your desktop PC, any stored Notes can be copied to the Notes part of Outlook on your PC. This is not switched on by default (see page 44 on ActiveSync to find out how to enable it).

Drawing with Notes

1 Draw a diagram.

2 Tap the Ink drawing tool so that it becomes deselected.

3 Using your stylus, drag and hold over a particular shape/area.

4 Tap and hold gives you a menu allowing you to create copies, etc. Select the appropriate option.

5 You can use the drag handles on the object to move or rotate it.

Drawing with Notes works in a similar way to handwriting, but there are a few little tricks to make your quick drawings more professional.

If, for example, you are drawing a map, if three lines should cross each other, a tap and hold of the stylus will bring up a formatting menu. Using this you can turn rough squares, circles, and boxes into perfect shapes.

You can also do some interesting things with the shapes, such as rotate or move them, etc.

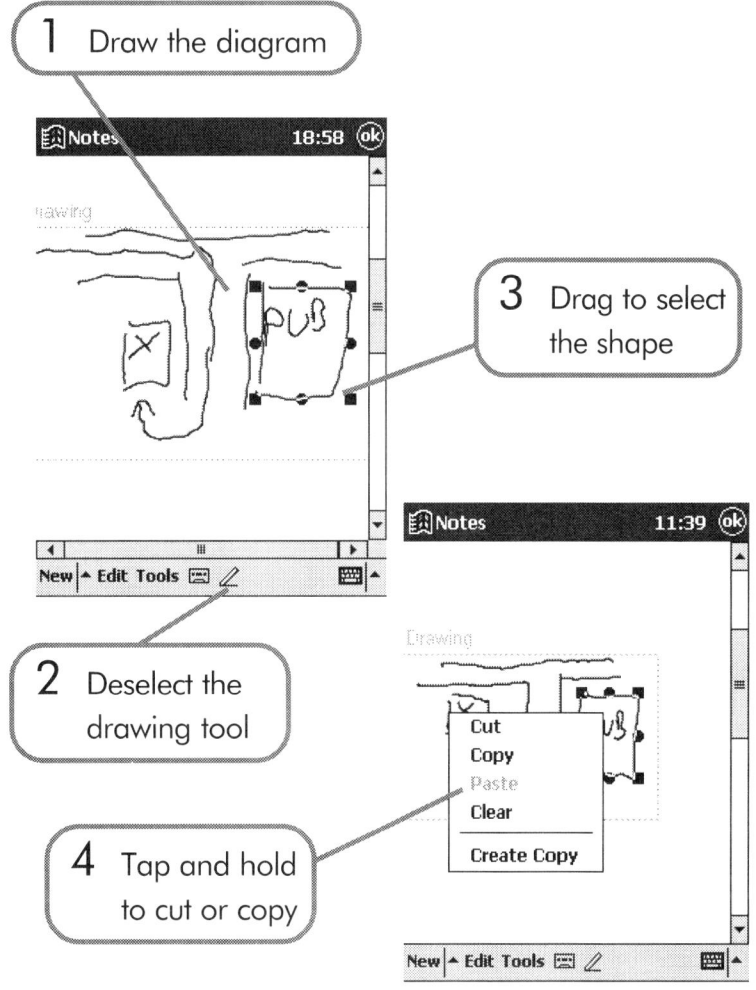

Voice-recorded Notes

The ability to use your Pocket PC as a voice recorder can come in very handy – it's great to record quick reminders or Notes. It is not uncommon for people to use the Pocket PC to record entire meetings and to e-mail them to others for their reference.

One way of activating the voice recorder in Notes is to use the hardware record button. The other is to use the Record icon.

Recording formats

The default recording format is *Mobile voice*. This is used as it provides really good compression and takes up far less space than the PCM (Pulse Code Modulation) formats used on PCs. Also, you cannot embed PCM Format recordings inside Notes.

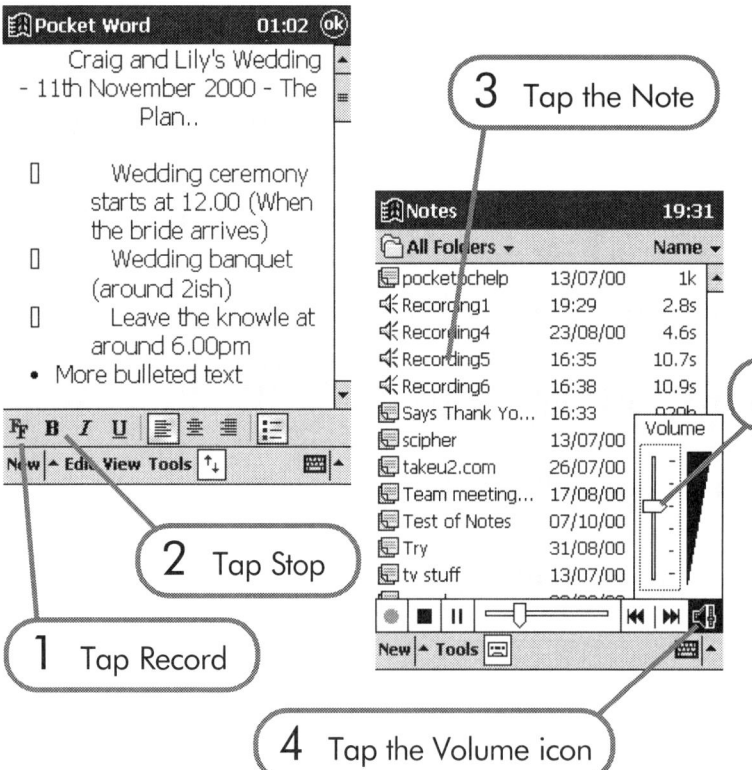

❏ To record a Note

1 Press the hardware record button or tap Record to start recording. The speaker icon will show that the device is recording.

2 Release the record button or tap Stop.

❏ Playing back a Note

3 In the List view tap the filename. The Play button will change to Pause when you are listening to a Note.

❏ Adjusting the volume

4 Tap the Volume icon.

5 Adjust the slider.

Take note

Devices vary in the sensitivity of their microphones. Experiment with different angles, noise levels, etc.

Basic steps

1 Open a blank Note.

2 Type in the text you want on your Note.

3 Tap ok.

4 Tap and hold on the Note and select Re-name/Move…

5 Give it a suitable name.

6 Move it to the *Templates* folder.

❑ To test it

7 Tap New.

8 Select the newly created template from the list.

Creating templates

If you regularly need to write a Note on a particular topic or always have to record similar details, then you can create a template and perhaps have it as the default for new Notes.

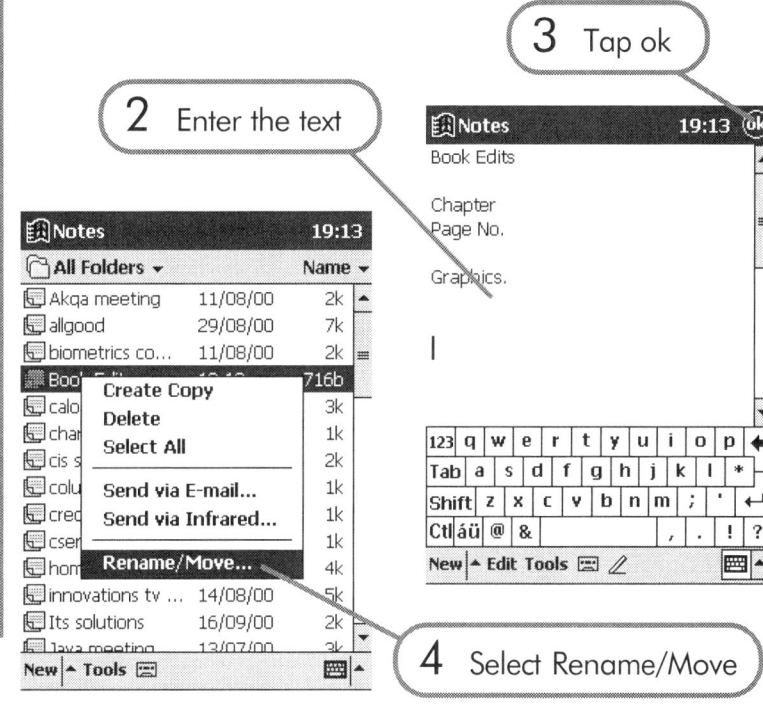

3 Tap ok

2 Enter the text

4 Select Rename/Move

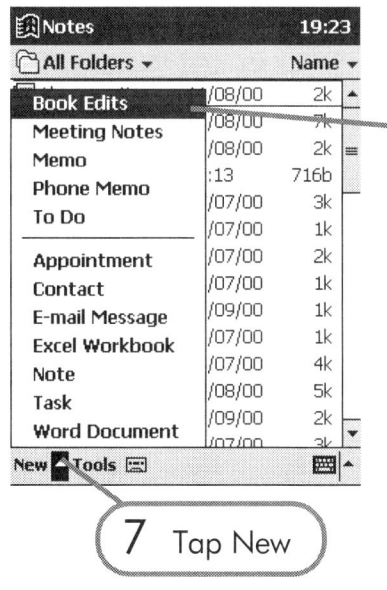

7 Tap New

8 Select the template from the New menu

5 Give it a name

6 Move it to Templates

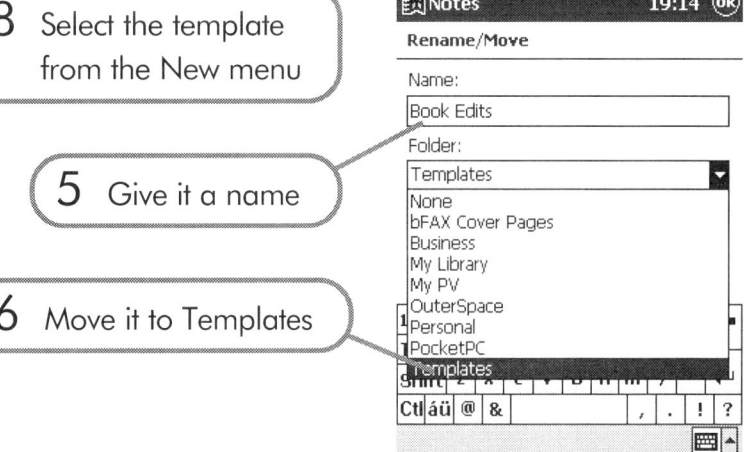

Pocket Word

This is a cut-down version of Microsoft Word, but still packed with the most commonly used features such as document templates, multiple font support, different font sizes, **bold,** *italics,* find and replace, and bulleted and numbered lists. The Undo facility and the ability to password-protect documents are also included. The Save icon is replaced by the ok button.

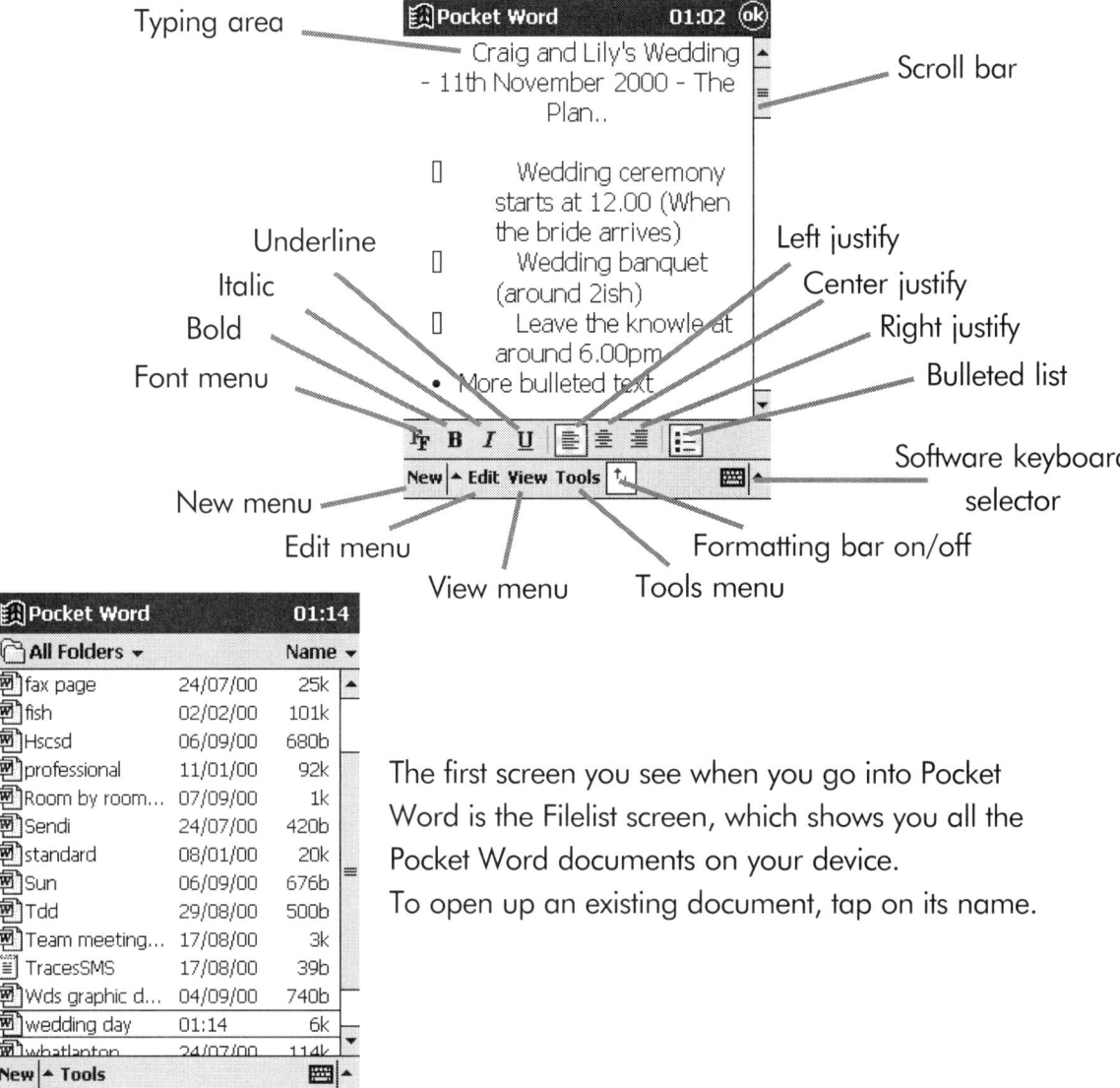

Typing area

Scroll bar

Underline

Italic

Bold

Font menu

Left justify

Center justify

Right justify

Bulleted list

Software keyboard selector

New menu

Edit menu

View menu

Tools menu

Formatting bar on/off

The first screen you see when you go into Pocket Word is the Filelist screen, which shows you all the Pocket Word documents on your device.

To open up an existing document, tap on its name.

Quitting without saving a document

1 In a document make a change to the text.

2 Instead of tapping ok tap New.

3 Select No to leave the document without saving the changes.

Or

4 Select Save As to save the edited document with a new name.

With no quit button in the applications on your Pocket PC it can be a little tricky at first to find out where the quit or don't save options are. Not all applications support these options – Notes is one that doesn't.

Pocket Word will prompt you if you try to start a new document after having made a change to the current one. This will only happen if the New menu button is enabled (see page 14).

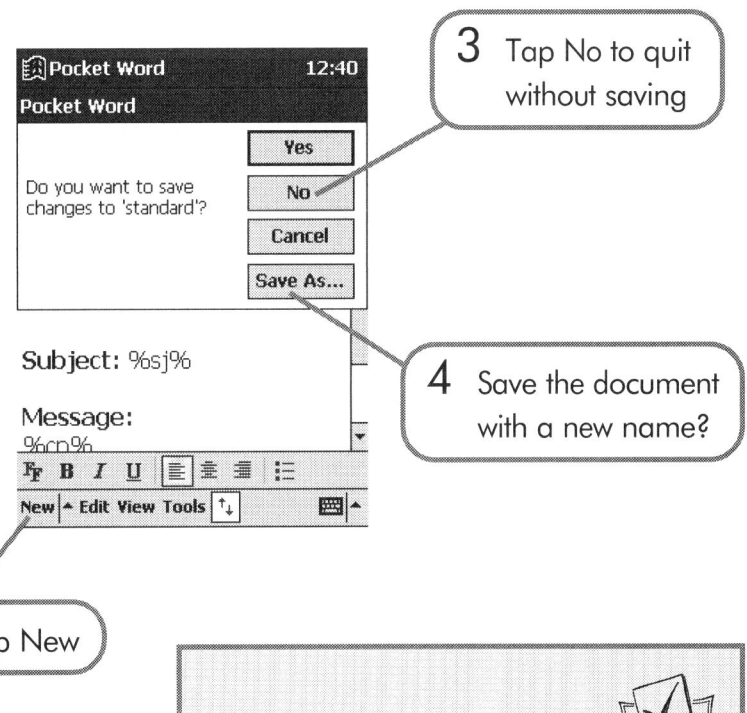

Take note

Pocket Word has no quit-without-saving option as standard.

3 Tap No to quit without saving

4 Save the document with a new name?

2 Tap New

Tip

If you want to get back to the previously saved version of a document, use the Revert to Saved option on the Tools menu.

The Edit menu

The Edit menu lets you change the appearance of text and format paragraphs – here we will add bullets to the paragraphs.

The Undo option comes in really handy if you've just made some typing errors or formatting changes that you wish to undo.

The View menu

To allow you to see more text on the screen, Pocket Word has several different zoom levels with which you can view your text. All of these options are found on the View – Zoom menu.

Other View menu options let you switch between the four modes of working – Writing, Drawing, Typing, and Recording.

❑ Formatting paragraphs

1 Highlight some text by tapping and dragging the stylus.

2 Tap Edit.

3 Tap Paragraph…

4 Tap Bulleted.

5 Tap ok.

❑ Zoom levels

6 Tap View, Zoom.

7 Select a Zoom level.

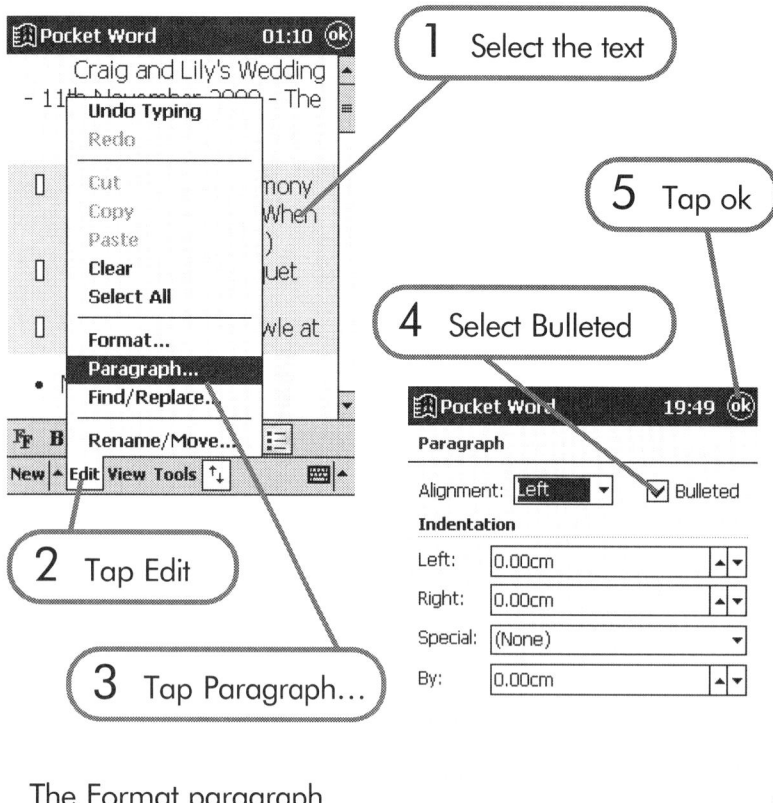

1 Select the text

2 Tap Edit

3 Tap Paragraph…

4 Select Bulleted

5 Tap ok

The Format paragraph screen has several options

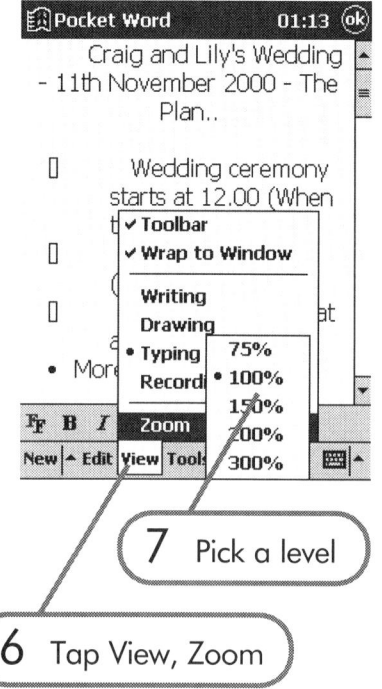

7 Pick a level

6 Tap View, Zoom

The Tools menu

This menu gives you different options for saving your Pocket Word documents, as well as letting you share your document with others either via infrared or e-mail.

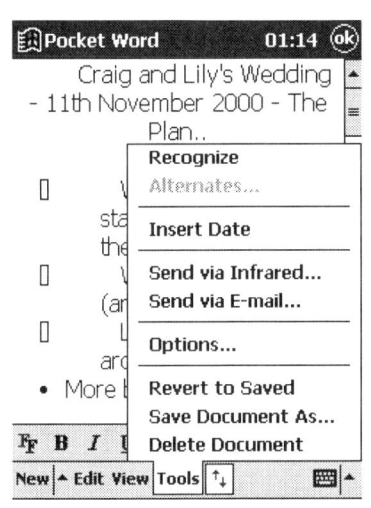

- **Recognize** converts handwriting to typed text;

- **Alternates** is used when the Recognizer doesn't convert your handwriting successfully;

- **Insert Date** puts the current date into the current cursor location in the document;

- **Send via Infrared/E-mail** lets you share the document with others (see pages 77 and 95);

- **Options** lets you choose where to save your documents (e.g., storage card if one is present);

- **Revert to saved** lets you go back to the previously-saved version of the current document;

- **Save Document As…** lets you give the current document a new name;

- **Delete Document** lets you erase the document from within Pocket Word.

The New menu

- **New menu button** – lets you create a new document;

- **New menu arrow** – gives you more new options including the ability to create a new document based on a template.

Writing mode

To get into the writing mode, select it from the View menu.

Use **Insert Space** if you need to make room for more text, or handwritten or drawn Notes.

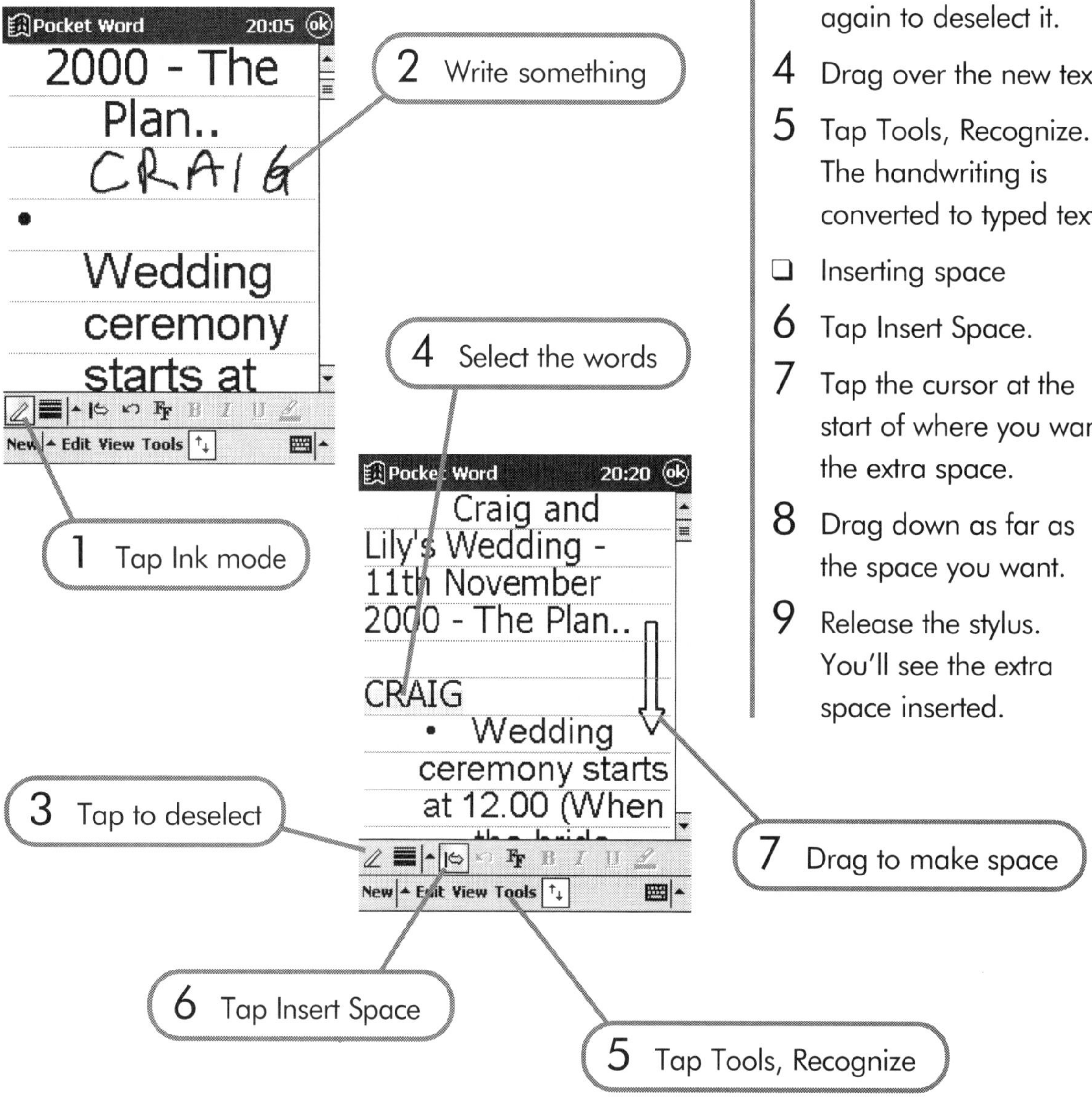

2000 - The
Plan..
CRAIG
●

Wedding
ceremony
starts at

> 2 Write something

> 1 Tap Ink mode

Craig and
Lily's Wedding -
11th November
2000 - The Plan..

CRAIG
  • Wedding
   ceremony starts
   at 12.00 (When

> 4 Select the words

> 3 Tap to deselect

> 6 Tap Insert Space

> 7 Drag to make space

> 5 Tap Tools, Recognize

Basic steps

1 Tap the Ink mode tool.

2 Handwrite something.

3 Tap the Ink mode tool again to deselect it.

4 Drag over the new text.

5 Tap Tools, Recognize. The handwriting is converted to typed text.

❑ Inserting space

6 Tap Insert Space.

7 Tap the cursor at the start of where you want the extra space.

8 Drag down as far as the space you want.

9 Release the stylus. You'll see the extra space inserted.

Basic steps

1 Tap View, Zoom and select a good zoom level (I've used 150%).

2 Tap the Ink mode tool to select it.

3 Draw a few shapes.

4 Tap the Ink mode tool to deselect it.

5 Tap the stylus near a shape and drag over it.

6 Tap and hold on the word 'Drawing' that is shown near your selected drawing.

7 Select the Shape menu.

8 Select a type of shape.

Drawing mode and shapes

In Drawing mode, several new options appear on the Pocket Word toolbar.

You can convert your rough sketches into regular shapes, just as you can in Notes.

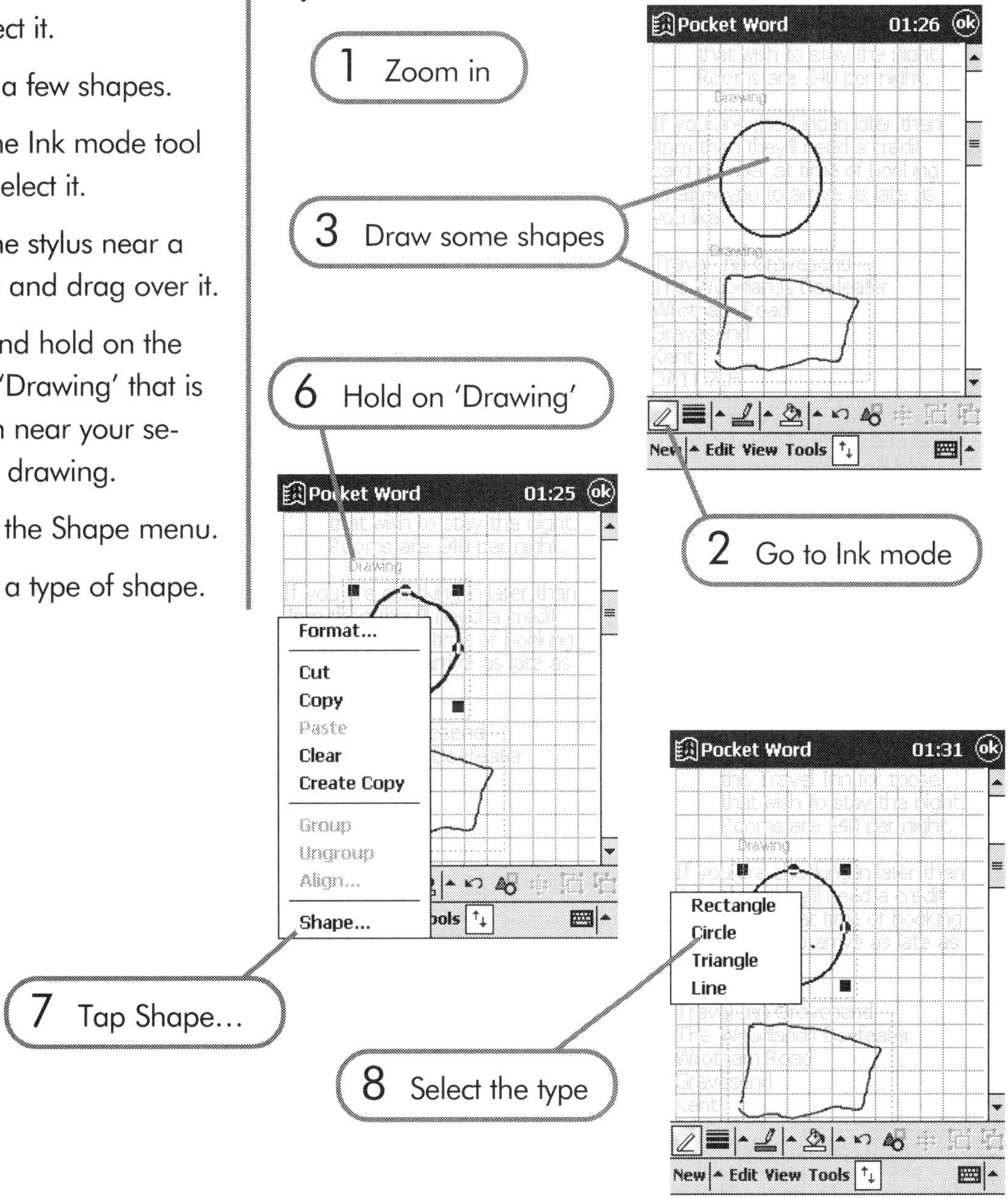

1 Zoom in

3 Draw some shapes

6 Hold on 'Drawing'

2 Go to Ink mode

7 Tap Shape...

8 Select the type

Format...

Cut
Copy
Paste
Clear
Create Copy

Group
Ungroup
Align...

Shape...

Rectangle
Circle
Triangle
Line

Coloring in shapes

When you've got a drawing on the screen you can fill it in with a color, there are 16 colors plus 'transparent' to pick from.

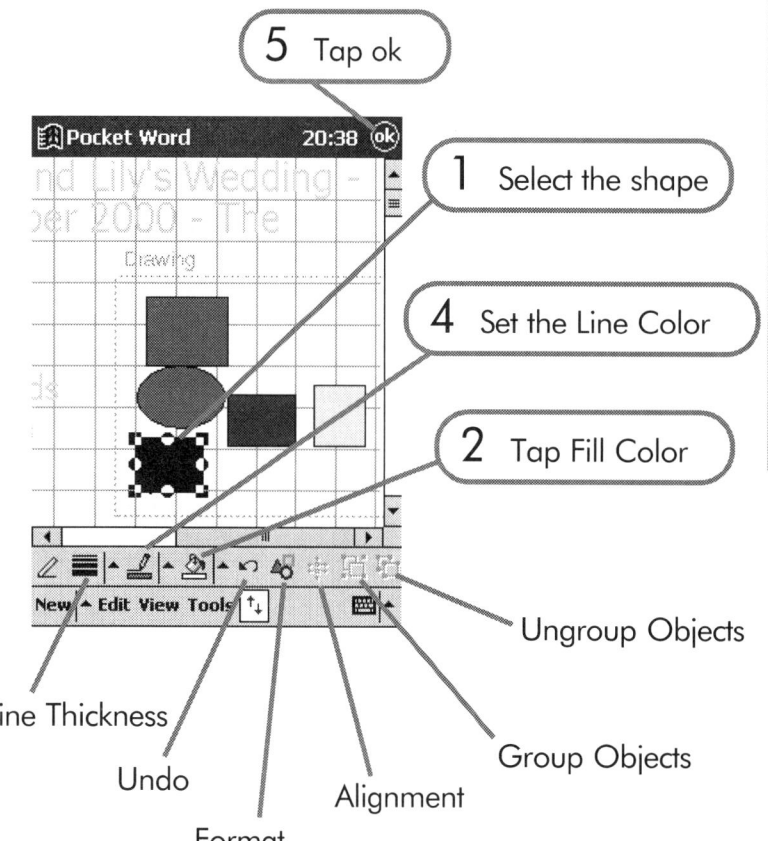

5 Tap ok

1 Select the shape

4 Set the Line Color

2 Tap Fill Color

Ungroup Objects

Line Thickness

Undo

Format

Alignment

Group Objects

1 Highlight the shape by tapping and dragging across it.

2 From the Drawing toolbar, select the Fill Color tool.

3 Select the appropriate color.

4 Set the color of the shape's outline using the Line Color tool.

5 Tap ok when done.

Take note

Desktop compatibility: Not all the functions of the desktop version of Word are supported on Pocket Word. Missing functions include password-protected documents, text within tables, headers and footers.

Basic steps

1 Tap somewhere in the document where you want to make the recording.

2 Tap View.

3 Tap Recording.

4 Tap the Record icon.

5 Tap Stop when finished.

6 Add a comment by the recording icon.

Recording mode

The voice recording function of Microsoft Pocket Word works very similarly to that in Notes discussed earlier.

If you put recordings in Word documents it's useful to put a little comment next to it to remind you what it's about.

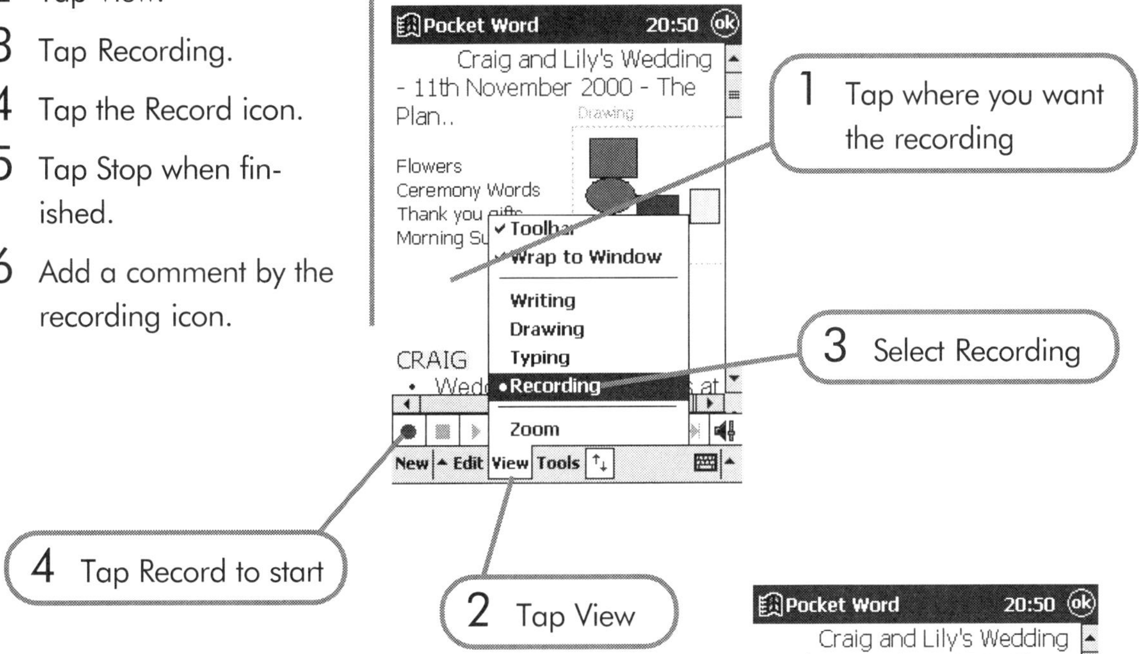

1 Tap where you want the recording

3 Select Recording

4 Tap Record to start

2 Tap View

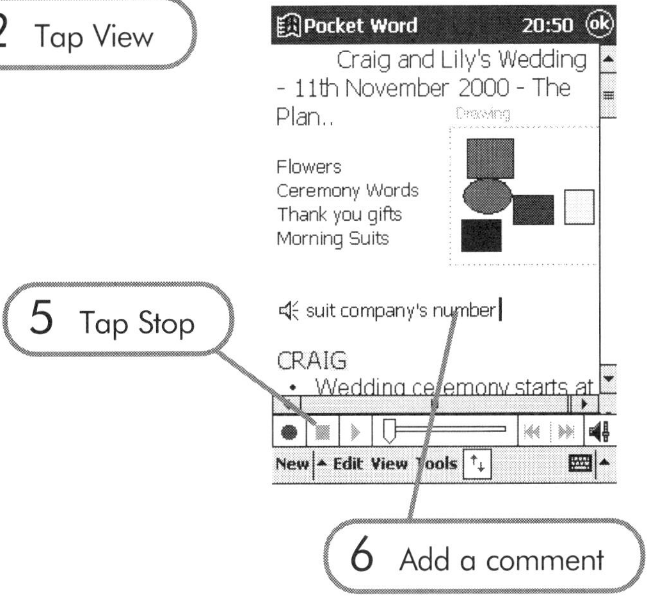

5 Tap Stop

6 Add a comment

Tip

Shortcut keys such as Ctrl C (Copy), Ctrl V (Paste) and Ctrl X (Cut) work in Pocket Word, although they aren't documented anywhere.

41

Summary

❑ You can create handwritten, typed, or voice Notes on your Pocket PC.

❑ Notes can be saved to a storage card, if one is present.

❑ Handwritten Notes can be converted to text using the Recognizer.

❑ Hand drawn sketches in Notes can be converted to regular shapes.

❑ Voice-recorded Notes are stored as separate files. The volume can be adjusted when playing them back.

❑ Voice Notes are normally stored in the Mobile voice format. This is more efficient than the Pulse Code Modulation format used on PCs.

❑ You can create templates for types of Notes that you will want regularly.

❑ Pocket Word has many of the functions of the desktop version. It can be used in Writing, Typing, Drawing, or Recording modes.

❑ In Pocket Word's Drawing mode, you can convert sketches to regular shapes, and change their fill and line colors.

❑ Voice recordings can be embedded in Pocket Word documents.

4 Communications

Desktop connectivity

When you purchased your Pocket PC it came with software called Microsoft ActiveSync, the purpose of which is to allow you to quickly and easily transfer information between your PC and your Pocket PC. This is most usually changing things such as Contacts, Calendar, Tasks, E-mail, Notes, and other information.

Microsoft ActiveSync has lots of features. With it, you can install other applications, backup and restore your data, and copy files and information to and from your Pocket PC. A lot of the work it does is taken care of behind the scenes. All-in-all, it is a very easy to use application.

After you've installed ActiveSync, when you plug in your Pocket PC to your PC it will detect that it is connected, and without you having to touch any keys or buttons it will synchronize the information between your PC and Pocket PC.

ActiveSync enables you to share information efficiently with your desktop PC

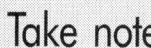

Take note

Pocket PCs differ in how they connect up to your PC. Some use USB (Universal Serial Bus) and others use a serial cable connection. Please refer to the manufacturer's documentation that came with your device for instructions on connecting the two.

Basic steps

1 Connect your Pocket PC to your PC.

2 On your PC, run the software's setup program. This might prompt you if there are optional components.

3 Work through the setup wizard, pressing Next at each step, then Finish at the last panel.

4 When asked if you want to install at the default location, it's best to say Yes.

5 After installation, you may be prompted to restart the device.

Installing a new application on a Pocket PC is almost identical to installing it on a PC. The software is usually supplied over the Internet or on a diskette or CD-ROM and will have a setup file (normally, but not always called setup.exe). Running this on your PC will copy the application to your Pocket PC. If the device isn't connected to the PC, the application will be installed when you next connect it.

When the software installation is complete, it will add an entry to the Programs menu on your Pocket PC.

2 Run the setup program

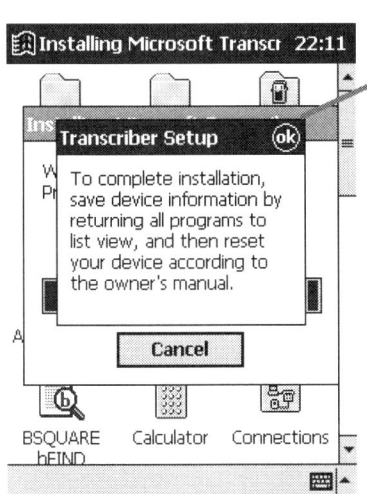

5 Reset if prompted

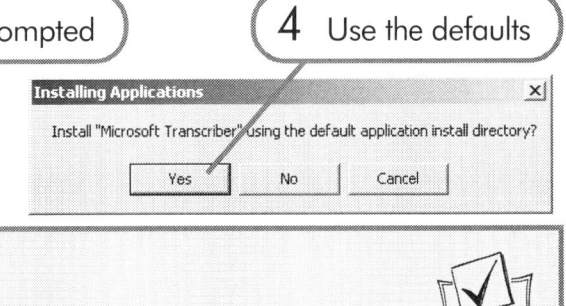

4 Use the defaults

Tip

If you are not sure which choices to make when installing software, accept the defaults, as they are best for most users.

Manual installation

Some vendors are releasing freeware and shareware applications on the Internet, and they are relying on the user being able to install these applications manually.

This process isn't quite as user friendly as the automatic method, but it can also be used to copy data files from your PC to your Pocket PC. Later in the chapter I'll show you how to have files copied automatically between your PC and Pocket PC.

Before you start, you need to know what processor family you have inside your Pocket PC. With a desktop PC, most processors are Intel or Intel-compatible; unfortunately this isn't the case with a Pocket PC.

Most vendors identify the names of the model of machine, but some rely on you to know which processor you have and therefore which version to download. I've included this table to help you understand which processor is in which machine.

Machine	Processor
Compaq iPAQ	SA1100
HP Jornada 540 series	SH3
Casio E115 / EM500	MIPS
Symbol PPT	MIPS

These type of files will usually have the file extension .*CAB* and are special files that you need to run on your Pocket PC to install them correctly.

Basic steps

1 Connect your Pocket PC to your desktop PC.

2 Open up the folder on your PC where you've downloaded the application.

3 Open up Microsoft ActiveSync – double-click the icon. You should now have two folders open on your PC screen.

4 On the Microsoft ActiveSync screen, double-click Explore.

continued...

Copying the files to your Pocket PC

With your Pocket PC connected to your desktop PC, you will need to locate the software you've downloaded onto your PC, and then navigate around your Pocket PC to ensure the files are copied to the correct location.

In this example I've downloaded a file to *d:\pocketpc* and I'm going to copy it to the Pocket PC so it can be installed.

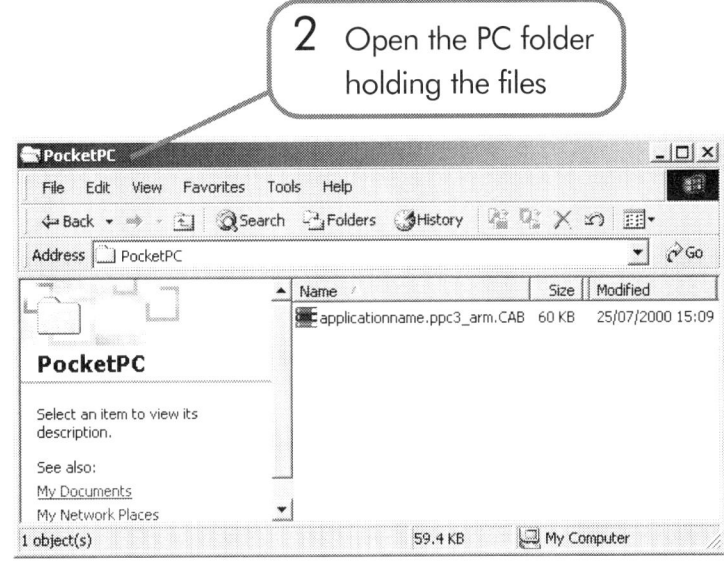

2 Open the PC folder holding the files

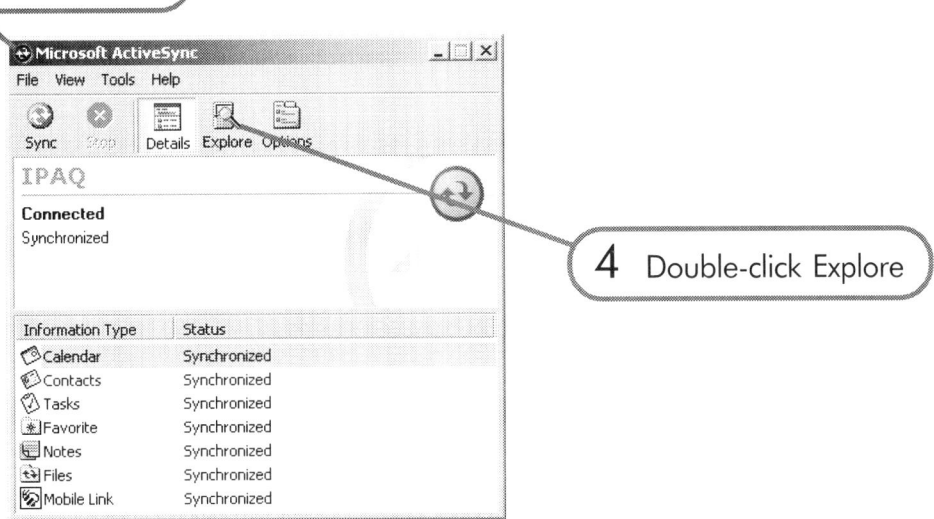

3 Run ActiveSync

4 Double-click Explore

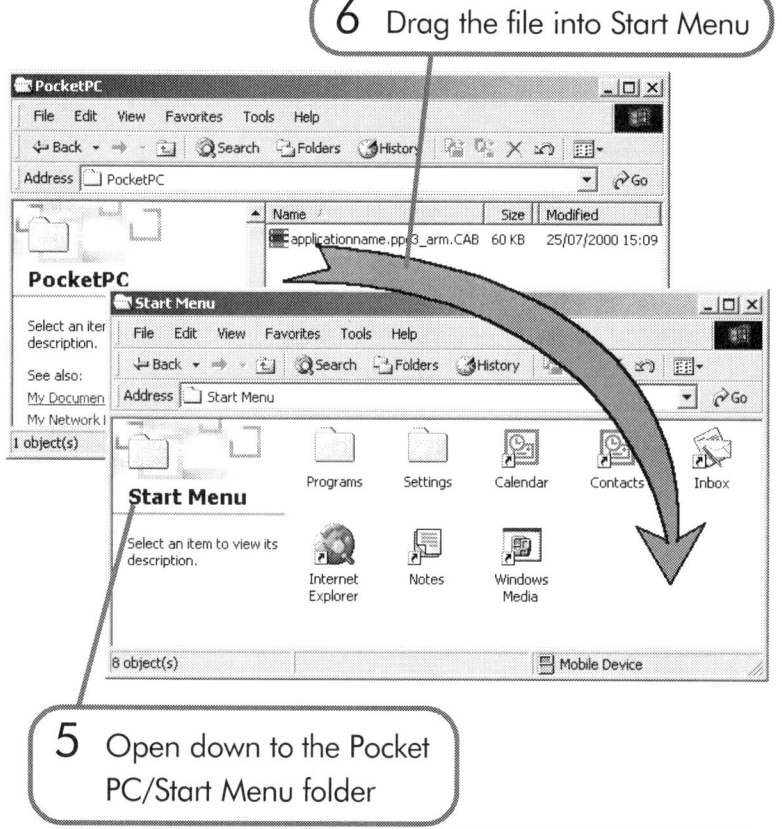

6 Drag the file into Start Menu

5 Open down to the Pocket PC/Start Menu folder

7 Tap Start, then tap the installation file

continued...

5 Open *My Pocket PC*, *Windows* and lastly the *Start Menu* folder.

6 With both windows displayed drag and drop the .CAB file from your PC to your Pocket PC. If you get a warning message saying this document cannot be converted click ok.

7 On your Pocket PC, tap Start – you will now see the .CAB file listed. Tap this and the software will be installed.

Copying data manually

At step 4, where you tapped the Explore button, you were in the *My Documents* folder on your Pocket PC. To install data files follow the process up to this step, then use drag and drop to put your data files into the *My Documents* folder.

For your data to appear in the Pocket PC applications it must be in *My Documents* or just one below it, e.g., *My Documents\work.*

48

Basic steps

1 Connect your Pocket PC to your PC.

2 Run ActiveSync on your PC.

3 Select Tools – Backup/ Restore.

4 Change the name of the backup file or its folder so that you don't override the previous backup.

5 Click OK.

6 Wait while the files are copied to your PC.

Backup and Restore

One task that is often overlooked with all computer systems is the backing up of data. A Pocket PC can be easily backed up on a PC – it's one of the features included in ActiveSync. If you ever lose some data or are unlucky enough to have your Pocket PC stolen, a backup will save you lots of time and frustration.

There are several backup options. These range from backing up every time you connect, through to the manual approach. It will depend on your working practice as to how often you wish to backup your device; I try and backup mine once a week.

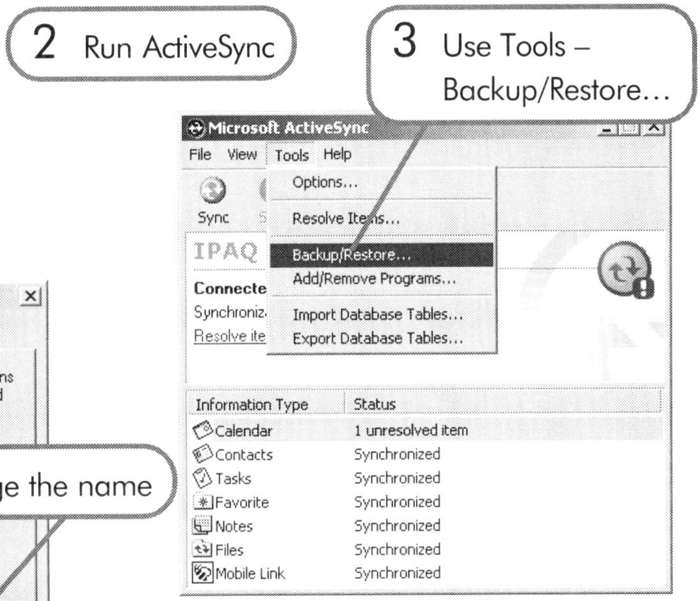

2 Run ActiveSync

3 Use Tools – Backup/Restore...

Microsoft ActiveSync

File View Tools Help

    Options...
Sync   Resolve Items...
IPAQ   Backup/Restore...
        Add/Remove Programs...
Connecte
Synchroniz   Import Database Tables...
Resolve ite   Export Database Tables...

Information Type	Status
Calendar	1 unresolved item
Contacts	Synchronized
Tasks	Synchronized
Favorite	Synchronized
Notes	Synchronized
Files	Synchronized
Mobile Link	Synchronized

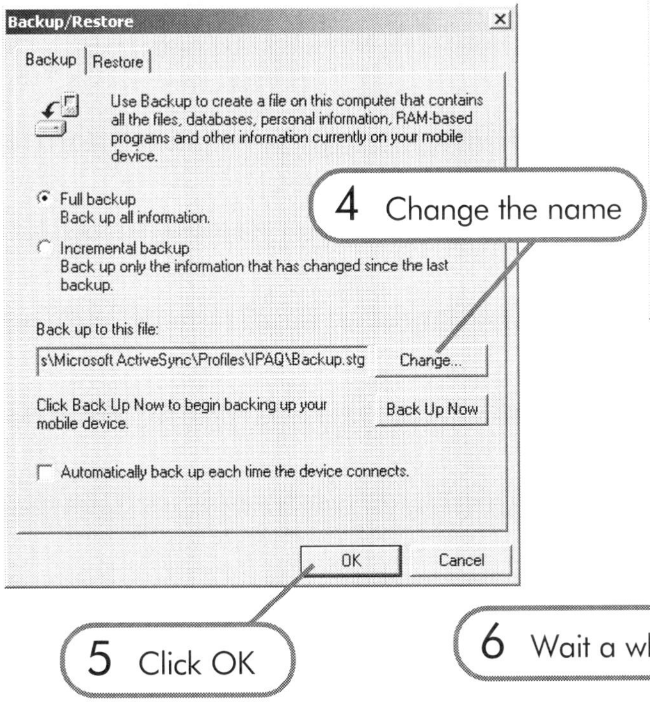

Backup/Restore

Backup | Restore |

Use Backup to create a file on this computer that contains all the files, databases, personal information, RAM-based programs and other information currently on your mobile device.

○ Full backup
  Back up all information.

○ Incremental backup
  Back up only the information that has changed since the last backup.

4 Change the name

Back up to this file:
s\Microsoft ActiveSync\Profiles\IPAQ\Backup.stg   Change...

Click Back Up Now to begin backing up your mobile device.   Back Up Now

☐ Automatically back up each time the device connects.

                    OK   Cancel

5 Click OK

Backup In Progress

Now backing up to 'Backup.stg'
Please do not use the device until backup is finished.

■■■■

Copying: \Program Files\Conduits Technologies Inc.\Pocke

                    Cancel

6 Wait a while

Restoring a backup

In the unlikely event that you need to restore a backup, the only restore option available in ActiveSync is to restore the whole device, erasing all the data currently stored on it. You will be asked several times to confirm the operation before it starts.

This example assumes you have a new Pocket PC or a completely blank one.

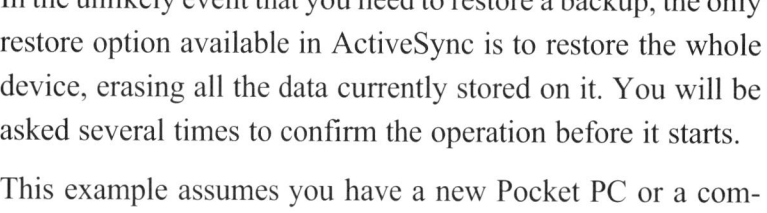

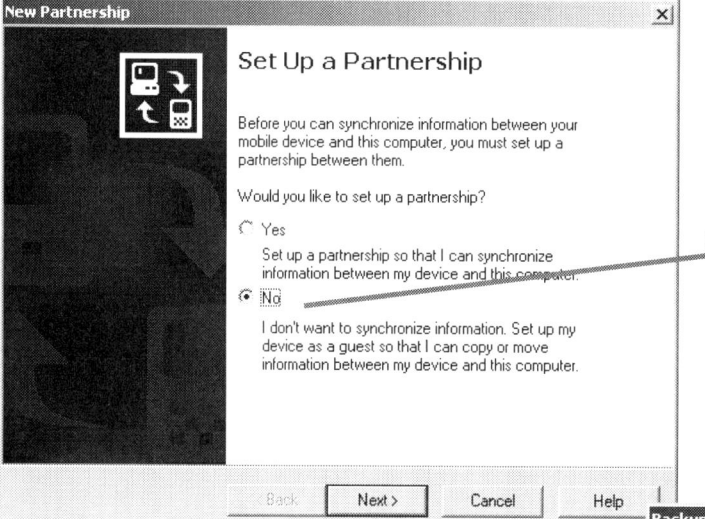

Basic steps

1 Connect up your Pocket PC.

2 The first time that you do this, the New Partnership wizard will run. Select No if you want to restore a backup.

3 In ActiveSync, select Tools – Backup/Restore then Restore Now.

2 Select No when restoring

3 Click Restore Now

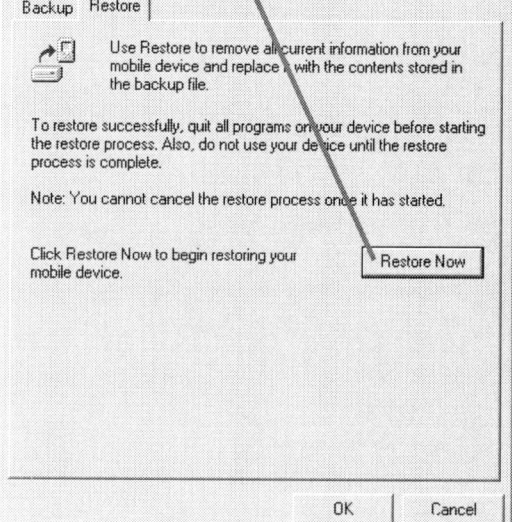

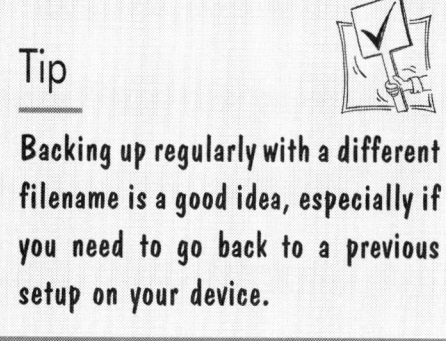

Tip

Backing up regularly with a different filename is a good idea, especially if you need to go back to a previous setup on your device.

4 Select the backup file you wish to restore by selecting the device name or by browsing for the .stg file, and click OK.

5 Click Restore.

6 If you have changed your Country settings you will get an error message when you try to restore. Change the Country settings on your Pocket PC back to what they were and try the restore again.

You will probably have only one device listed here

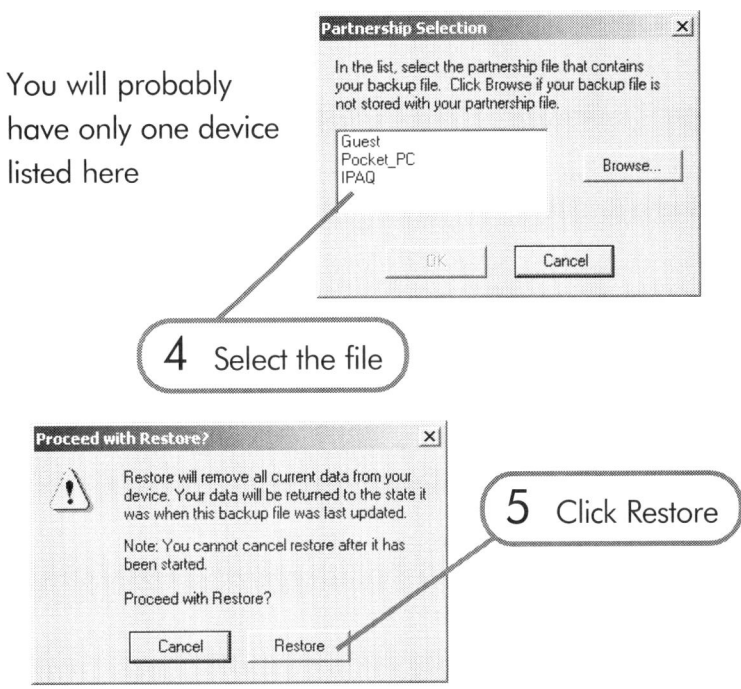

4 Select the file

5 Click Restore

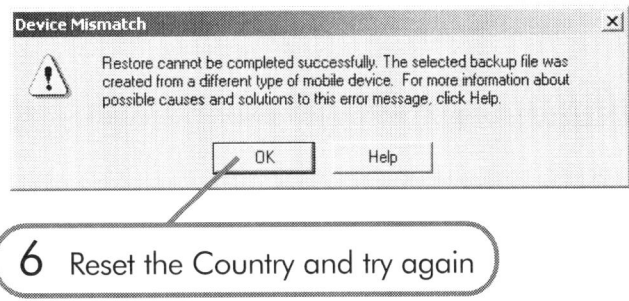

6 Reset the Country and try again

Take note

If you backed up with UK settings and try to restore with the default settings of USA you'll get an error message, titled 'Device Mismatch.' Don't panic!

Tip

Anyware Consulting (http://hometown.aol.com/anyware) sells an application called H/PC Vault, that will allow you to restore individual files from your backup to your Pocket PC.

Synchronization

ActiveSync manages all aspects of the transfer and synchronization of data between your Pocket PC and desktop PC.

You may wish to change some of the synchronization options from their default settings. The most commonly changed are the e-mail synchronization and the number of weeks of calendar appointments that are copied from your PC to Pocket PC.

Calendar

To save space on your Pocket PC, ActiveSync copies the next six months' worth of appointments, but only the previous two weeks' worth. Here's how to change this.

Basic steps

1 On your PC, open ActiveSync.

2 Select Calendar.

3 Select Options.

4 Change the number of weeks the calendar synchronizes.

5 Click OK.

3 Open the Calendar Options

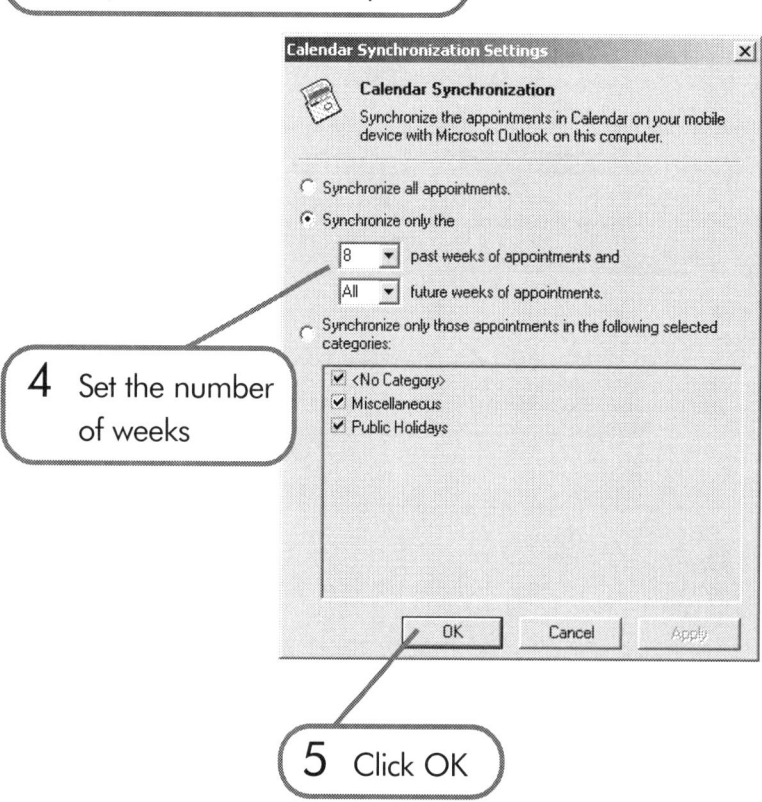

4 Set the number of weeks

5 Click OK

Take note

After two weeks have passed, the older meetings are removed from your Pocket PC, but they remain on your PC.

Data synchronization

The desktop icon for my synchronization folder (above) and the open folder (below)

To have data automatically copied across from your Pocket PC to your desktop PC you need to enable the **File** option (see the next page). When you do this, a special folder is created on the desktop of your PC, called '*[name of your device] My Documents*', e.g., '*Pocket PC My Documents.*' Double-clicking on this icon will reveal a copy of the files that are on your device.

● If you save files to this folder, they will automatically appear on your device when you next synchronize.

● If you delete files from this folder, they will disappear from your Pocket PC when you next synchronize.

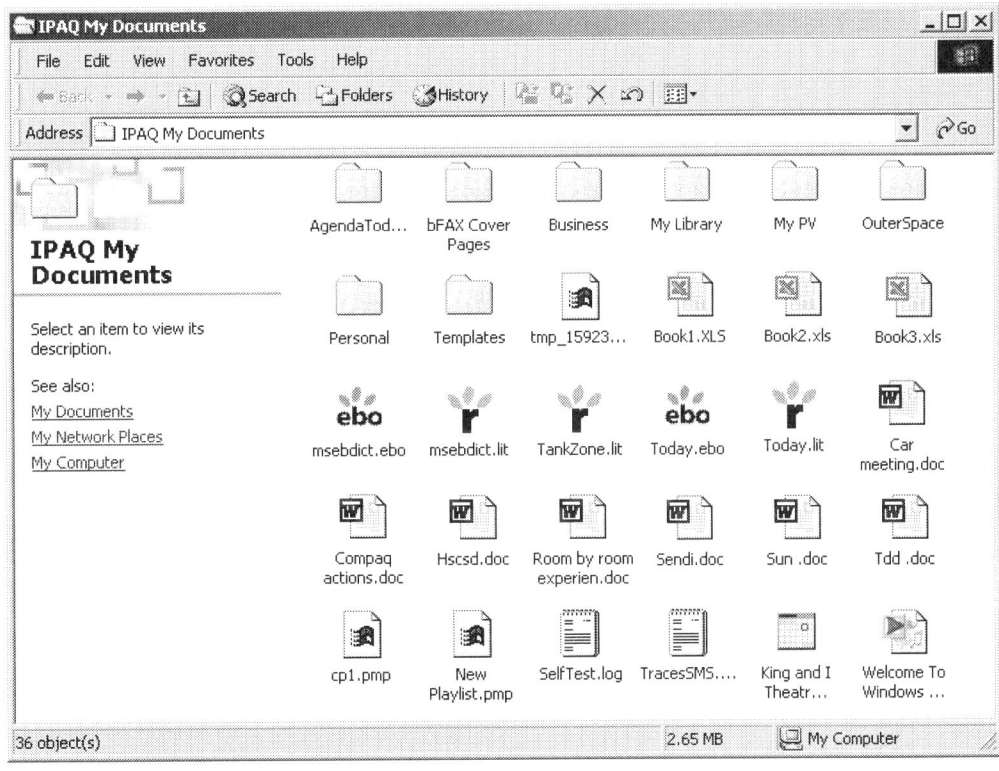

Enabling File synchronization

File synchronization is one of the ActiveSync options, and as the default is 'off,' you will need to turn it on. Do it while you are selecting the applications to synchronize.

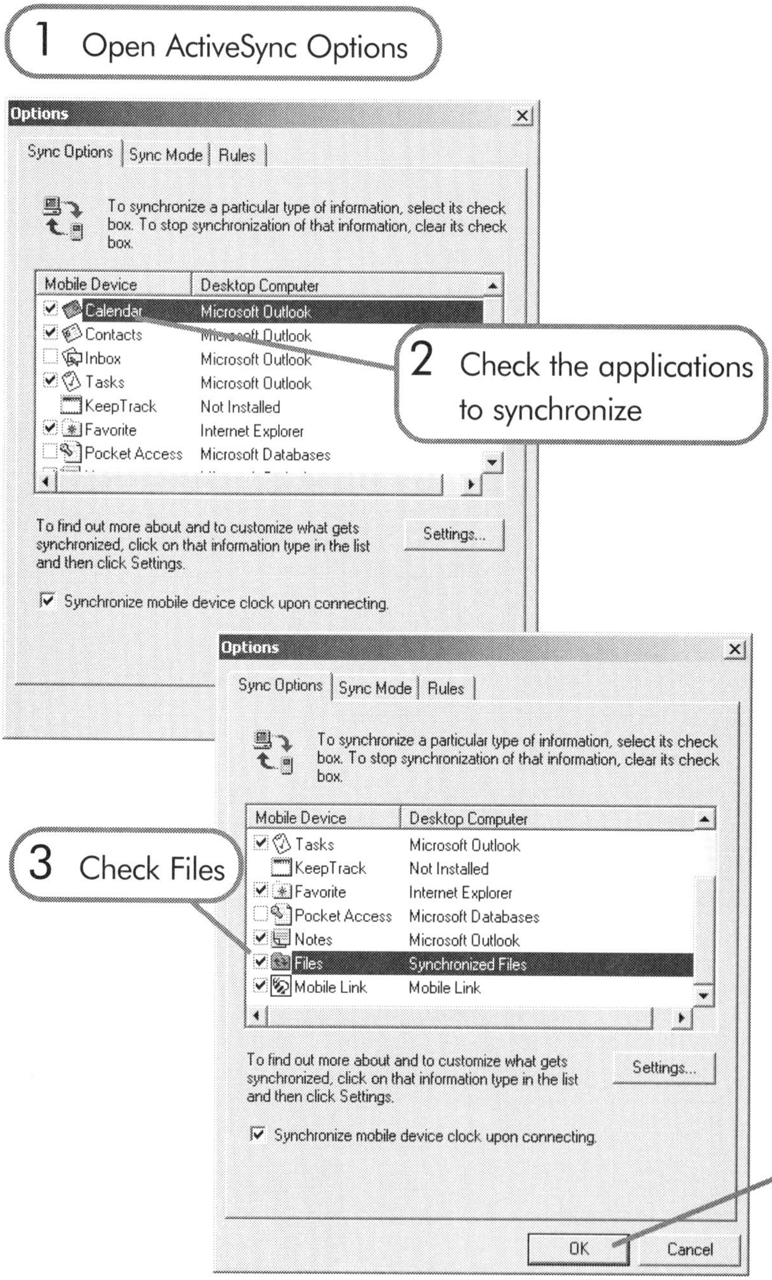

1 Open ActiveSync Options

Options

Sync Options | Sync Mode | Rules

To synchronize a particular type of information, select its check box. To stop synchronization of that information, clear its check box.

Mobile Device	Desktop Computer
☑ Calendar	Microsoft Outlook
☑ Contacts	Microsoft Outlook
☐ Inbox	Microsoft Outlook
☑ Tasks	Microsoft Outlook
KeepTrack	Not Installed
☑ Favorite	Internet Explorer
☐ Pocket Access	Microsoft Databases

2 Check the applications to synchronize

To find out more about and to customize what gets synchronized, click on that information type in the list and then click Settings. **Settings...**

☑ Synchronize mobile device clock upon connecting.

Options

Sync Options | Sync Mode | Rules

To synchronize a particular type of information, select its check box. To stop synchronization of that information, clear its check box.

3 Check Files

Mobile Device	Desktop Computer
☑ Tasks	Microsoft Outlook
KeepTrack	Not Installed
☑ Favorite	Internet Explorer
☐ Pocket Access	Microsoft Databases
☑ Notes	Microsoft Outlook
☑ Files	Synchronized Files
☑ Mobile Link	Mobile Link

To find out more about and to customize what gets synchronized, click on that information type in the list and then click Settings. **Settings...**

☑ Synchronize mobile device clock upon connecting.

4 Click OK

OK | Cancel

1 On the PC, open ActiveSync and select Options.

2 On the Sync Options tab, select the applications you'd like to synchronize between your PC and Pocket PC.

3 Scroll down and tick Files to enable data synchronization.

4 Click OK.

❑ On the next synchronization e-mail data will be synchronized.

Take note

If receive a large number of e-mails, then your device can get very full if you synchronize several days' worth of e-mail.

Ethernet cards

If you have a high-speed Internet connection at home or work, you may wish to connect up your Pocket PC over a high-speed connection, such as an Ethernet networking card.

A lot of computer departments have particular rules and guidelines for connecting devices up to the corporate network, so always seek assistance of a member of that department when dealing with any network issues you may have.

Before you start configuring the networking adaptor on your Pocket PC there are several items that you'll need to check with your computer department. Is there an available port for your Ethernet connection and does it operate at the same speed as the adaptor for your mobile device? You should also ask if they support DHCP (Dynamic Host Configuration Protocol) and if you have a WINS (Windows Internet Name Service) server on your network. DHCP and WINS servers will greatly simplify the task of connecting your Pocket PC up to the network.

Connecting over Ethernet

I'll cover the easy way first and then look at the way to handle the details that you may need if you are experiencing problems.

Once you have set up a network connection to your PC you will be able to perform the functions such as synchronizing and installing software much quicker than over a serial link.

Setting up a wireless LAN is very similar to a regular LAN, except you have the added bonus of not having to find any connectors to plug your cables into.

I've shown the use of both the Compaq Wireless LAN and Provim Wireless cards on the following pages, but any supported Ethernet card – wired or wireless – will work.

2 Start Network
Connections

5 Tap ok

Settings   01:51 (ok)

Network Connections

The system uses these credentials to access
remote network resources. If these
credentials fail you will be prompted for a new
set of credentials to access the network
resource.

User name: craigp

Password: ********

Domain:

Adapters | Identification

123	1	2	3	4	5	6	7	8	9	0	-	=	←
Tab	q	w	e	r	t	y	u	i	o	p	[	]
CAP	a	s	d	f	g	h	j	k	l	;	'
Shift	z	x	c	v	b	n	m	,	.	/	↵
Ctl	áü	`	\						↓	↑	←	→

4 Enter your details

3 Tap Identification

6 Start Connections

Settings   00:01

AvantGo   Modem   Network
Connect

PC

7 Run ActiveSync

8 Select the Network
Connection

9 Check the name
and tap Connect

Personal | System | Connections

Connecting to Desktop

Checking for partnership with this
computer. Please wait...

Cancel

Connection Status

Connected, synchronizing...

241/242: Searching for updated Web
pages...

☐ Disconnect when complete

Cancel Sync   Disconnect

The connection can be
broken if necessary

1 Plug a supported
Ethernet Card into your
Pocket PC.

2 Tap Start, Settings,
Network Connections.

3 Go to the Identification
tab.

4 Enter your User name
and Password for the
network, and the Do-
main name if required.

5 Tap ok.

❏ To connect to your PC

6 Tap Start, Programs,
Connections.

7 Tap ActiveSync.

8 Select the Network
Connection from the
drop-down list.

9 Check the Connect To
machine name and tap
Connect.

❏ The Pocket PC will
establish the connection
and transfer the files.

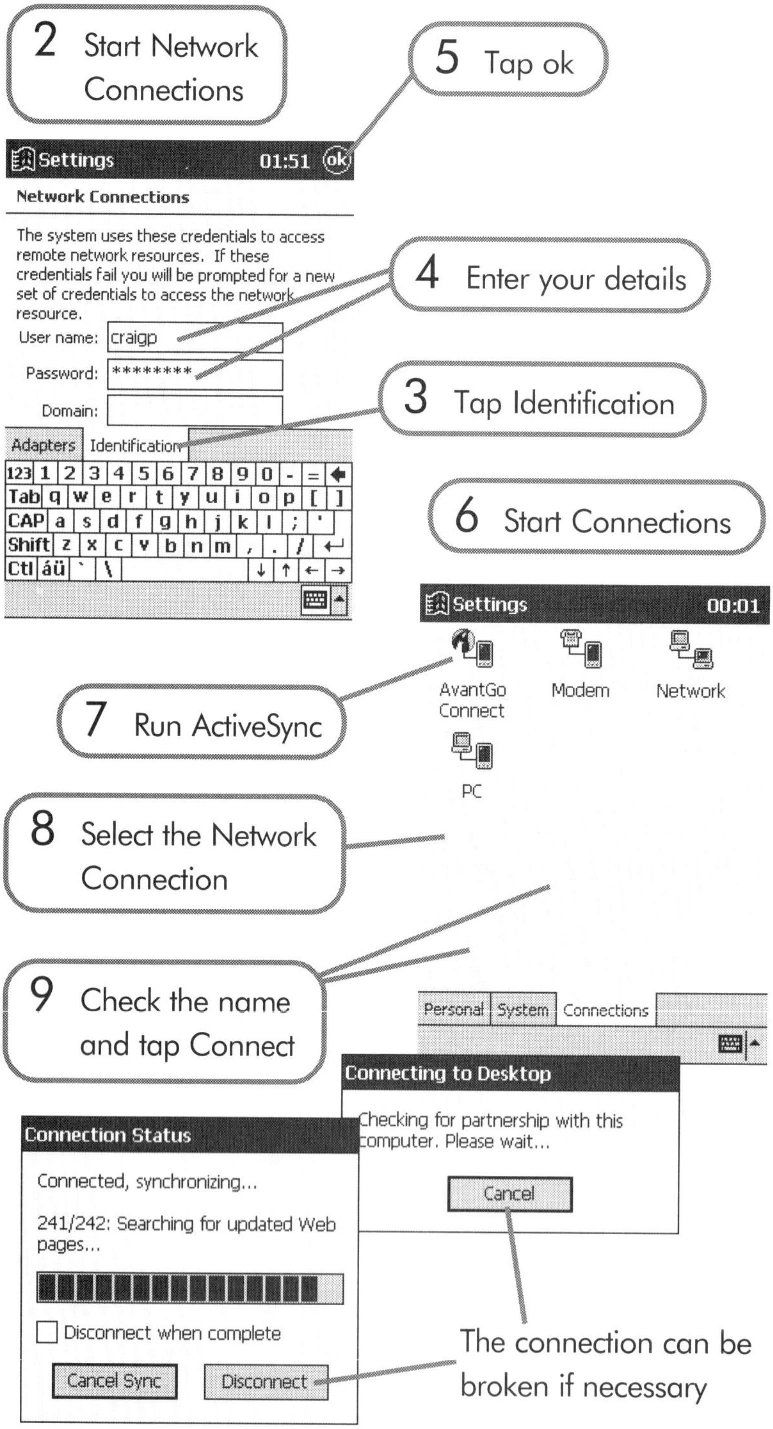

Basic steps

1 Plug a supported Ethernet card into your Pocket PC.

2 For a fixed IP Address, tap Use specific IP address and enter the address and the subnet mask. Leave the default gateway blank unless advised otherwise.

3 Tap the Name Servers tab.

4 Enter the numbers for the DNS and WINS servers if used.

5 Tap ok.

6 Complete the Identification tab in Network Connections, as before.

Tip

Network cards take a lot of power, so it is best to always use an AC adaptor when you want to use them in your Pocket PC.

Manual setup

You need to find out, then enter the following details:

● The IP address of your PC (the one with ActiveSync).

● Your network's subnet mask and default gateway.

● IP address of any WINS or DNS servers, if used.

● Whether your Pocket PC will use a fixed IP address or be allocated one each time using DHCP. If using a fixed IP address, you need to get it from the IT department.

● The port on your network to connect your device to.

● The user name and password of the PC you wish to access.

● Your machine's network name, which could be something obscure like CPMLT111100 or your name – it depends on how the IT department set up your PC.

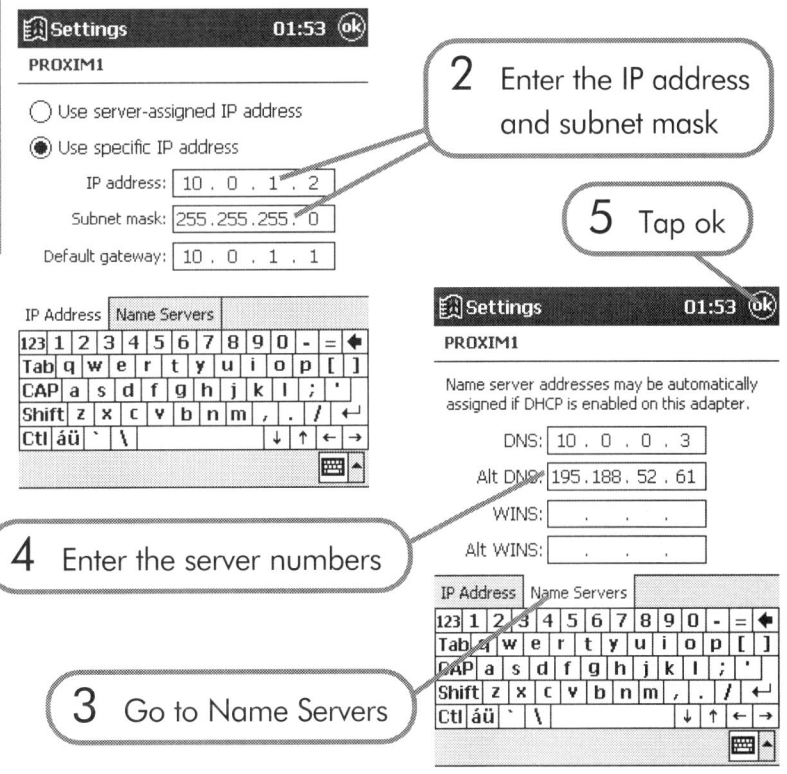

Connecting to the Internet

Basic steps

1 Tap Start, Programs, Connections.

2 Tap Modem settings near the bottom of the screen.

3 Tap New Connection...

Before you can connect to the Internet you will need:

● A modem and telephone line;

● An Internet Service Provider (ISP)

● The dial-up telephone number of your ISP and your login name and password.

To enable you to connect to the Internet from your Pocket PC we will be using a built-in feature, the connections application.

Having connected to several different ISPs, I have found that there are slight differences in how the connection actually works, so if the first method doesn't work for you don't despair, the second method should get you connected.

Dial-up connections

In this example, I'm using a Plug-in Compact Flash modem; later in this chapter, I show you how to get connected using a mobile phone and infrared. This method assumes that your ISP doesn't require you to know such details as the DNS (Domain Name Servers) settings or for you to login manually.

Take note

Not all Pocket PCs support plug-in modems. To ensure compatibility you should check with your hardware vendor.

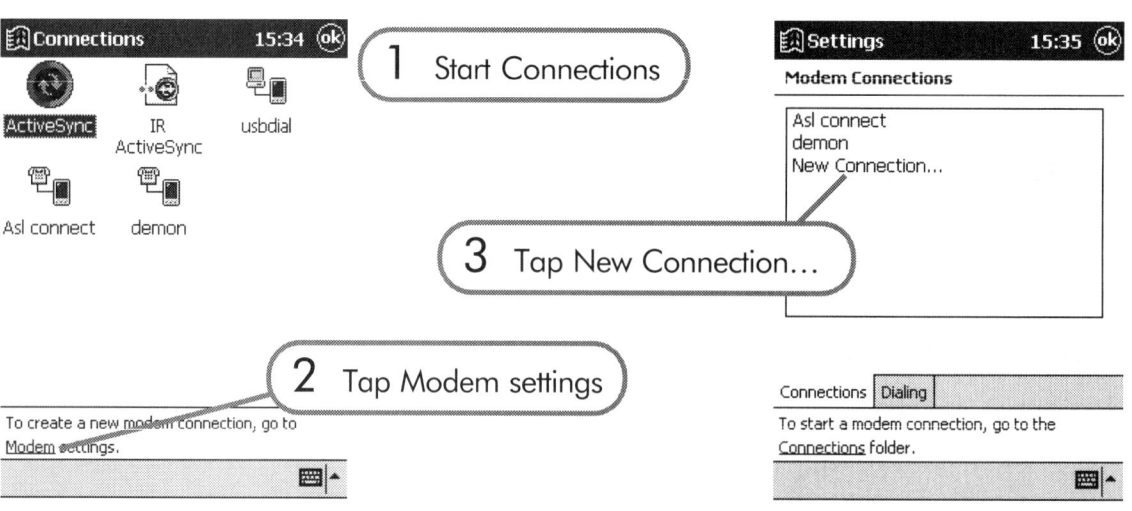

1 Start Connections

3 Tap New Connection...

2 Tap Modem settings

4 Enter a Name for the connection.

5 Select the modem if it isn't displayed.

6 Make sure the Baud Rate: is set to the highest your modem can manage, e.g., 57,600 for a 56K modem, and tap Next.

7 Enter the area code/ phone number to dial into your ISP and tap Next.

8 Set the Cancel and Wait options, then tap Finish.

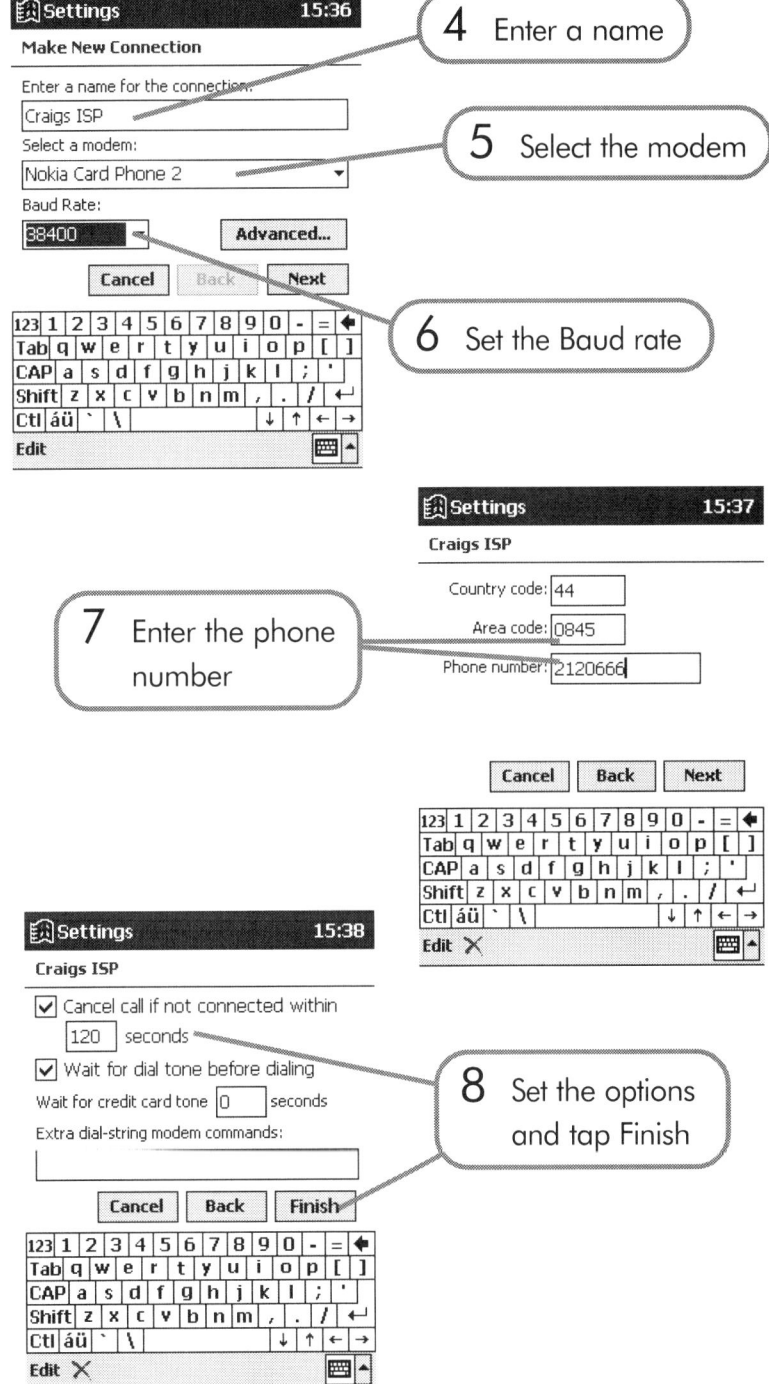

Tip

If you are going to be connected with your modem for long periods, it is recommended that you plug in AC power.

Manual connection

If your ISP doesn't support the easy way, then you'll have to login manually each time. Here's how to set that up.

Your TCP/IP settings will be different to those shown below as each ISP has its own unique DNS settings, and some of these companies assign them automatically – if in doubt try it first, and then check with your Internet Service Provider if you are having connection troubles.

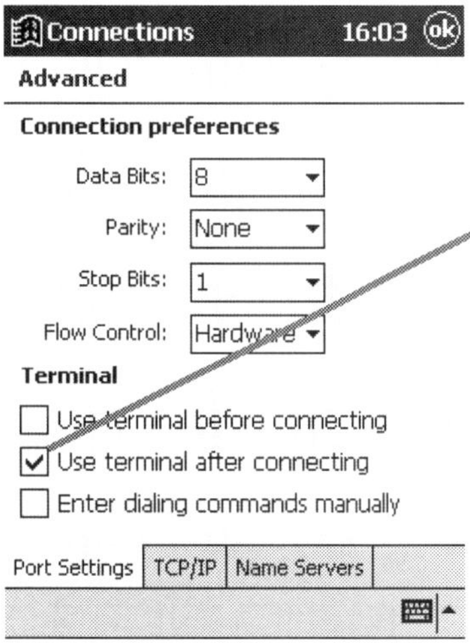

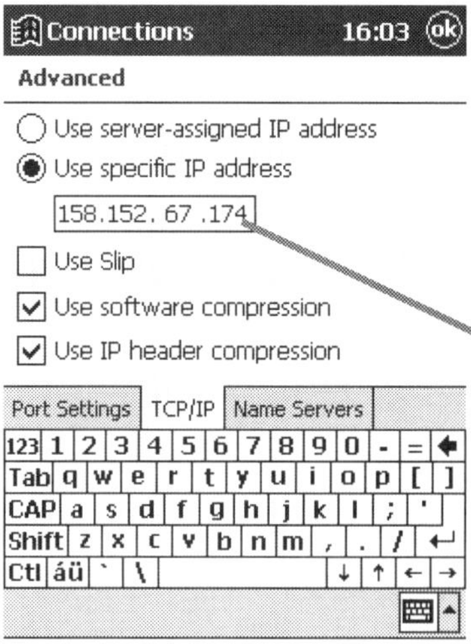

1 Follow steps 1 to 6 on pages 58 and 59, but at the Connection dialog box tap the Advanced button.

2 Check Use terminal after connecting.

3 Tap the TCP/IP tab and enter your details.

4 Enter the numbers given to you by your ISP in the Name Servers tab – usually just the DNS and Alt (Alternative) DNS settings boxes – and tap ok.

5 Tap ok and complete as on page 59.

📖 Connections   16:03 (ok)

Advanced

Connection preferences

Data Bits:	8 ▼
Parity:	None ▼
Stop Bits:	1 ▼
Flow Control:	Hardware ▼

Terminal

☐ Use terminal before connecting
☑ Use terminal after connecting
☐ Enter dialing commands manually

Port Settings | TCP/IP | Name Servers

2 Turn on Use terminal after connecting

📖 Connections   16:03 (ok)

Advanced

○ Use server-assigned IP address
◉ Use specific IP address
    158.152. 67 .174
☐ Use Slip
☑ Use software compression
☑ Use IP header compression

Port Settings | TCP/IP | Name Servers

3 Enter the TCP/IP tab details

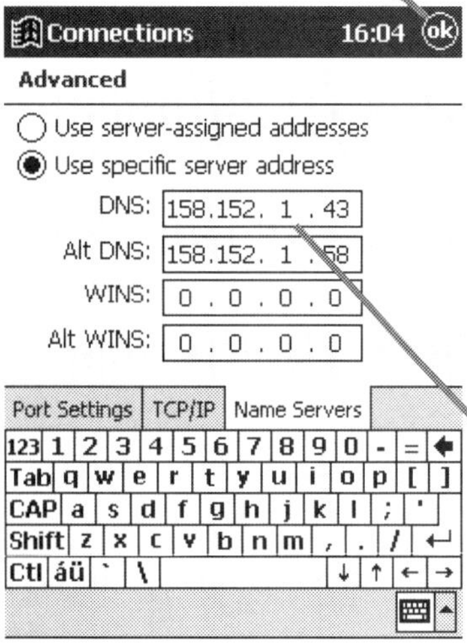

---

5 Tap ok

📖 Connections   16:04 (ok)

Advanced

○ Use server-assigned addresses
◉ Use specific server address
    DNS: 158.152. 1 . 43
    Alt DNS: 158.152. 1 .58
    WINS: 0 . 0 . 0 . 0
    Alt WINS: 0 . 0 . 0 . 0

Port Settings | TCP/IP | Name Servers

4 Enter the Name Servers numbers

Basic steps

1 Tap Start, Programs, Connections.

2 Tap on the connection you have just created.

3 Enter your User name and Password.

4 Check the Phone number and the Dial from location.

5 Tap Connect.

6 When the connection is completed, tap Hide Status to remove the message box. You can now browse the web or check your e-mail.

❑ I'm lucky enough to have an ISP that supports Microsoft PAP/CHAP user authentication. The user name and password are passed onto the ISP when I dial in, so that I'm logged in quickly and efficiently.

Testing the connection

Here is where it can sometimes go wrong! If you get connected and the line drops shortly after (usually 15–20 seconds), then check out the next section.

If you don't get the 'User Authenticated' then the login didn't complete properly.

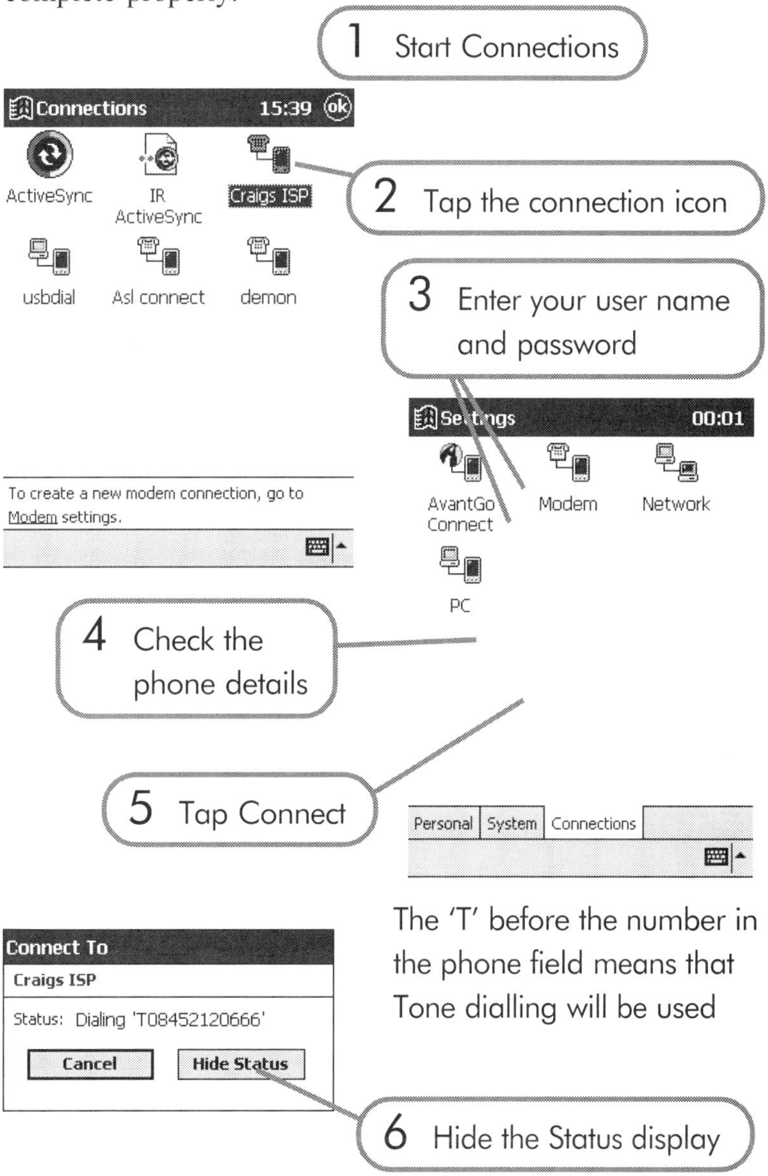

1 Start Connections

2 Tap the connection icon

3 Enter your user name and password

4 Check the phone details

5 Tap Connect

The 'T' before the number in the phone field means that Tone dialling will be used

6 Hide the Status display

Manual login

If your ISP doesn't support automatic login, you will have to do it manually. You must have set up for manual connection (see page 60) to do this.

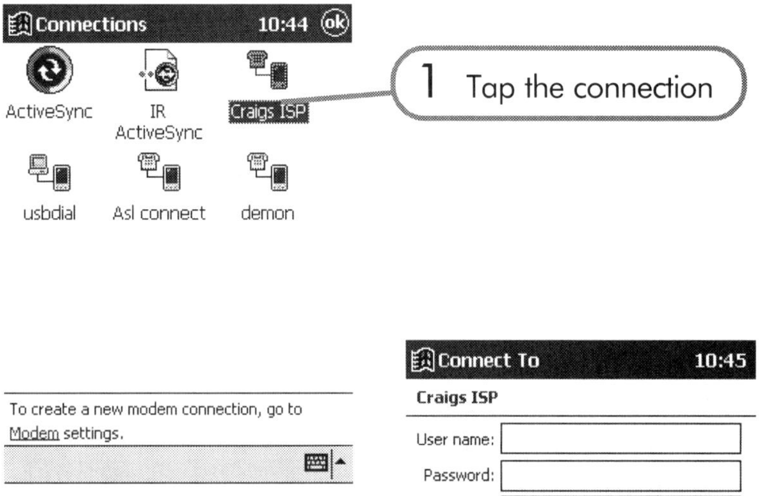

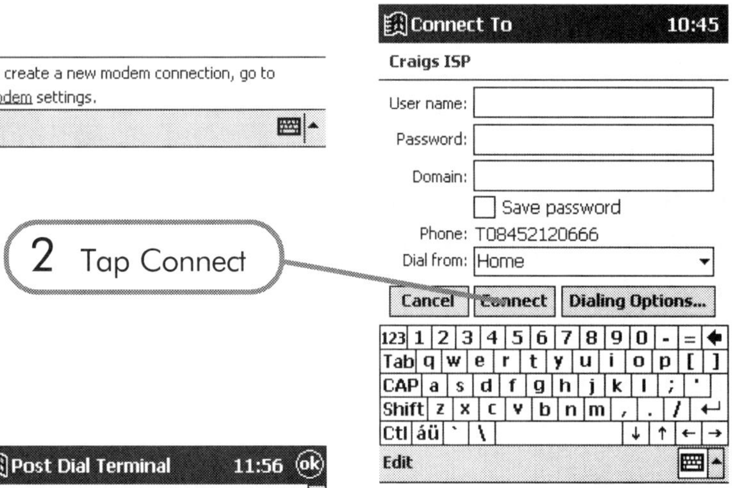

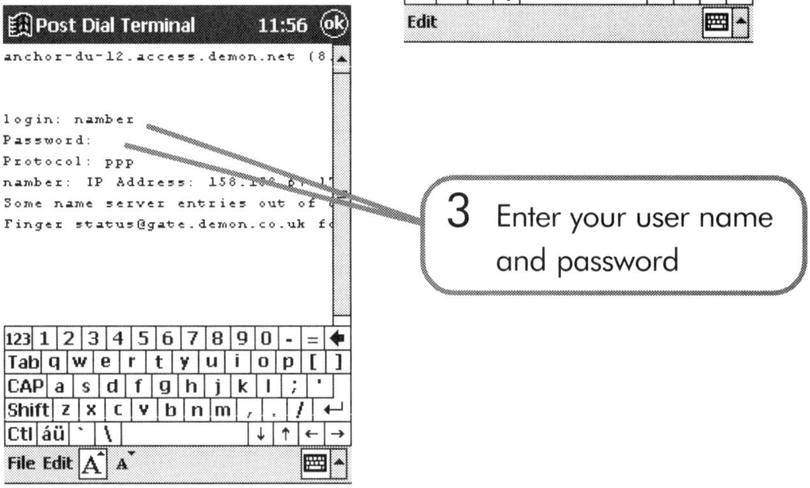

Connections   10:44 (ok)

ActiveSync   IR ActiveSync   Craigs ISP

usbdial   Asl connect   demon

> 1 Tap the connection

To create a new modem connection, go to Modem settings.

> 2 Tap Connect

Connect To   10:45

Craigs ISP

User name:
Password:
Domain:
☐ Save password
Phone: T08452120666
Dial from: Home

Cancel   Connect   Dialing Options...

123 1 2 3 4 5 6 7 8 9 0 - = ←
Tab q w e r t y u i o p [ ]
CAP a s d f g h j k l ; '
Shift z x c v b n m , . / ↵
Ctl áü ` \   ↓ ↑ ← →
Edit

Post Dial Terminal   11:56 (ok)

anchor-du-12.access.demon.net (8

login: namber
Password:
Protocol: ppp
namber: IP Address: 158.
Some name server entries out of
Finger status@gate.demon.co.uk f

> 3 Enter your user name and password

123 1 2 3 4 5 6 7 8 9 0 - = ←
Tab q w e r t y u i o p [ ]
CAP a s d f g h j k l ; '
Shift z x c v b n m , . / ↵
Ctl áü ` \   ↓ ↑ ← →
File Edit A A

Basic steps

1 Tap the connection icon.

2 Leave the User name and Password fields blank and tap Connect.

3 You will usually be presented with a blank screen, bring up the software keyboard and press [Enter] then login with your user name and password at the prompts.

4 Tap the ok button in the top right hand corner of the screen when you see 'garbage' appear – it's just the connection at work.

Wireless connections

With the growing speed of cellular connections, getting connected without wires is easier than ever before. Where in the world you live and the data capabilities of your mobile phone provider will govern how fast you can connect wirelessly.

In this first example I'm using a Nokia high speed PCMCIA card in a Compaq iPAQ machine with its optional jacket. This gives me a wirefree connection to the Internet or corporate network. Depending on the cellular network that you are using, a plug-in card and drivers may or may not be available for your Pocket PC. I'm connecting using the cellular operator Orange in the UK, in these examples.

This particular card and operator requires a couple of special settings to ensure that I connect at the highest possible speed. Follow the process for setting up any plug-in modem.

Modem connections and cellular phones

A few ISPs require special settings to allow your Pocket PC to talk to them. The settings that need to be manually entered are called DNS or Domain Name Servers.

A DNS machine is one of the magical secrets of the World Wide Web, and with so many Web servers on the Internet today, without their relatively easy to remember names you'd have to know the unique number of each server to be able to see them.

If every time you wanted to access a Web site you had to enter addresses like **http://194.128.1.1**, then it's highly unlikely that the World Wide Web would have been so popular. DNS machines translate names such as **www.pocketpchelp.com** to those unique numbers, so you don't need to remember them.

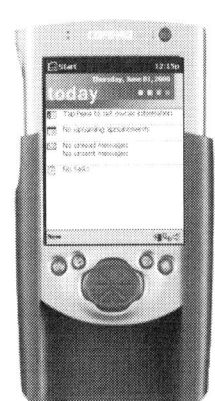

Compaq iPAQ with
its optional jacket

Take note

As with other modem connections you should check with the hardware vendor and your cellular operator to ensure compatibility. Extra Pocket PC software may be required.

DNS server entries

For the Internet Service Providers that don't automatically set these numbers up here's how to do it the manual way. These DNS entries are called the IP (Internet Protocol) addresses of the DNS servers.

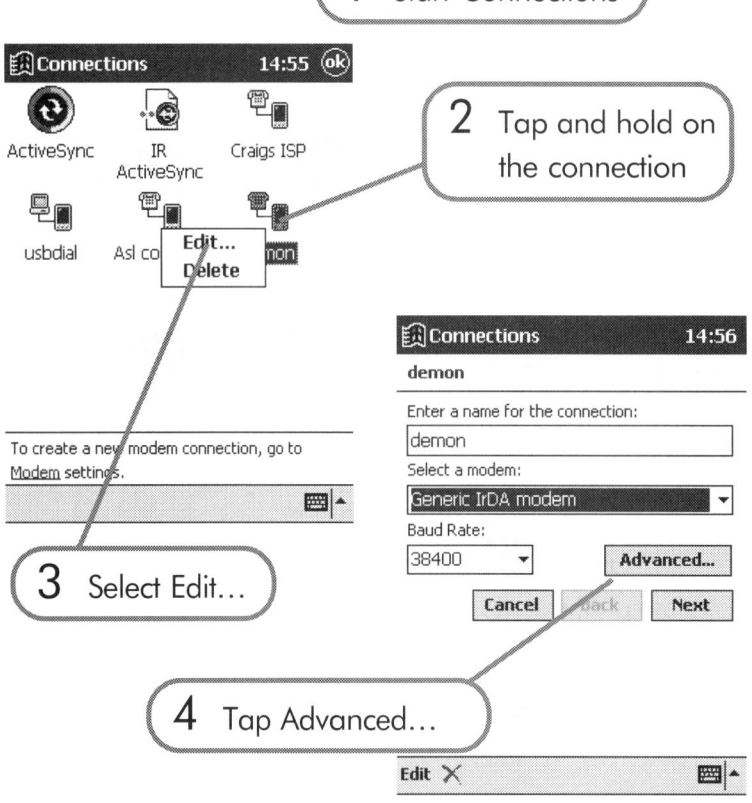

1 Start Connections

2 Tap and hold on the connection

3 Select Edit...

4 Tap Advanced...

1 Tap Start, Programs, Connections.

2 Tap and hold on the Connection icon you wish to change.

3 Tap the Edit... option.

4 Tap the Advanced... button.

5 Tap the Name Servers tab.

6 Tap the Use specific server address box

7 Enter the IP Addresses given to you by your Internet Service Provider in the DNS and Alt DNS fields.

8 Tap ok when done.

9 Tap Next twice then tap Finish.

Tip

Call your ISP's support department or check their Web site to get the IP addresses of the Domain Name Servers.

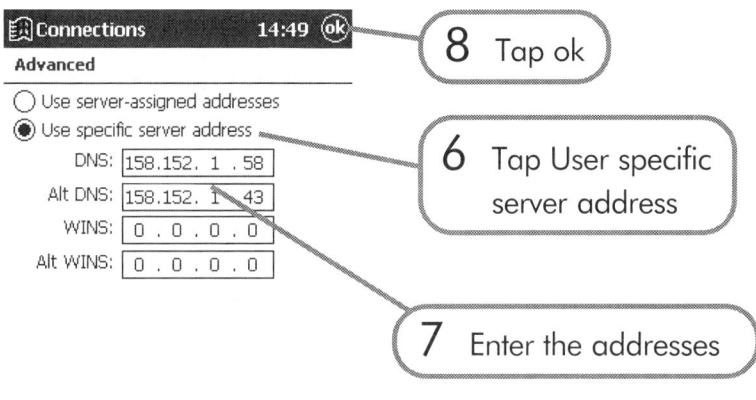

8 Tap ok

6 Tap User specific server address

7 Enter the addresses

The TCPIP screen allows you to switch off compression or specify a specific IP address.

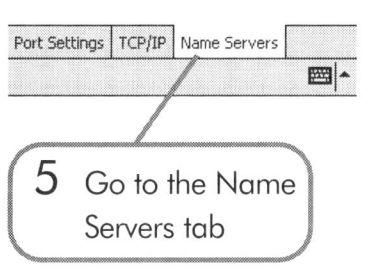

5 Go to the Name Servers tab

Sometimes it is necessary to manually specify the Domain Name Servers (or DNS) that your connection must use to resolve web sites correctly.

Connections 14:48 (ok)

Advanced

(•) Use server-assigned IP address
( ) Use specific IP address

158.152. 67 .174

[ ] Use Slip
[✓] Use software compression
[✓] Use IP header compression

Port Settings | TCP/IP | Name Servers

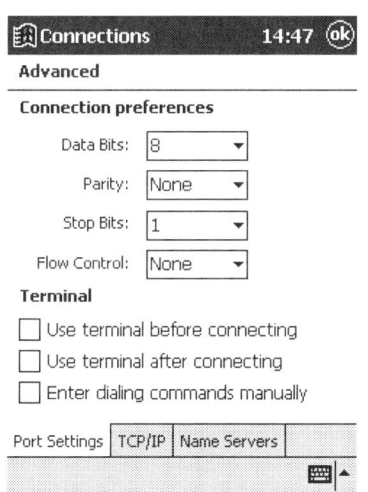

The Port Settings is the screen where you can set options such as using the terminal window to dial in manually.

Take note

If connecting to a corporate network, you may need to enter details in the WINS Server fields instead or as well as the DNS Fields.

Pocket Internet Explorer

Pocket Internet Explorer (IE) is a fully featured Web browser – just because the screen is small, doesn't mean that you can't browse the Web on your Pocket PC.

Address Bar   Recently viewed pages

Go button

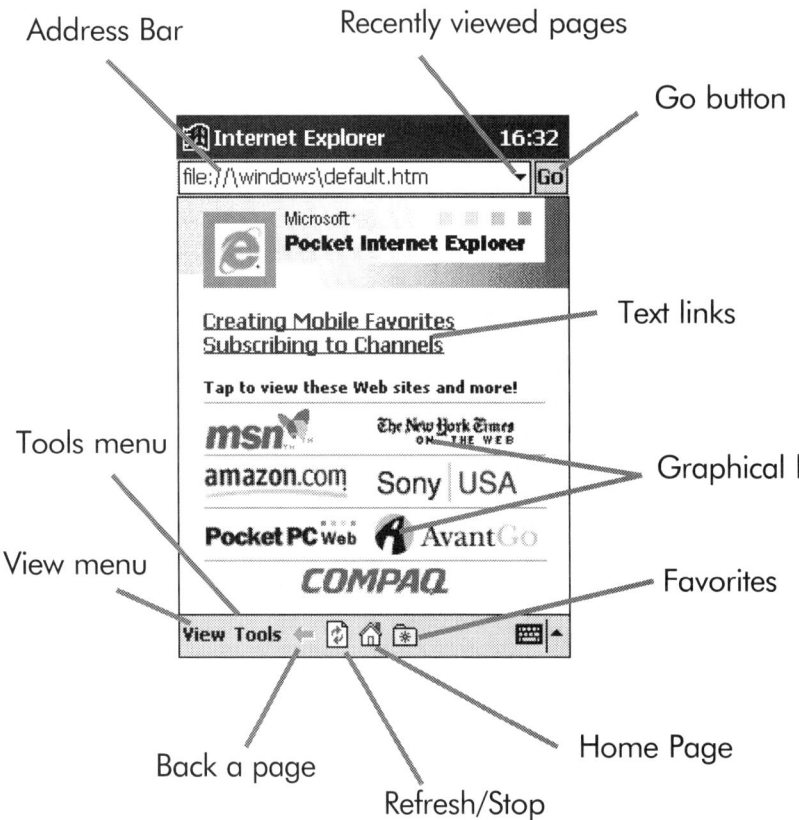

Text links

Graphical links

Tools menu

View menu

Favorites

Back a page

Refresh/Stop

Home Page

Tip

On some machines, the Address Bar, where you would normally type in the Internet address, is hidden. To enable it, tap View, Address Bar.

Take note

The Refresh icon changes to the Stop icon when IE is busy downloading.

Tip

Images on the Pocket IE Home Page are hyperlinks and you can tap on them to take you to other pages.

66

Fit to Screen

1 Tap Start.

2 Tap Internet Explorer.

3 Tap View.

4 Tap Fit to Screen.

❑ Fit to Screen can be switched off to show the Web page in its full size but you will then have to use the scroll bars to see all the content correctly.

When viewing Internet sites on a desktop PC the screen is much bigger and this fact hasn't gone unnoticed to Microsoft. When they designed Pocket Internet Explorer, they built in a unique feature that intelligently resizes the content being displayed and re-sizes it as best it can to fit the screen.

Here's how to use it.

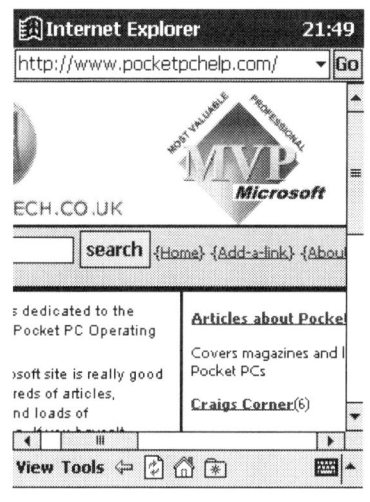

2 Start Interent Explorer

Fit to screen is disabled so the picture is quite large

Take note

Not all Web pages work with Fit to Screen – graphics are typically displayed very small.

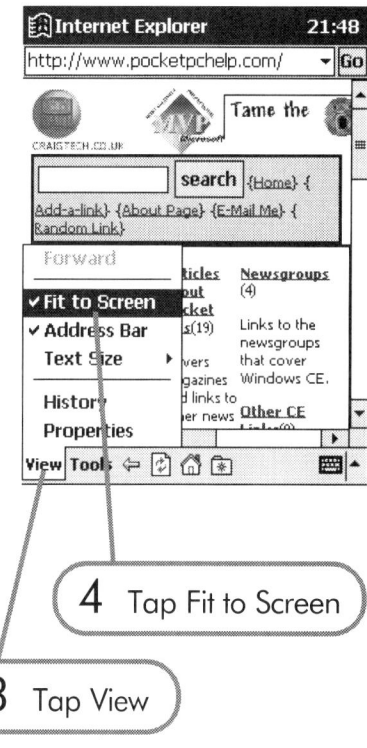

4 Tap Fit to Screen

3 Tap View

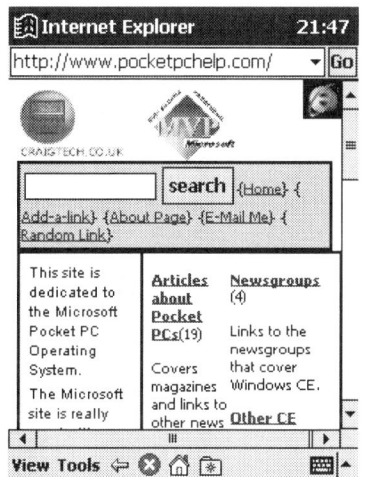

Screen is nicely resized with fit to screen enabled

Mobile Favorites

The Favorites option within Pocket Internet Explorer is very powerful – unlike previous versions of Internet Explorer for Windows CE this one allows you to synchronize your desktop Favorites with your device. Synchronizing Favorites has lots of advantages – I find the most useful is that I don't have to remember whether I saved the Favorite on my Pocket PC or desktop PC.

Another feature is that when viewing Internet sites on your PC, if you save one as a Mobile Favorite then its content is copied to your Pocket PC the next time you synchronize with your PC.

1 On your PC using Internet Explorer browse to any Web site.

2 Click the Create Mobile Favorite button.

3 Give the page a name or description.

4 If the page gets updated regularly, you can schedule how often it should be updated.

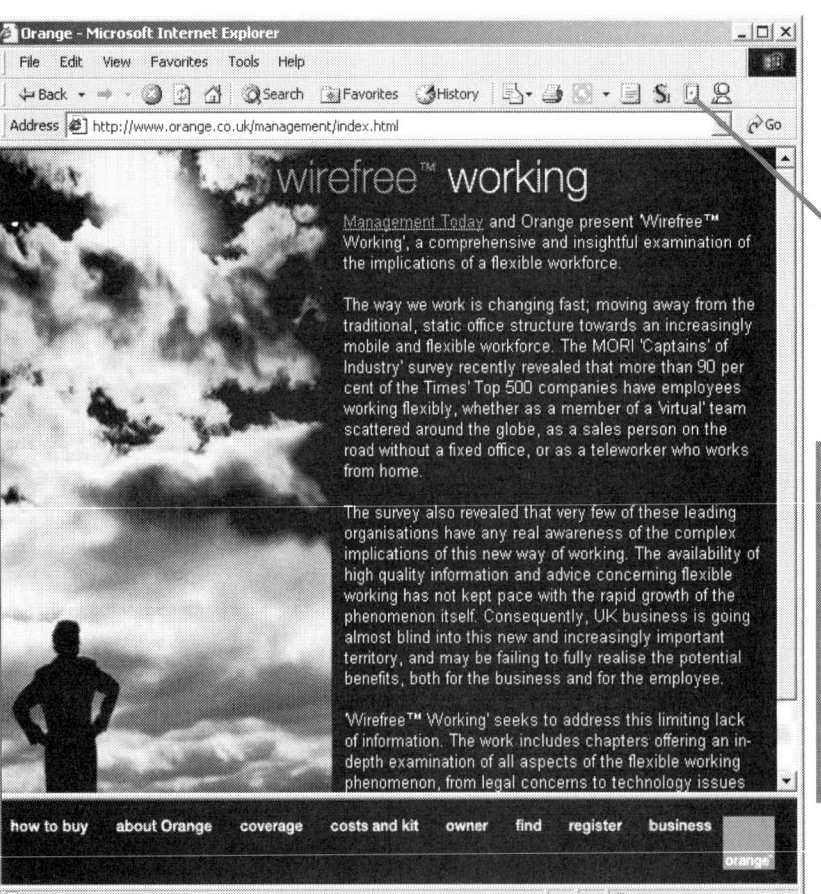

2 Click Create Mobile Favorite

Take note

You can read Mobile favorites even when you are not connected to the Internet.

5 Click OK.

6 On the next synchronization of your Pocket PC, when you tap the Favorites icon in Pocket Internet Explorer you'll see the recently added link in bold.

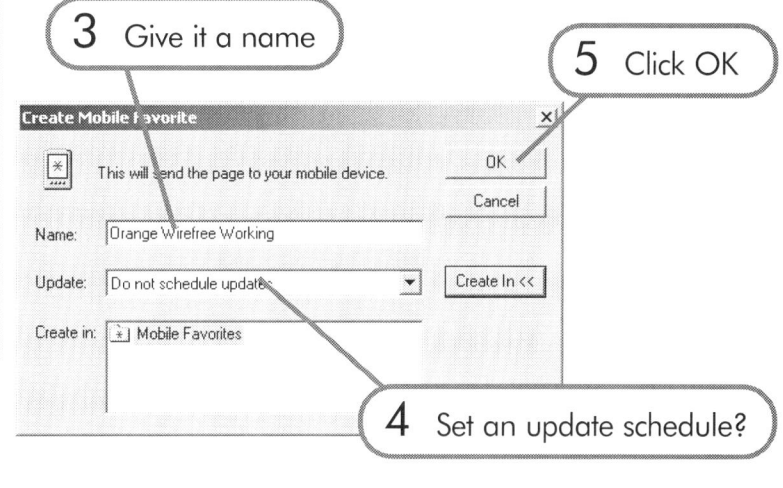

3 Give it a name

5 Click OK

Create Mobile Favorite

This will send the page to your mobile device.

OK

Cancel

Name: Orange Wirefree Working

Update: Do not schedule update

Create In <<

Create in: Mobile Favorites

4 Set an update schedule?

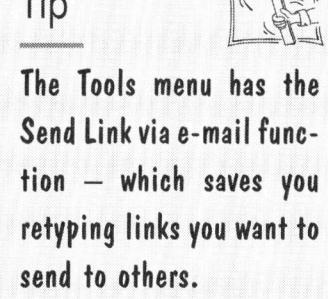
Content listed in bold means it can be browsed offline – older links are also listed, but cannot be browsed

6 View it on your Pocket PC

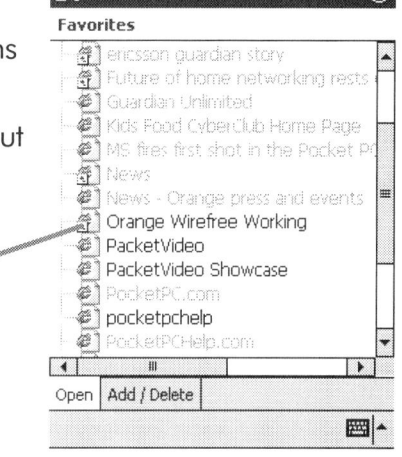

Internet Explorer   16:44 ok

Favorites

ericsson guardian story
Future of home networking rests
Guardian Unlimited
Kids Food CyberClub Home Page
MS fires first shot in the Pocket PC
News
News - Orange press and events
Orange Wirefree Working
PacketVideo
PacketVideo Showcase
PocketPC.com
pocketpchelp
PocketPCHelp.com

Open | Add / Delete

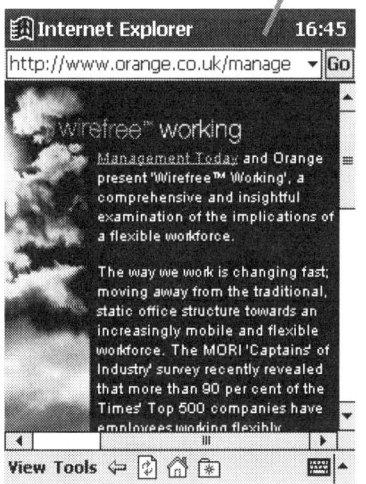

Internet Explorer   16:45

http://www.orange.co.uk/manage ▼ Go

wirefree™ working

Management Today and Orange present 'Wirefree™ Working', a comprehensive and insightful examination of the implications of a flexible workforce.

The way we work is changing fast; moving away from the traditional, static office structure towards an increasingly mobile and flexible workforce. The MORI 'Captains' of Industry' survey recently revealed that more than 90 per cent of the Times' Top 500 companies have employees working flexibly

View Tools

Internet options

In the **General** options you can choose to delete temporary files, clear the History of links you've visited and change your home page.

The **Connections** options is where you would set up your Pocket PC to allow it to connect automatically to the Internet via a dial-up connection, or to use a proxy server. These are normally used by companies – check with your computer helpdesk for the settings if you need to set this option.

In the **Advanced** options, you can turn cookies on or off, or turn off pictures and/or sounds for faster browsing.

Take note

If you delete the Temporary Internet files, you can't get them back.

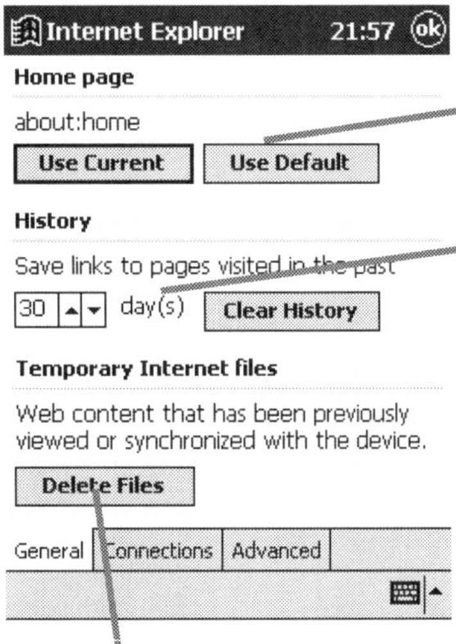

Where do you want to start your browsing?

How many days do you want to keep track of pages?

Let sites write cookies to your device?

Delete files to free up some space?

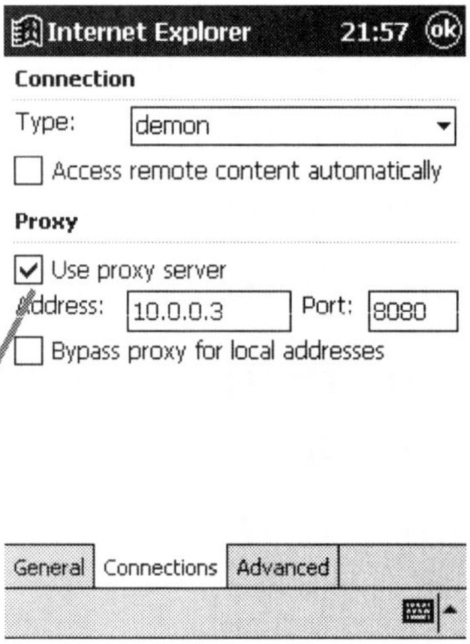

Do you use a proxy server?

Text-only browsing is quicker

Basic steps

❏ Enabling AvantGo in ActiveSync

1 Run ActiveSync on your PC and select Options.

2 On the SyncOptions tab, check AvantGo and click OK.

3 On your Pocket PC, launch Internet Explorer and tap 'More web sites' in the lower right hand of the screen.

4 A screen will appear asking for your e-mail address, so that you can be sent instructions on how to setup AvantGo. Enter your address in the box.

continued...

AvantGo provides a free news and information service for Pocket PC users; here's how to set it up and customize it to suit your requirements.

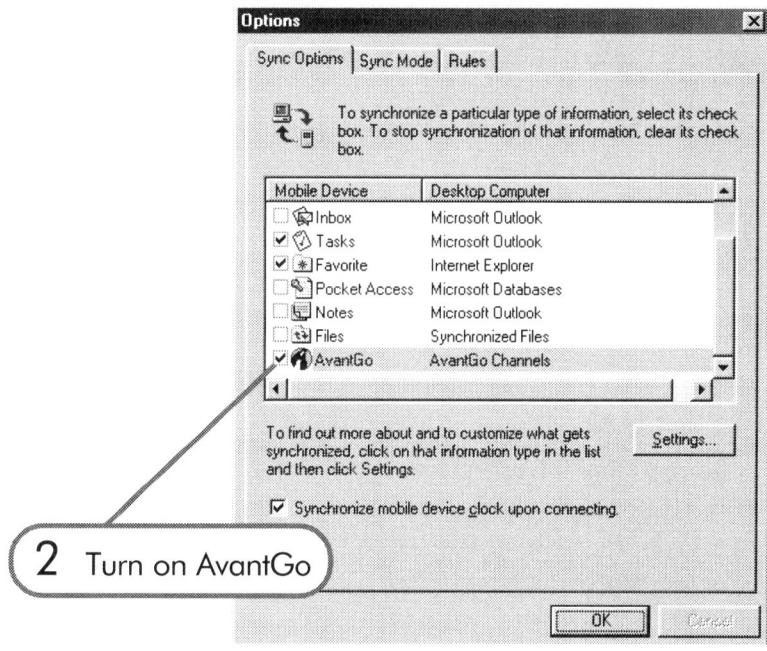

2 Turn on AvantGo

3 Run Internet Explorer

4 Enter your address

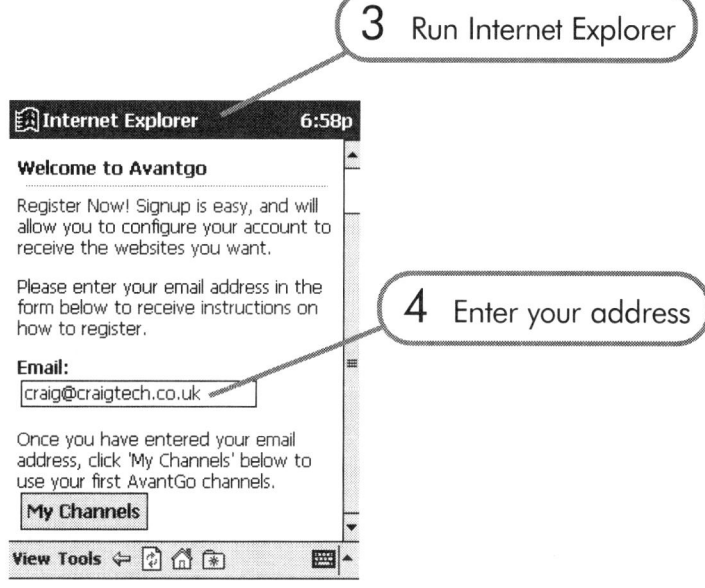

Take note

If you try and access AvantGo pages on your device when it's synchronizing you will see the busy screen. Wait for the synchronization to finish.

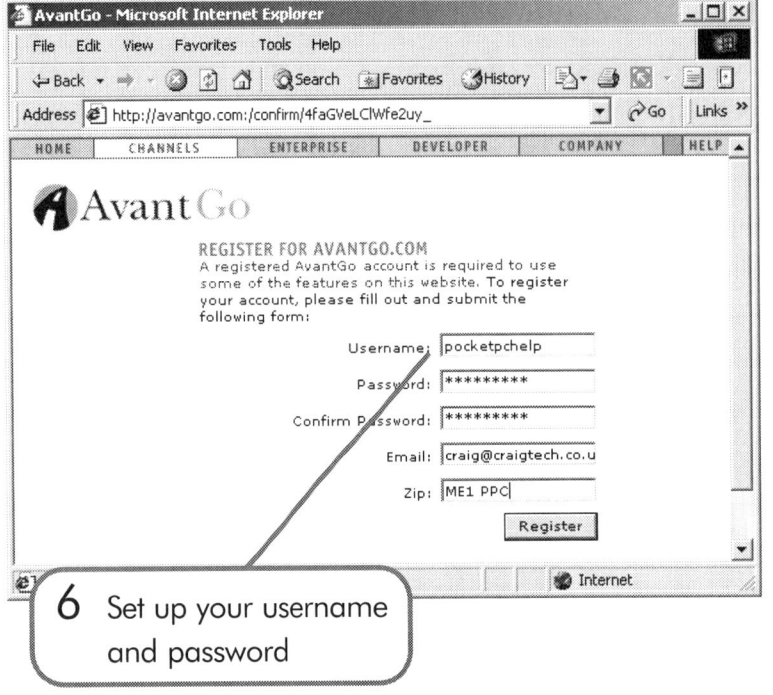

6 Set up your username and password

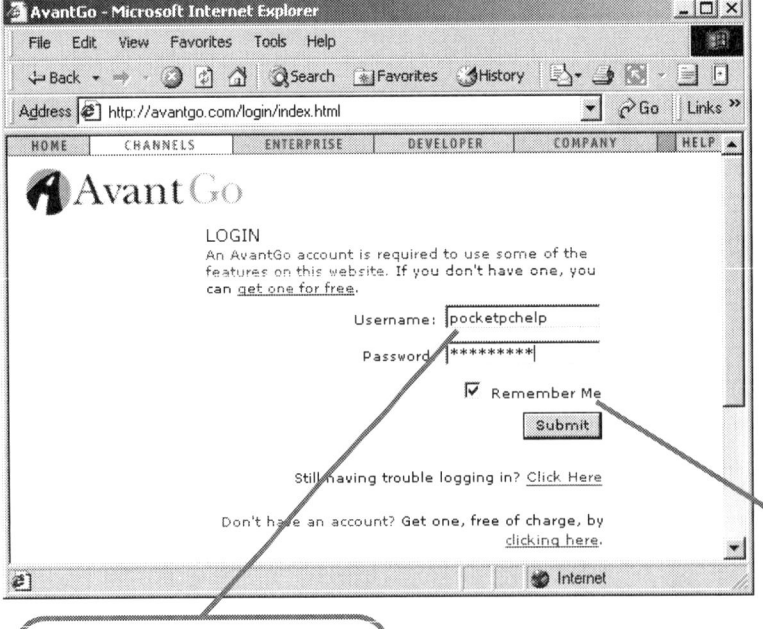

7 Login to the main site

continued…

5 Synchronize with your PC, by tapping the Synchronize button in ActiveSync.

❑ The picking of channels is done from the Web browser on your PC.

   You should have had an e-mail giving you instructions on how to perform the next part of the setup process.

6 Clicking on the link in the e-mail should take you to a registration screen similar to the one here – enter a username and password of your choice.

7 Once you've setup a username and password, then you are ready to login to the AvantGo site and pick your channels.

If you check Remember Me, you won't have to login when you return to the site

8 Click the Edit button in the My Account section.

9 Follow the links to select channels.

AvantGo has well over 1,000 channels to choose from

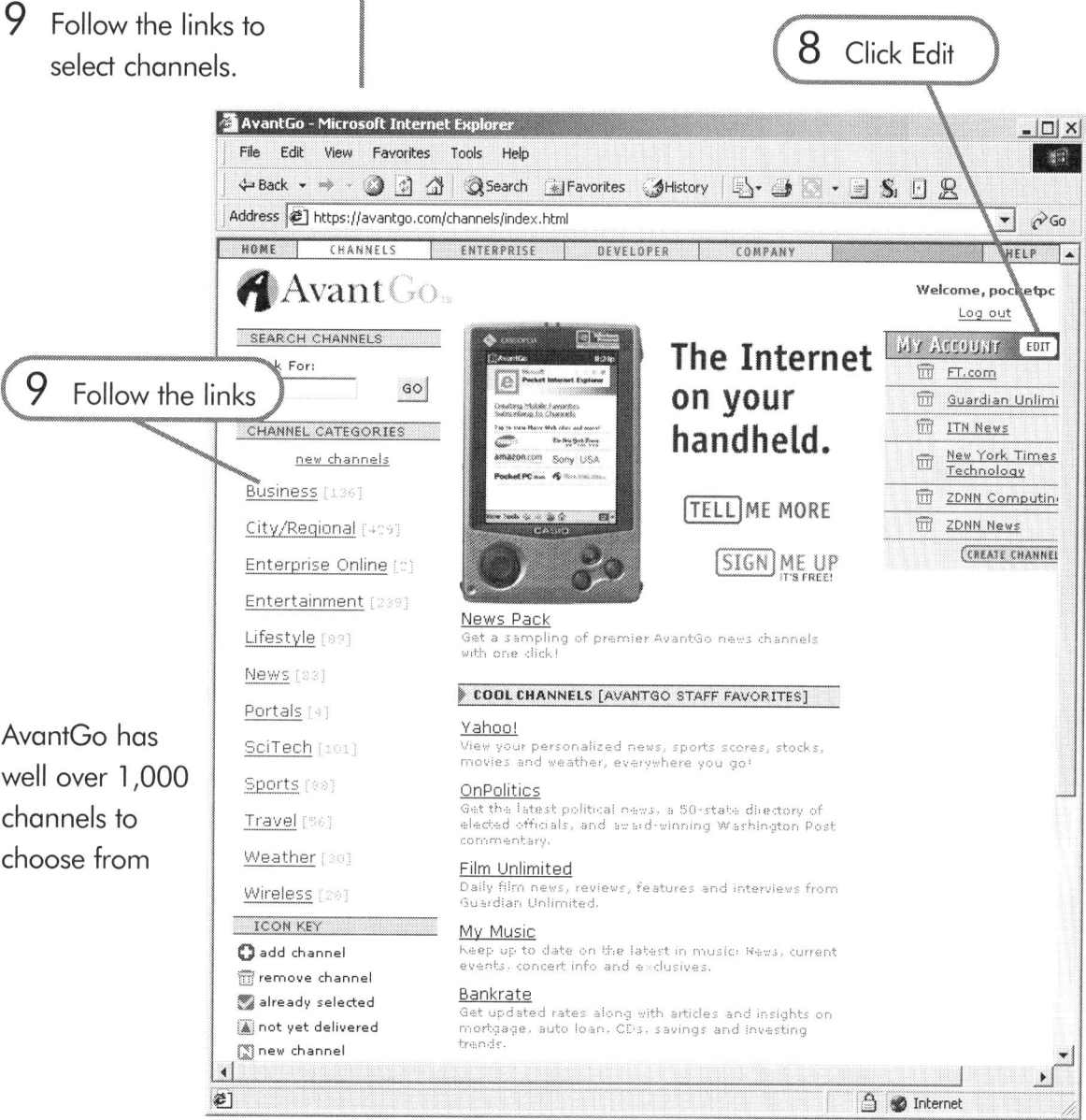

8 Click Edit

9 Follow the links

AvantGo ActiveSync settings

To ensure that you get all the channels you've selected we have to change the username and password that you are going to use when you synchronize with AvantGo, here's how.

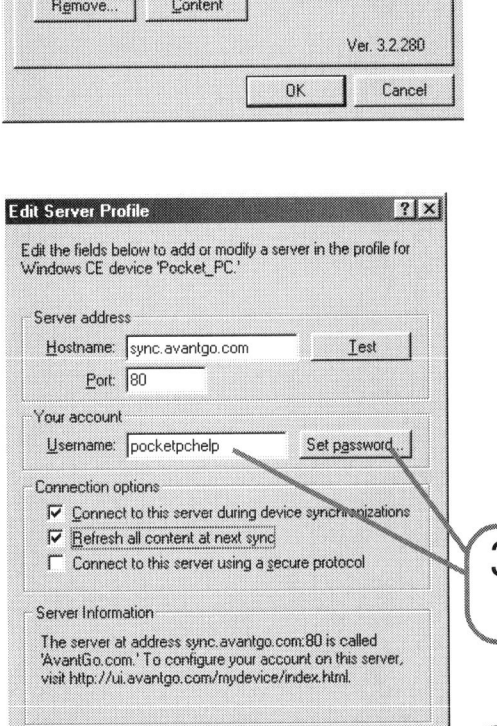

1 Open AvantGo's Options panel

2 Click Properties...

3 Enter your username and pasword

4 Click OK

1 In ActiveSync, click on AvantGo, then Options and Settings.

2 Click Properties...

3 Enter your username and set the password.

4 Click OK three times to return to the main ActiveSync page.

5 Synchronize with your device again.

6 Return to your Pocket PC.

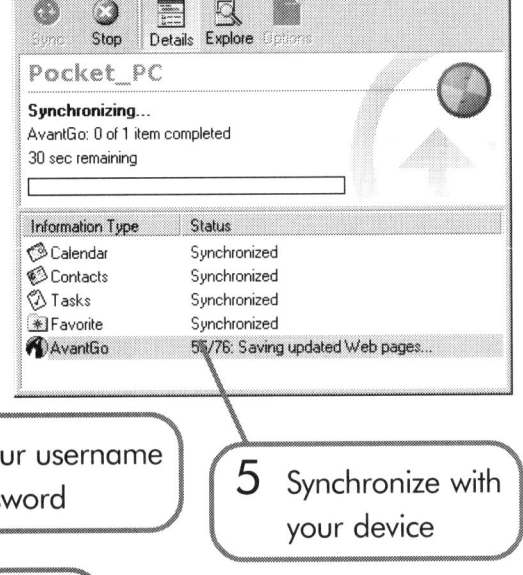

5 Synchronize with your device

AvantGo displaying your selections

During the process of setting up my channels on the AvantGo Web site I picked various sites and these will be shown on my Pocket PC when the synchronization process is complete.

Viewing AvantGo channels

Tapping on a selection, will display information and news. In our example we tapped on the MSN Mobile link.

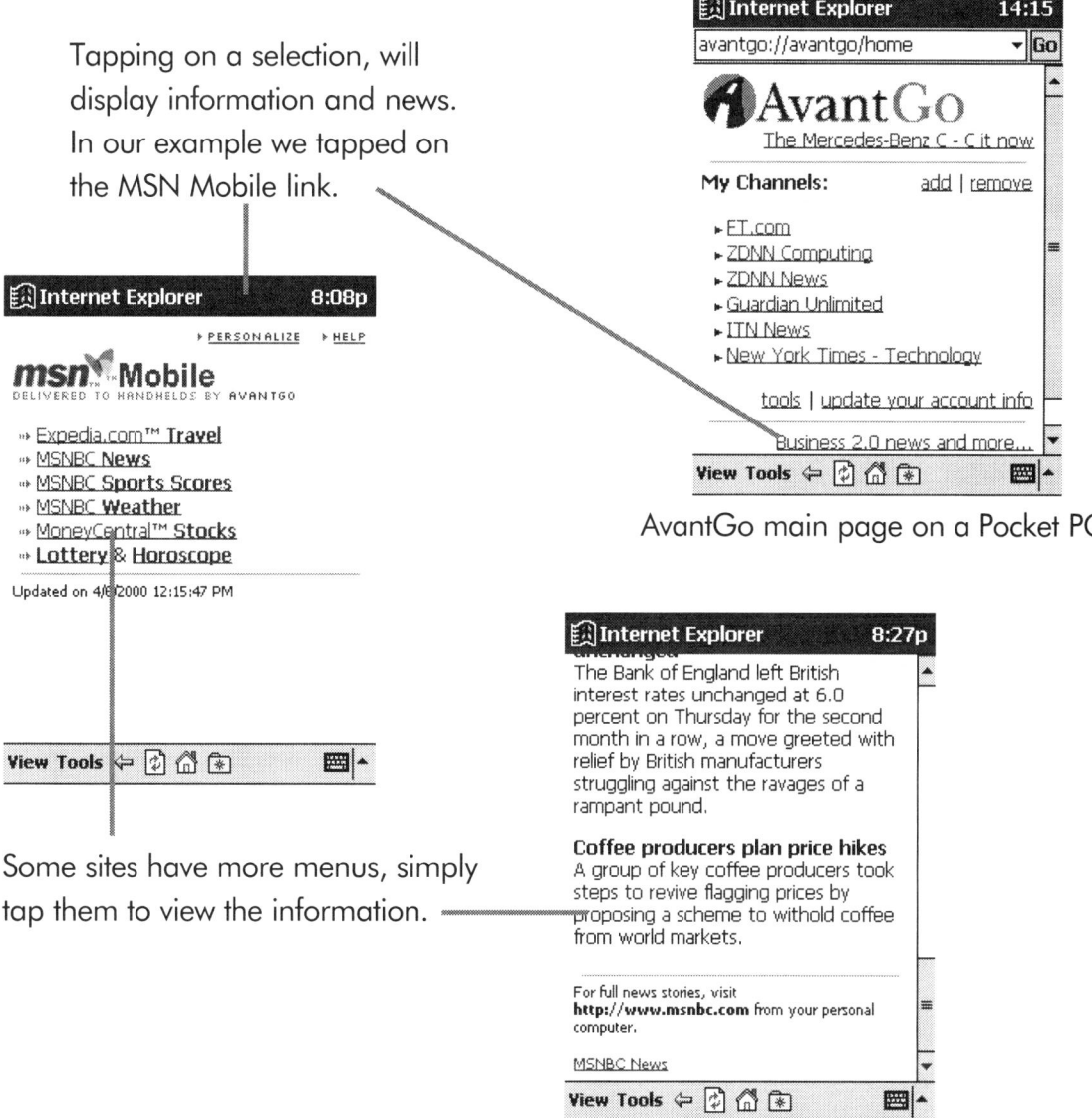

AvantGo main page on a Pocket PC

Some sites have more menus, simply tap them to view the information.

75

Synchronizing using a modem

If you have a modem connection to the Internet directly from your Pocket PC, then synchronizing AvantGo content via the modem is possible with just these steps.

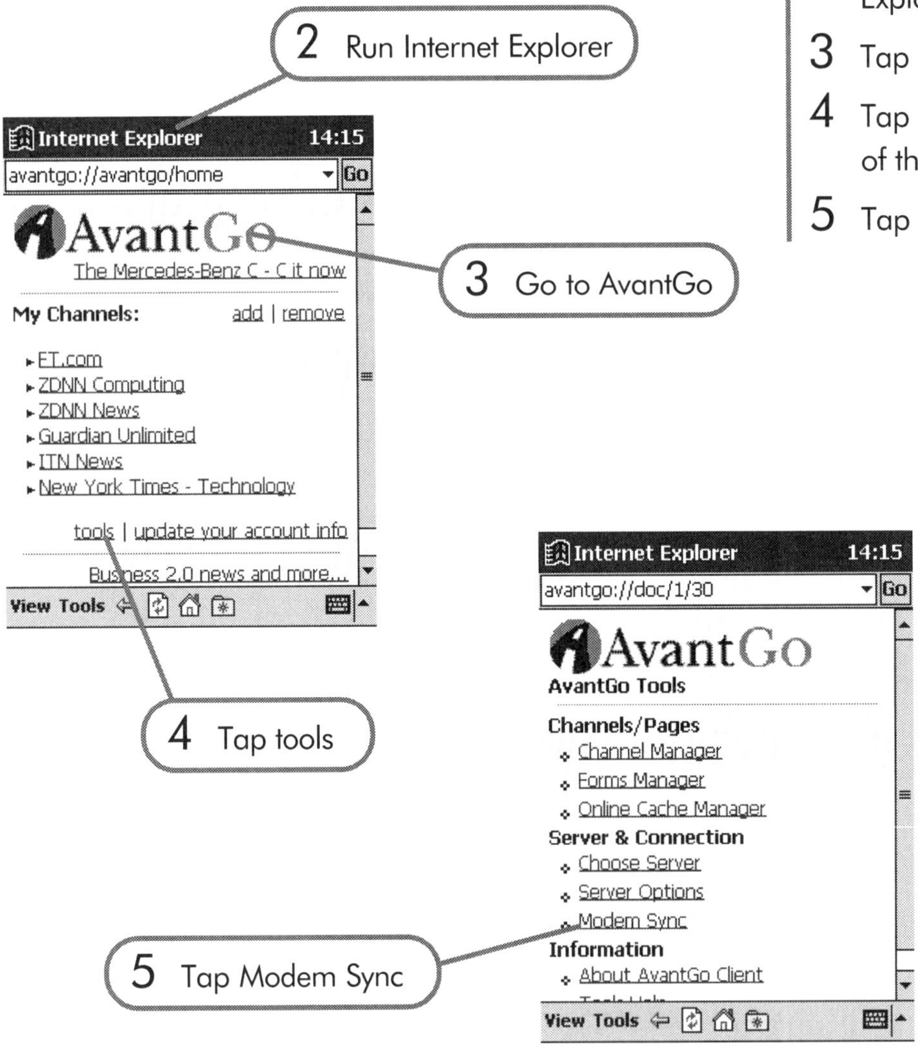

1 Connect up to your Internet Service Provider.

2 Open Pocket Internet Explorer.

3 Tap AvantGo.

4 Tap tools at the bottom of the AvantGo screen.

5 Tap Modem Sync.

2 Run Internet Explorer

Internet Explorer   14:15

avantgo://avantgo/home ▾ **Go**

AvantGo

The Mercedes-Benz C - C it now

My Channels: add | remove

- ►FT.com
- ► ZDNN Computing
- ► ZDNN News
- ► Guardian Unlimited
- ► ITN News
- ► New York Times - Technology

tools | update your account info

Business 2.0 news and more...

View Tools ⇦ 🔁 🏠 ⊛   ⌨

3 Go to AvantGo

4 Tap tools

Internet Explorer   14:15

avantgo://doc/1/30 ▾ **Go**

AvantGo

AvantGo Tools

Channels/Pages
- ❖ Channel Manager
- ❖ Forms Manager
- ❖ Online Cache Manager

Server & Connection
- ❖ Choose Server
- ❖ Server Options
- ❖ Modem Sync

Information
- ❖ About AvantGo Client

View Tools ⇦ 🔁 🏠 ⊛   ⌨

5 Tap Modem Sync

Basic steps

Sending via infrared

❑ On the sending device

1 Highlight the items to be sent.

2 Tap and hold on the items and from the menu select Send via Infrared…

❑ On the receiving device

3 Tap Tools, Receive via Infrared.

4 Line up the infrared ports of the two devices and the contacts start transferring.

5 If the devices aren't lined up within 60 seconds you will be prompted to try again.

You can use infrared to transfer information between your Pocket PC and another Pocket PC – as long as they are within line of sight!

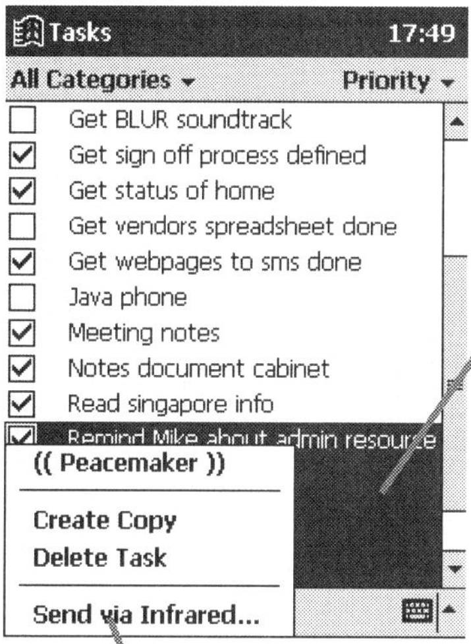

```
📖 Tasks                    17:49
All Categories ▾         Priority ▾
☐  Get BLUR soundtrack
☑  Get sign off process defined
☑  Get status of home
☐  Get vendors spreadsheet done
☑  Get webpages to sms done
☐  Java phone
☑  Meeting notes
☑  Notes document cabinet
☑  Read singapore info
☑  Remind Mike about admin resource
   (( Peacemaker ))
   ──────────────────────
   Create Copy
   Delete Task
   ──────────────────────
   Send via Infrared...        ⌨▴
```

> 1 Highlight the items

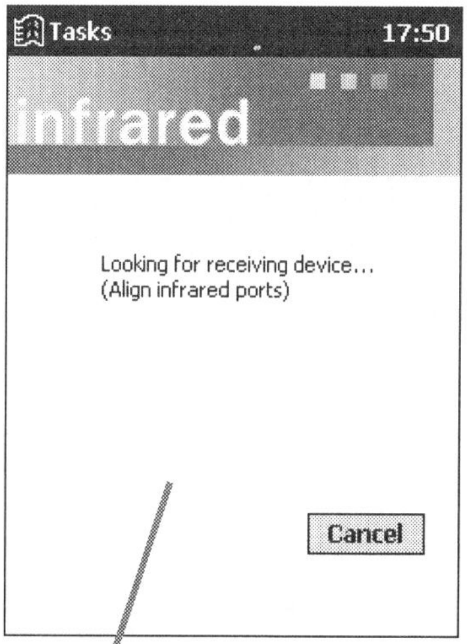

```
📖 Tasks                    17:50
               ■ ■ ■
infrared


        Looking for receiving device...
        (Align infrared ports)




                          Cancel
```

> 2 Select Send via Infrared…

> 4 Line up the devices

```
📖 Contacts                 23:48
               ■ ■ ■
infrared



     Sending 152 of 161 contact(s)...
     craigtech

   ████████████████

                  Cancel
```

The status screen when sending contacts via Infrared

Take note

Some devices have the PeaceMaker Infrared transfer utility from Conduits Technologies Inc. This lets you beam contact details between Windows CE devices and 3Com Palm Pilots.

Summary

- ❏ ActiveSync allows you to transfer information between your desktop PC and your Pocket PC.

- ❏ New Pocket PC software is installed through your PC, using the ActiveSync link.

- ❏ You can copy files from your desktop PC through a dedicated folder.

- ❏ ActiveSync lets you backup your Pocket PC onto your PC. Restore overwrites existing files on your device.

- ❏ Synchronization ensures that the same up-to-date information is present on your desktop and Pocket PC.

- ❏ An Ethernet card will allow you to link up to a local area network.

- ❏ If you have a modem and an ISP, you can connect to the Internet on your Pocket PC.

- ❏ Dial-up connections are usually simple to set up, although you must have the necessary details from your ISP.

- ❏ You may be able to establish a wireless connection to your LAN or the Internet through a cellular phone.

- ❏ Pocket Internet Explorer has the best features of the desktop version. Fit to Screen helps to overcome the problem of the small screen.

- ❏ You can mark sites as Mobile Favorites when browsing on your PC, then transfer their data to your Pocket PC for reading off-line.

- ❏ Configure the Internet options to suit yourself.

- ❏ AvantGo offers channels for mobile device users.

- ❏ You can send data via infrared to another Pocket PC.

5 Calendar

Calendar views

Calendar is one of the most used applications on Pocket PCs. In this chapter you learn how to create, delete, and move appointments as well as invite people to meetings.

When you first launch the Calendar application, you are presented with a view showing the current day. To navigate around Calendar you have several different options. You can jump to a particular date, scroll through month by month, as well as viewing day, week, month or year on the screen. There is also an Agenda view which just shows you meetings that you have booked on that particular day in a compact view.

Switching between Calendar views can be done two ways:

●   Tap the View menu and select the desired View;

Or

●   Press the Calendar hardware button to scroll through the different modes.

Day view

The Day view is the main view displayed on the screen when you go into the Calendar application. By default it shows the day split into one hour slots. The Options screen (see page 83) lets you change this and other preferences.

Most appointments show up in blue (the colour to signify busy). When creating or viewing appointments, you have various options and these are shown in the Day view as appropriate.

Calendar in Day view

Go to Today – get back to today's entries by tapping this

Month and year

Agenda view

Next Week

Previous Week

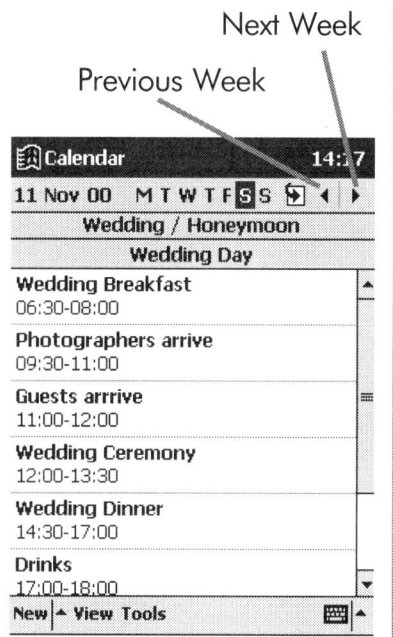

Calendar in Agenda view

At first glance the Agenda view looks quite similar to the Day view, though can make you think your whole day is booked full of meetings! It gives a compact view of all the appointments for the day, removing the gaps between them and displaying as much information as possible on a single view.

Week view

The Week view is great for giving you a quick view of any particular week. It shows all-day events as well as individual meetings. You can create and move appointments in Week view.

In Week view you will see lots of boxes that show you a lot of information – albeit somewhat cryptically. If you tap once with your stylus on any of the small boxes indicating a meeting then the area at the top of the screen will change to show you a summary of that meeting.

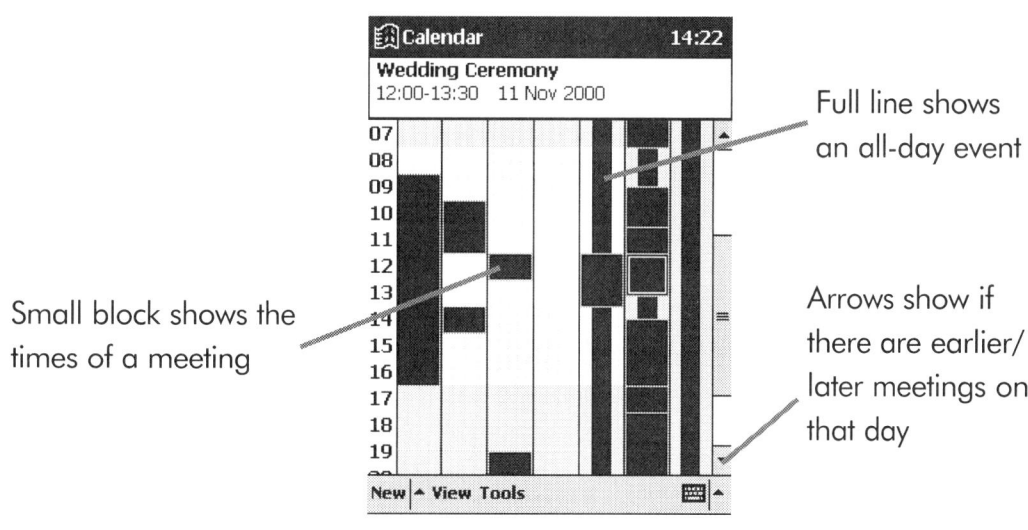

Full line shows
an all-day event

Small block shows the
times of a meeting

Arrows show if
there are earlier/
later meetings on
that day

Calendar in Week view

Month view

The Month view is very similar to other views in the calendar application in that it has been designed to give you as much information as possible in an uncluttered way. The icons follow a nice, simple pattern that's easy to follow, once it's been explained. Here's what they mean:

- ☐ Blue outlined box – all-day event

- ■ Full blue square – meetings in morning and afternoon

- ◤ Triangle pointing to top left – meetings in morning

- ◢ Triangle point to lower right – meetings in the afternoon

- ◪ Box with any other symbol – all-day event, plus meetings

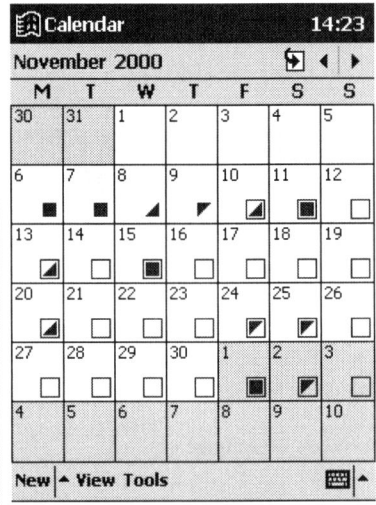

Calendar in Month view

Year view

Because the Pocket PC has a high-resolution screen, it's capable of displaying a year's calendar on the screen at one time.

Tapping on any date will take you to the Day view.

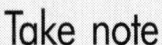

Calendar in Year view

Tip

Tapping on any given day in the Month view will take you to the Day view for that day.

Take note

It's also possible to have all-day event entries with individual meetings also displayed.

Calendar Options

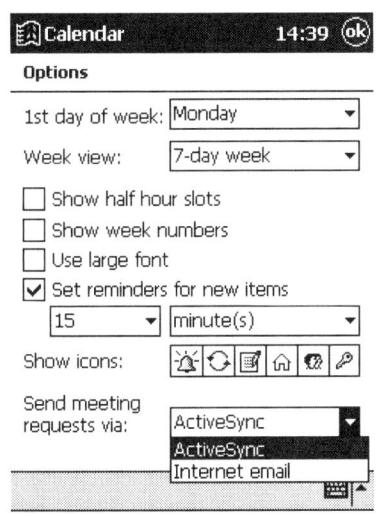

Tap Tools, Options to reach this screen and set the options to suit yourself

Back/forward a day

Go to selected date

Go to a day

The Options screen in the calendar application lets you set various preferences to suit your needs. These include which day of the week you'd like to set as the first day (either Monday or Sunday), how many days would you like to display in the week view, etc.

Calendar symbols

Icons can be displayed next to Calendar entries to represent the type of meeting and give you extra information. These icons take up quite a lot of space, but they can be easily switched on or off as required.

🔔	A reminder has been set
↻	Recurring appointment
📝	Note attached
⌂	Location marked
✆	Attendees required
🔑	Private meeting

Navigating around Calendar

There are various ways of moving around in the calendar application. The most common one is using the left and right arrows to skip between weeks or months, but there are others.

You can also tap on month name, year, or week number to bring up other options if you need to book meetings more than a few weeks ahead.

Making appointments

There are several ways of creating and editing appointments on your Pocket PC, these can either be done by using the tap-and-hold feature or the new menu. Both methods take you to the New Appointment dialog box, which is where you can enter the various details of the appointment.

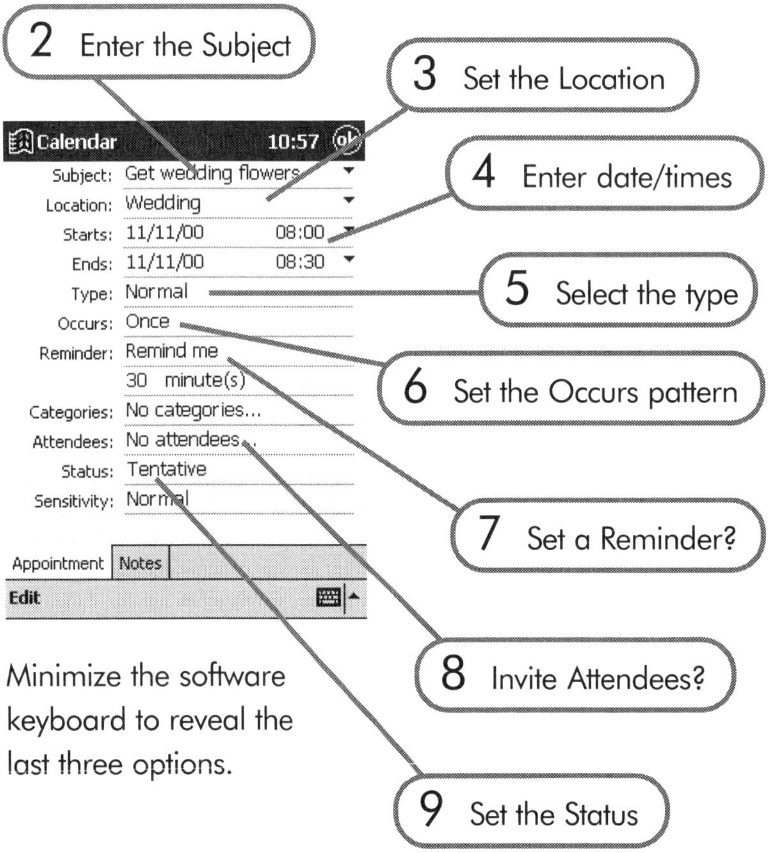

2 Enter the Subject

3 Set the Location

4 Enter date/times

Calendar	10:57
Subject:	Get wedding flowers
Location:	Wedding
Starts:	11/11/00 08:00
Ends:	11/11/00 08:30
Type:	Normal
Occurs:	Once
Reminder:	Remind me
	30 minute(s)
Categories:	No categories...
Attendees:	No attendees...
Status:	Tentative
Sensitivity:	Normal

Appointment | Notes

Edit

5 Select the type

6 Set the Occurs pattern

7 Set a Reminder?

8 Invite Attendees?

Minimize the software keyboard to reveal the last three options.

9 Set the Status

Take note

The sensitivity option lets you select if the meeting is classed as Private or not.

1. Navigate to the relevant day and select New Appointment.

2. At the New Appointment dialog box, enter the Subject.

3. Enter a Location or select one from the drop-down box.

4. Enter the Start and End dates and time.

5. Select the Type (either *Normal* or *All-day*).

6. If this item Occurs regularly tap the drop-down box and select a pattern. If a suitable one is not listed tap the <Edit pattern ....> line to add a new one.

7. Turn on and set the time for a Reminder if wanted.

8. If you are inviting others, tap Attendees to view your contacts.

9. Set the Status as required.

Appointment categories

❑ To view the Categories

1 Tap View, Categories.

2 Go to the Add/Delete tab.

3 Give your new category a name.

4 Tap the Add button.

❑ Filtering appointments

5 Tap View, Categories.

6 Select the categories to filter on. Appointments not in those categories will disappear from the view!

❑ To display all your appointments

7 Tap View, Categories.

8 Remove all the checks from the boxes.

When you create appointments, you can assign a category to it. Categories let you group types of appointments to allow you to view them selectively later.

● The View Category button isn't displayed until you've actually entered an appointment with a category selected.

Filtering categories is the easiest method of breaking down a large list of contacts/appointments especially if you work on lots of projects. By just viewing appointments in a particular category you can reduce the amounts of detail on the screen.

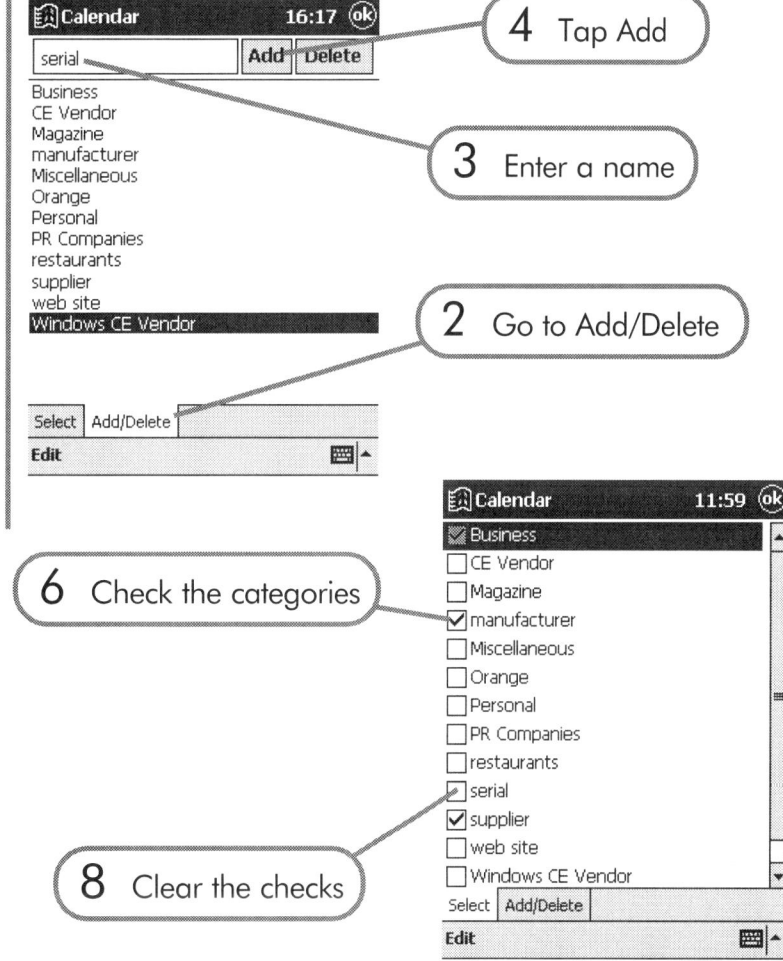

4 Tap Add

3 Enter a name

2 Go to Add/Delete

6 Check the categories

8 Clear the checks

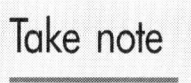
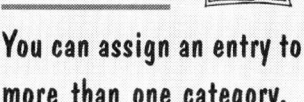

Appointment Notes

You can add a note to any meeting or appointment. It can be one of any of the types supported within the Notes application, such as voice recording. In my example I've attached a handwritten note, and a voice note, as well as some text.

1 Enter a new appointment.

2 Tap the Notes tab.

3 Bring up the keyboard to enter a typed note.

4 Tap the Voice recorder and then use the voice controls to record/ playback any notes.

5 Tap the pencil tool to write a note or draw a sketch on the screen.

6 Tap ok.

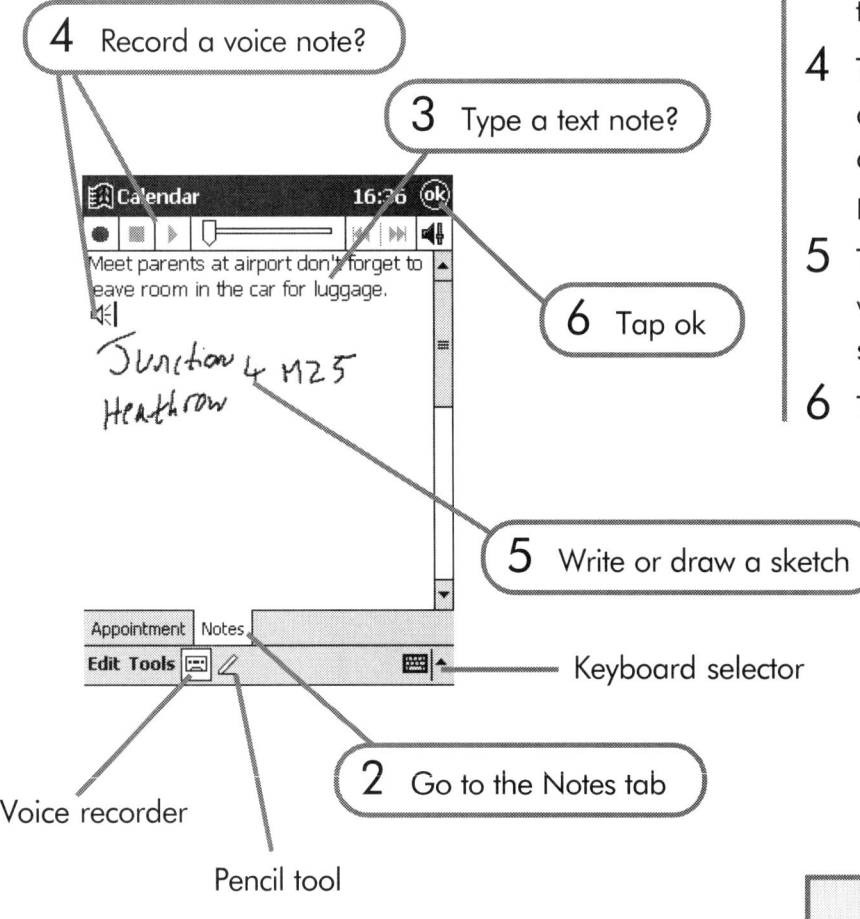

4 Record a voice note?

3 Type a text note?

6 Tap ok

5 Write or draw a sketch

Keyboard selector

Voice recorder

Pencil tool

2 Go to the Notes tab

Take note

Any Notes are automatically deleted if the appointment is deleted.

Adjusting meeting times

1 In Day view, tap the top half of the screen.

2 At the Appointment dialog box, change the start and/or end time.

❑ Moving appointments

3 In Day view, tap on the bar to the left of the appointment description and drag to move it to the new time.

4 In Week view, tap onto the appointment and drag it to another day in the same week – you cannot drag appointments into another week.

Meeting times are frequently changed, so here are a couple of ways of changing/moving appointments.

When you tap an appointment, drag bars appear. These let you alter an appointment without having to type in the new times.

You can change the start and/or end time of a meeting, either in Day View, as shown here, or in Week view.

If you don't need to change the duration then moving an appointment is even simpler.

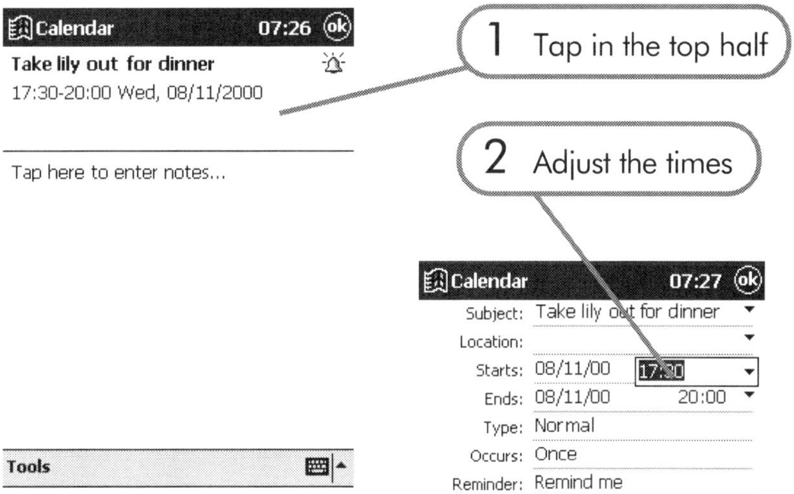

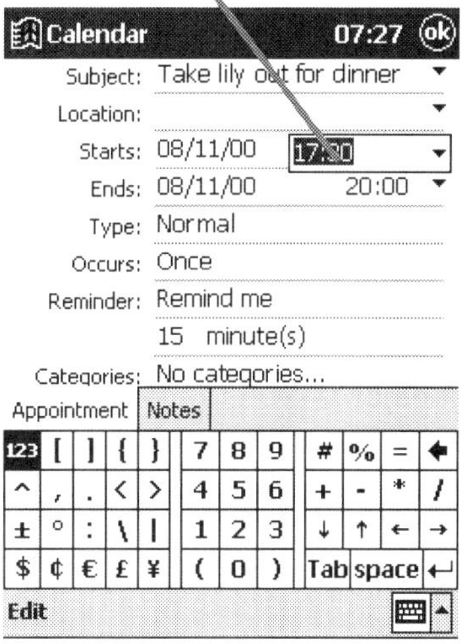

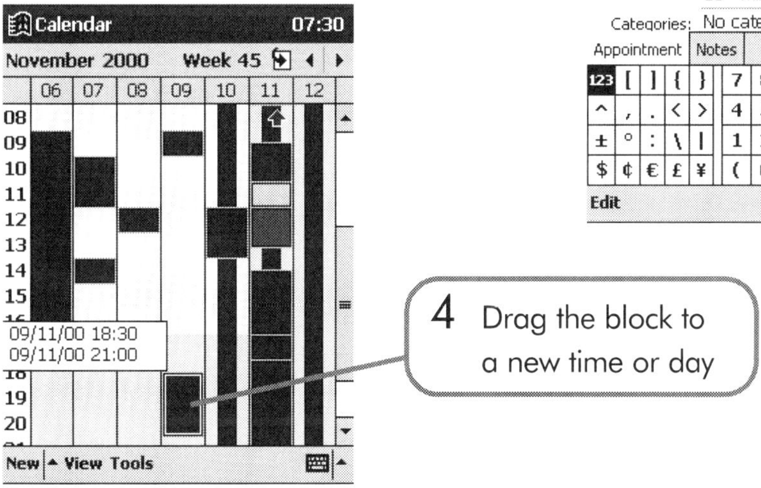

1 Tap in the top half

2 Adjust the times

4 Drag the block to a new time or day

Summary

❑ The Calendar can be viewed by Day, Week, Month, Year or in the Agenda view.

❑ Use the Calendar Options to customize the Calendar to suit your way of working.

❑ You can make an appointment in Day or Week view. The appointment has many spaces for details – though you don't have to fill them all in if you don't want to!

❑ By assigning appointments to categories, you can filter the display to show only those of certain categories.

❑ Notes of any type can be added to appointments.

❑ You can easily adjust the time or date of a meeting in either Day or Week view.

6 Contacts and Tasks

Contacts

The Contacts application is where you keep names, addresses and other contact details. Contacts has been designed to show you the information you need at a glance and to allow you to customize the information you view on a per-contact basis.

Utilizing the tap and hold menu system allows you to e-mail others and also to share contacts with other people via infrared.

Quick search bar

Categories

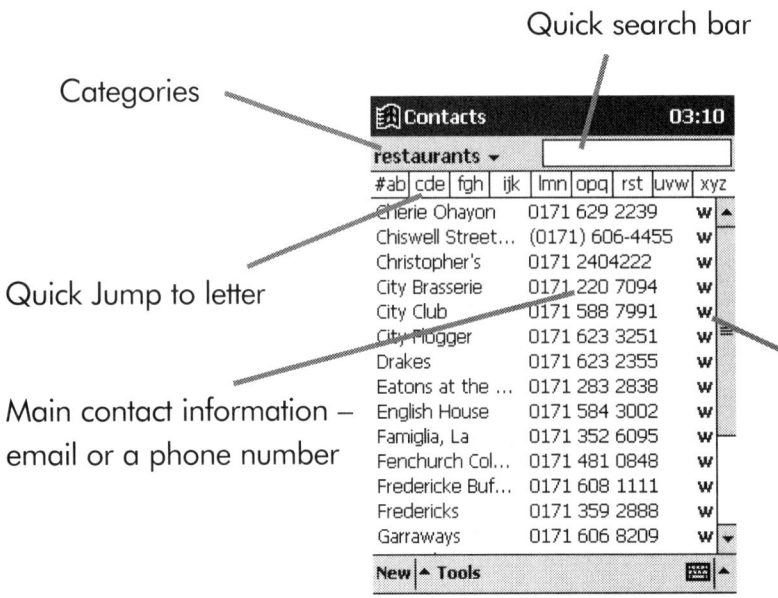

Quick Jump to letter

Main contact information – email or a phone number

Tip

Pressing the hardware button for Contacts will scroll through your Categories.

w = work phone number (see page 92)

Reset list

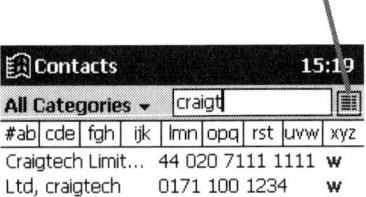

Quick searching

Using the quick search box at the top of the Contacts screen you can quickly and easily find contacts. It works by looking for both the first and last names and so regardless of how your information is entered a quick search will show the contact.

To display all contacts again tap the Reset list button.

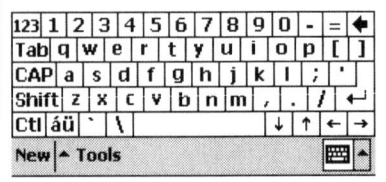

Creating a Contact

Basic steps

1 Tap New.

2 Enter the name and other details.

3 Scroll down to see more fields.

4 If you want to categorize the contact tap the Category field.

5 Check the categories as needed.

6 Tap ok to exit from the category screen.

7 Tap Notes and enter a notes if wanted.

8 Tap ok save the information and exit.

When creating a new contact on your Pocket PC you have quite a lot of options available. Some of them require you to scroll down as they are hidden below the software keyboard. As with other applications on your Pocket PC, it's possible to categorize your contacts, add notes as well as the commonly used fields such as e-mail addresses, Web sites, home/fax numbers as well home and work mailing addresses.

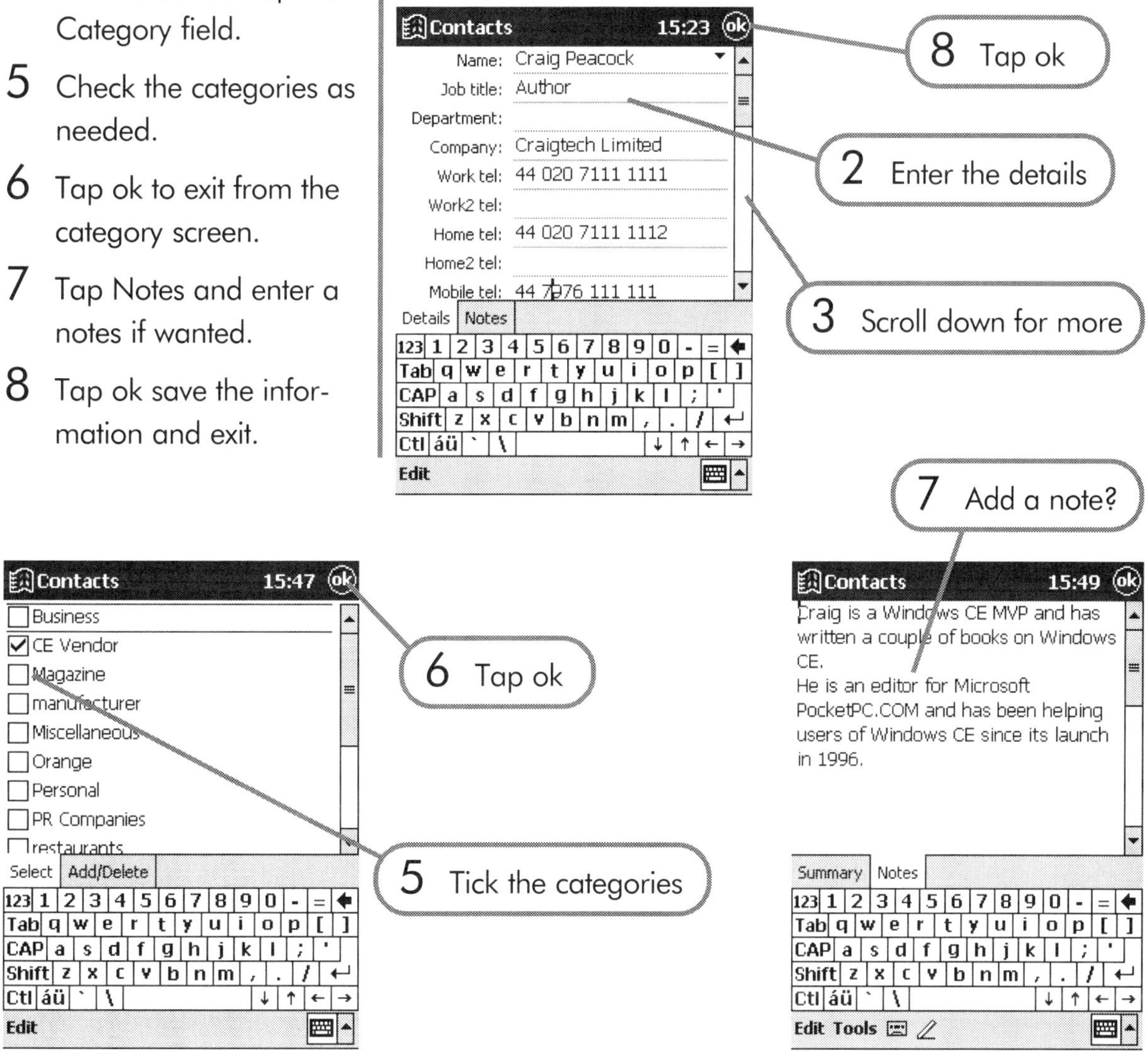

8 Tap ok

2 Enter the details

3 Scroll down for more

7 Add a note?

6 Tap ok

5 Tick the categories

Customizing Contacts

On a per-contact basis, you can decide which of the main methods of contacting someone you wish to show. This procedure is a little fiddly and works on a bit of trial-and-error approach.

Once you've picked an option, that is the one that will be displayed for the contact until you change it.

1 Tap the stylus on the letter shown at the end of a contact.

2 While holding down the stylus move it to the left and down in a small arc shape.

3 Release the stylus and the menu should open – select the default method of contacting this person.

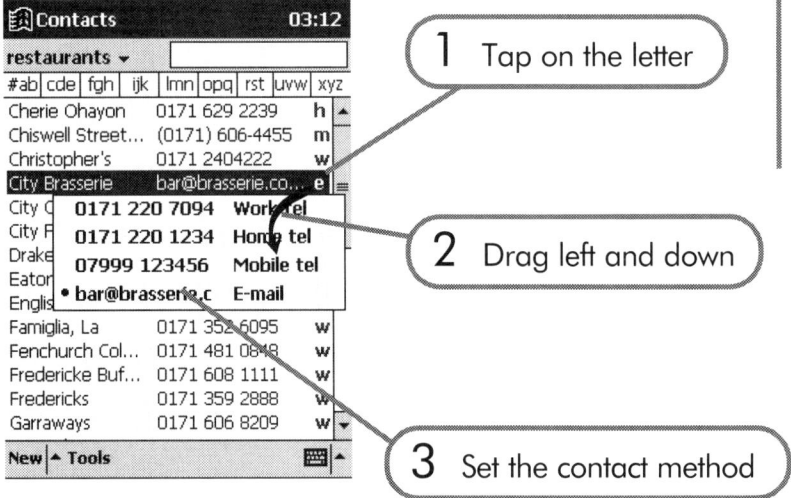

1 Tap on the letter

2 Drag left and down

3 Set the contact method

Contact method codes
h = home phone
m = mobile phone
w = work phone
e = e-mail

File As

In the Contacts in Microsoft Outlook on your PC, there is a 'File As' field, where the default setting is to display information as last name, first name.

However you decide to display information in this File As field will be reflected in the Name field on your Pocket PC.

Basic steps

1 In the Contacts screen tap the drop down arrow to the right of the All Categories word.

2 Select the appropriate category from the list.

Or

3 Select More… .

4 Tap the appropriate category then tap the ok button when done.

❑ Using the hardware button

5 The first time you press the Contacts hardware button, the Contacts application is loaded. If you press it when you are in Contacts, it will scroll through your categories one at a time in alphabetical order. There is an All Categories group which is always listed near the top of the list.

When you have a large number of contacts it is often quicker to navigate and find them when you've split them into categories. In *Creating a contact* I showed you how to associate a contact with a particular category. In this section I'll show you how to select those categories.

You can navigate between categories in two ways.

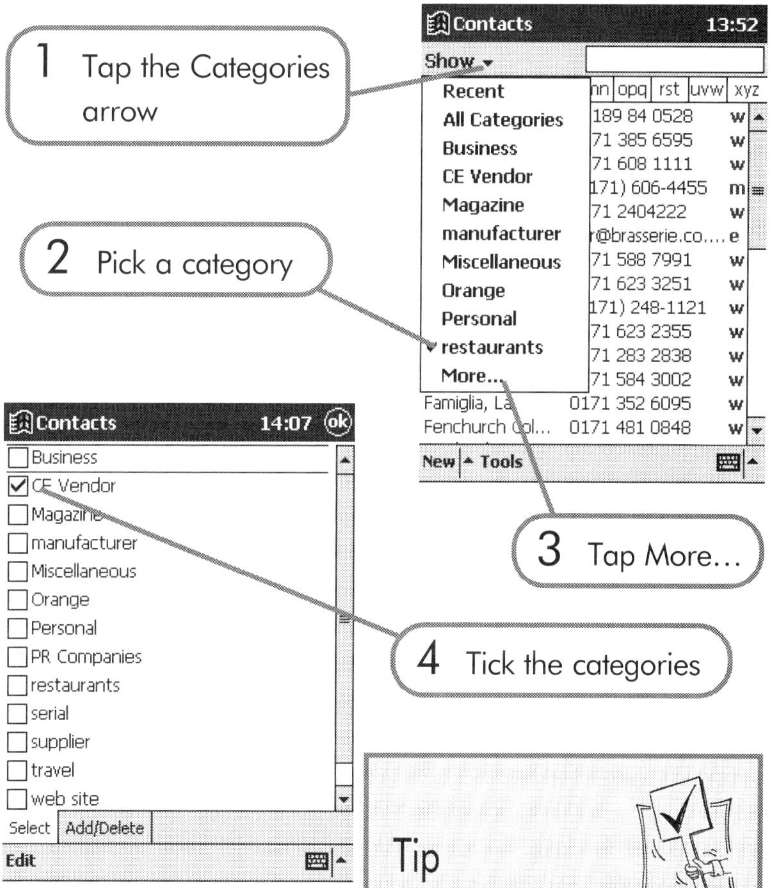

1 Tap the Categories arrow

2 Pick a category

3 Tap More…

4 Tick the categories

In the More… screen you can select multiple categories

Tip

To jump to a particular letter in the Contacts application tap the letter on the index bar at the top of the screen.

Adding and deleting Categories

When you are in the More… option in the Contacts screen there is an Add/Delete page, in which you can create new categories on the device.

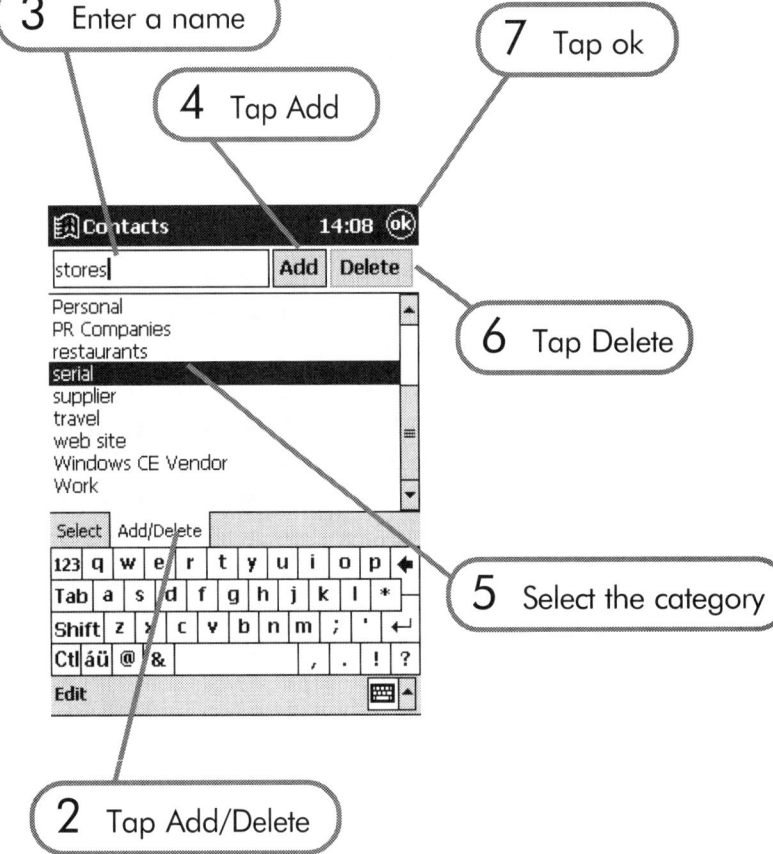

③ Enter a name

④ Tap Add

⑦ Tap ok

⑥ Tap Delete

⑤ Select the category

② Tap Add/Delete

1 In Contacts, tap More… at the bottom of the drop-down Categories list.

2 Switch to the Add/ Delete tab.

❏ Adding a category

3 Enter a new name for a category.

4 Tap Add.

❏ Deleting a category

5 Select the unwanted category.

6 Tap Delete.

7 Tap ok when done.

Take note

Once you've added some categories you need to edit contacts, as relevant, to associate them with the corresponding categories.

Basic steps

1 Go to the Contacts list view.

2 Tap and hold on the contact you wish to send an e-mail to.

3 Select the Send E-mail to Contact... option.

4 Inbox will be opened and you can compose and send your e-mail.

Tip

For more information on Inbox and e-mail please refer to Chapter 7.

Sending an e-mail

When you are in the Contacts application the tap and hold menu can be incredibly handy. It is possible to e-mail a contact directly from the Contacts screen. This can save a lot of time, as instead of going into Inbox and composing a new e-mail first, you can use these steps to have the system automatically launch Inbox and address the e-mail to your recipient.

1 Go to the list view

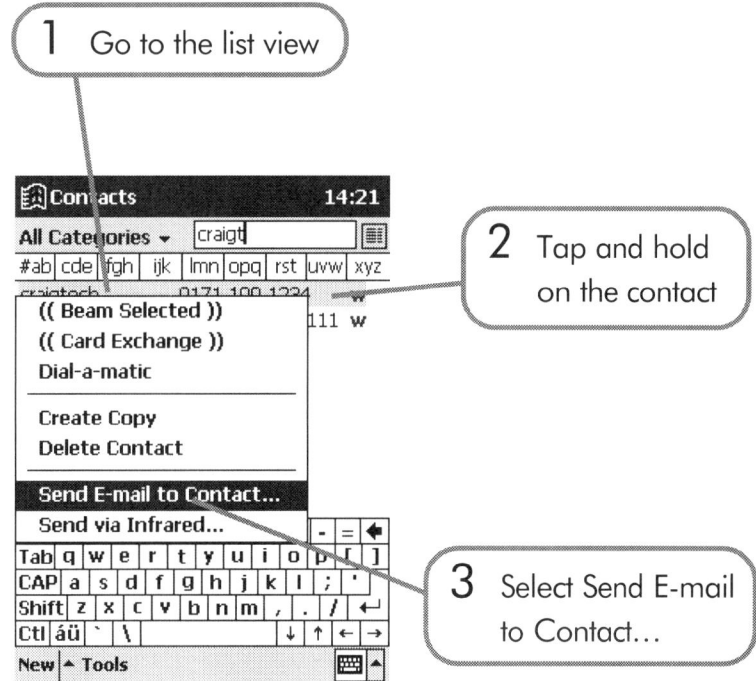

2 Tap and hold on the contact

3 Select Send E-mail to Contact...

Tip

Tap and hold on the Contact displays extra options.

Creating tasks

In the Tasks application there are a couple of ways to create tasks. The first method that is shown here is the full version; the quick entry method is shown opposite.

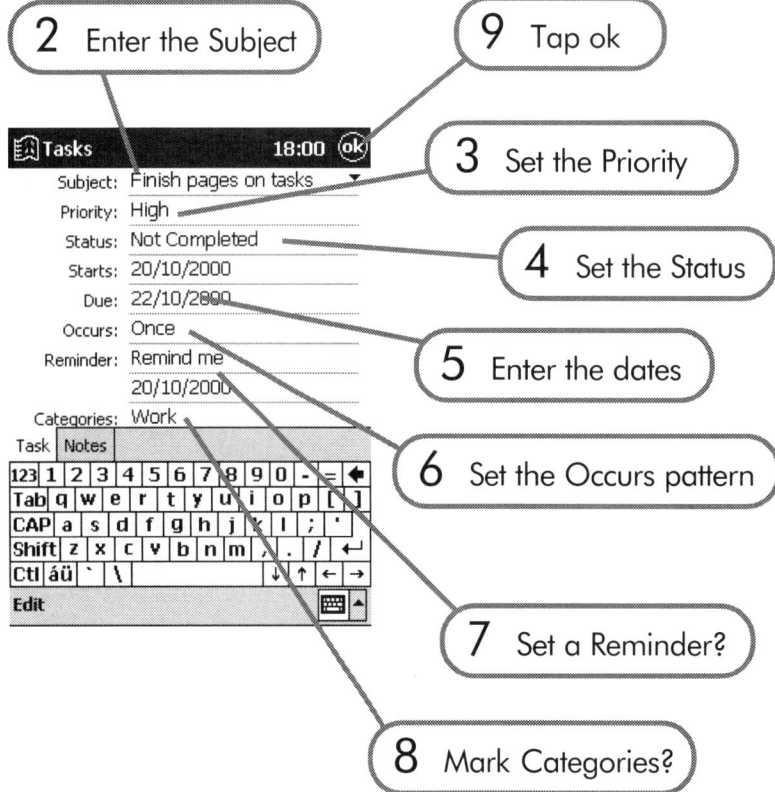

2 Enter the Subject

9 Tap ok

3 Set the Priority

4 Set the Status

5 Enter the dates

6 Set the Occurs pattern

7 Set a Reminder?

8 Mark Categories?

Basic steps

1 Tap New.

2 Give the task a Subject description.

3 Set the Priority if appropriate.

4 Set the Status to suit.

5 Enter the Starts and Due dates for the task.

6 If the task Occurs regularly, select the pattern.

7 Turn on the Reminder and set the date, if wanted.

8 Select the Categories if appropriate.

9 Tap ok when done.

Take note

You can set a date to be reminded, but not the time of day for your reminder.

Tip

On the Notes page you can enter either voice, typed or handwritten notes.

Basic steps

❑ Sorting the list

1 Tap the Sort By arrow.

2 Select the order.

❑ To turn on the Quick Entry bar

3 Tap Tools and tap Option Bar in its menu.

❑ Making a Quick Entry

4 Tap into the bar and type the subject.

Sorting tasks

There are various options available to you when sorting tasks all of which are available from the **Sort By** drop-down menu.

Status Tasks either completed or not completed

Priority High Priority tasks are shown at the top of the list with low priority at the bottom

Subject Alphabetical order of subject

Start/Due Date In order of Start or Due dates, if given – if no dates are set, the items appear below.

Quick Entry bar

If you switch on the Quick Entry bar, you can enter tasks by simply tapping into the bar and entering a subject.

Take note

To mark a task as complete, tap the box to its left.

Tap to set high or low priority

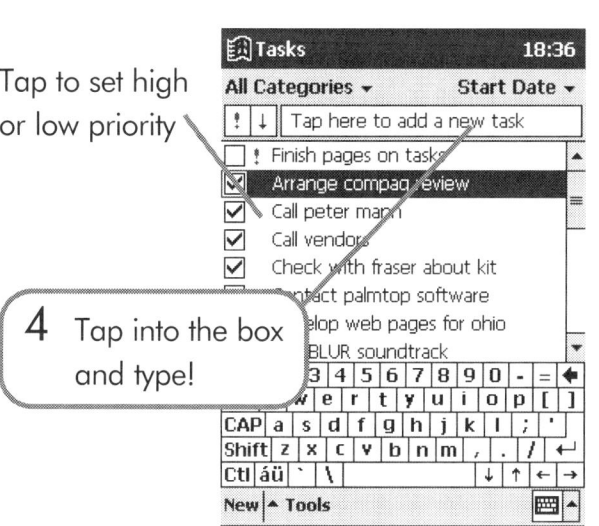

4 Tap into the box and type!

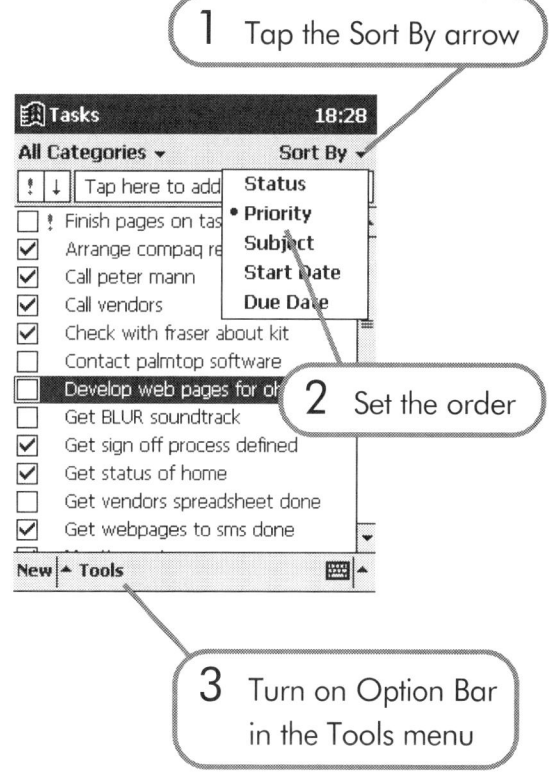

1 Tap the Sort By arrow

2 Set the order

3 Turn on Option Bar in the Tools menu

Summary

- ❑ The Contacts application will hold the names, e-mail and street addresses, phone numbers, and other details of people.

- ❑ When creating a new contact, you can give as much detail as you need.

- ❑ You can set the main contact method for each person in the list view, from the alternatives: home, mobile or work phone, or e-mail address.

- ❑ If you assign Categories to contacts, you can then filter the list to display only those that belong to selected categories.

- ❑ You can start to send an e-mail to someone from within the Contacts application.

- ❑ Tasks helps you to keep track of current jobs. The display of tasks can be sorted into status, priority, subject, or date order.

7 E-mail

Inbox

Inbox is the Pocket PC's e-mail application. It is very similar to Outlook on the PC, and has many of the same features and options.

Inbox on the Pocket PC is an extension of your desktop e-mail system, and not a replacement for it. If you are using a modem and download e-mail messages from your ISP you are in fact downloading a copy of the messages – the originals are left on the server. It is only when you next connect up your PC to collect e-mail, that the messages are actually moved from the server to your PC.

There are so many ways of configuring corporate e-mail servers that it is possible that yours may not work exactly as described here, but this is the most common method.

IMAP4 versus POP3

POP3 e-mail servers work by keeping all the messages in one folder and when you download your e-mails they are copied straight into Inbox. If you receive a large number of e-mails on your device and move them to folders to make them easier to manage when you get back to your desktop PC you'll have to go through the process again – which is very frustrating.

IMAP4 is a method used by some corporate e-mail systems to allow their staff to view e-mails directly on the server.With IMAP4 e-mail, you file messages into folders on your device, then when you next synchronize your e-mail Inbox tells the server to move the messages on the server, saving you valuable time when you return to a desktop PC.

E-mail jargon

POP3   Post Office Protocol 3, for receiving Internet e-mail.

SMTP   Simple Mail Transport Protocol, for sending e-mail.

LDAP   Lightweight Directory Access Protocol, for looking up e-mail addresses.

IMAP   Internet Mail Application Protocol, for receiving e-mail.

Service   the settings on your Pocket PC for a connection to an Internet Service Provider.

Take note

Many ISPs use different servers for sending and receiving e-mails.

100

 Configuring Inbox POP3 for Internet access

1 Tap Start, Programs, Inbox, Services, New Service.

2 Select the Connection from the list.

3 Enter the details of your POP3 mail server.

4 Enter your User ID and Password. If you don't want to type your password in every time, tick Save password.

5 Tap Next.

6 Enter the SMTP host details.

7 Enter your e-mail address in the Return address box.

8 Tap Next.

continued...

You'll need several key pieces of information before you can set up and test your e-mail connection. If you don't have these to hand, check your Internet Service Provider's Web site or give their technical support department a call. You need:

● Your e-mail address;

● Your e-mail login name and password;

● The name of your ISP's server for *receiving* e-mail, often referred to as the 'POP3 mail server.'

● The name of your ISP's server for *sending* e-mail, known as the 'SMTP server.'

You must have a working modem or Ethernet connection to your Internet Service Provider to test the next section.

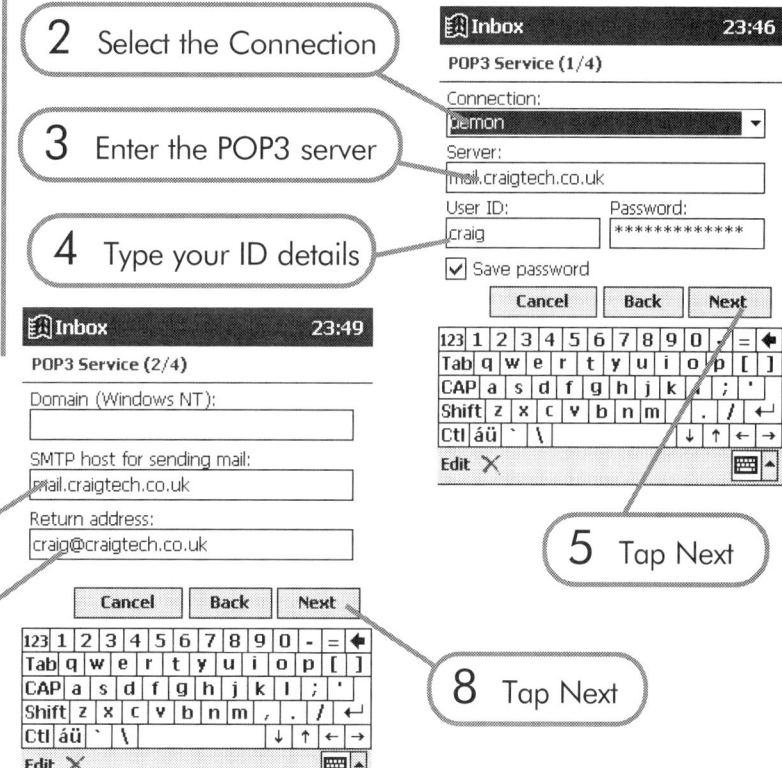

2 Select the Connection

3 Enter the POP3 server

4 Type your ID details

5 Tap Next

6 Enter the SMTP host

7 Type your address

8 Tap Next

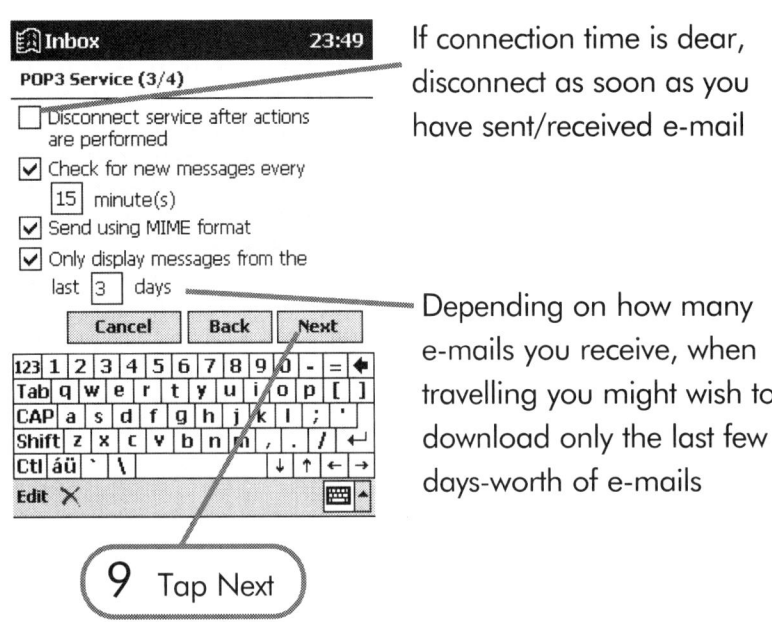

If connection time is dear, disconnect as soon as you have sent/received e-mail

Depending on how many e-mails you receive, when travelling you might wish to download only the last few days-worth of e-mails

9 Tap Next

continued...

9 At stages 3 and 4, leave the settings at the defaults unless you have specific preferences – tap Next.

10 Tap Finish when you are done, then tap ok.

The first 100 lines of an e-mail will normally be enough for the message, though not for an attachment – you can get a full copy later

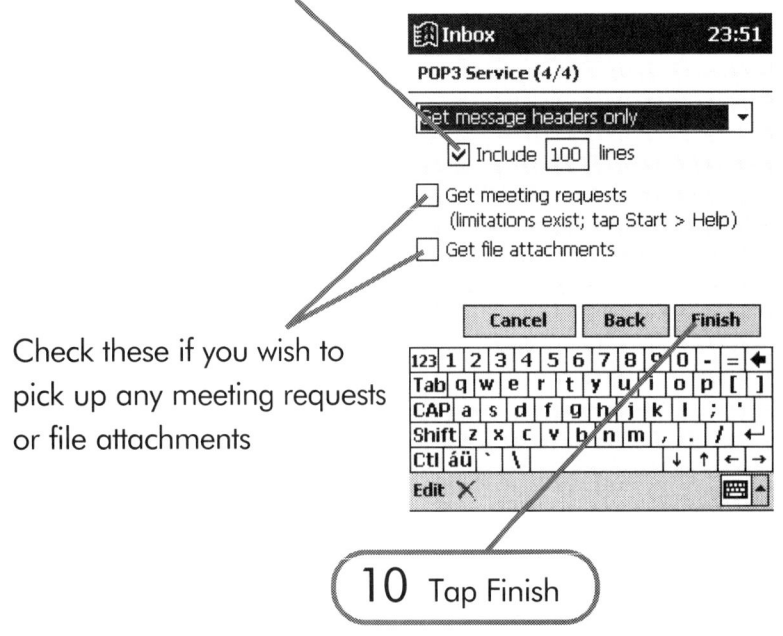

Check these if you wish to pick up any meeting requests or file attachments

10 Tap Finish

Tip

If you enable Inbox in ActiveSync, you can connect your Pocket PC to your PC at home in the morning and copy across your e-mails automatically so that you may read and reply to them during the day. Go to the ActiveSync options screen (see page 44), put a check in the Inbox checkbox and you're all set.

Basic steps

1 Tap the Tools, New Folder... option.

2 Give the folder a name.

3 Tap ok.

The commonly performed functions that you may wish to use on the e-mails in your Inbox, can all be found on the tap and hold menu. Shortly you will see how to move a message to a new folder. But, before you can move any messages you first need to create a folder, so let's start with that.

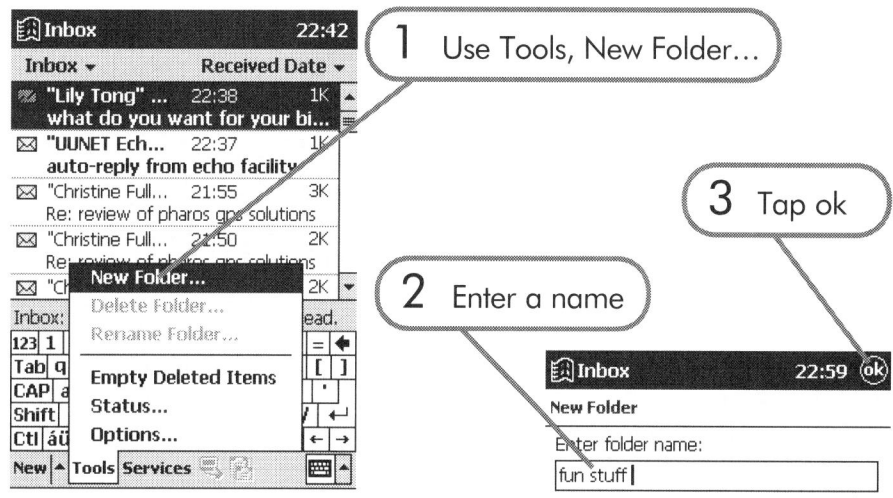

1 Use Tools, New Folder...

2 Enter a name

3 Tap ok

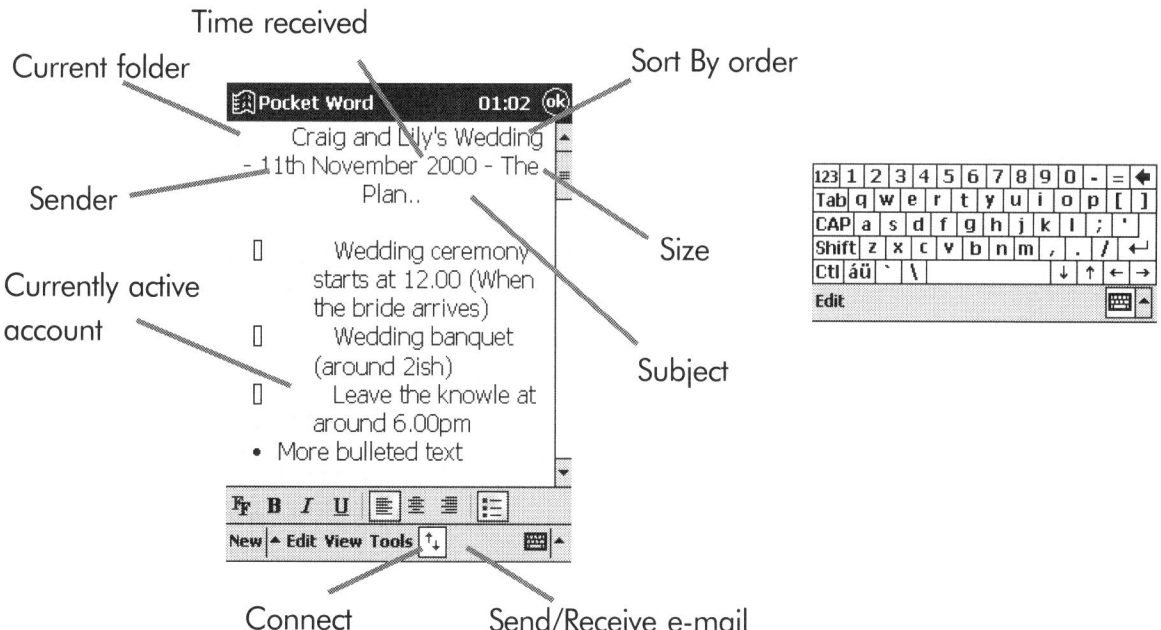

Time received

Current folder

Sort By order

Sender

Size

Currently active account

Subject

Connect

Send/Receive e-mail

Moving messages

Some e-mails can be deleted immediately after reading them; others you want to keep for future reference. If you leave them in the Inbox, it will soon get very cluttered, but it's very simple to move messages from one folder to another.

1 Tap and hold on a message.

2 Select Move to…

3 Select the target folder.

4 You will asked to confirm that you want to move the message – tap Yes.

5 The name of the current folder is shown just beneath the title bar. When you tap on this, a folder list will appear – tap on the name of a folder to navigate to it.

1 Tap and hold on the message

2 Select Move to…

5 Pick the folder from the drop-down list

3 Select the folder

Take note

With the default settings only a small part of most messages will be copied down to your device – so be careful if you move messages.

1 Notice the Get Full Copy icon 🐾 next to the attachment type icon – a Word document in the example.

2 Tap the Edit menu and select Get Full Copy.

Or

3 On the main Inbox screen, tap and hold on the message and select Get Full Copy.

4 When the e-mail has been downloaded the Get Full Copy icon will have vanished from the bottom left of the screen.

With a lot of other portable devices, it's not possible to download and run attachments but with your Pocket PC this process is quite simple.

If you open a message and see a paperclip, then it has an attachment. It's quite likely that you will have to download a full copy of the message to see the attachment, here's how.

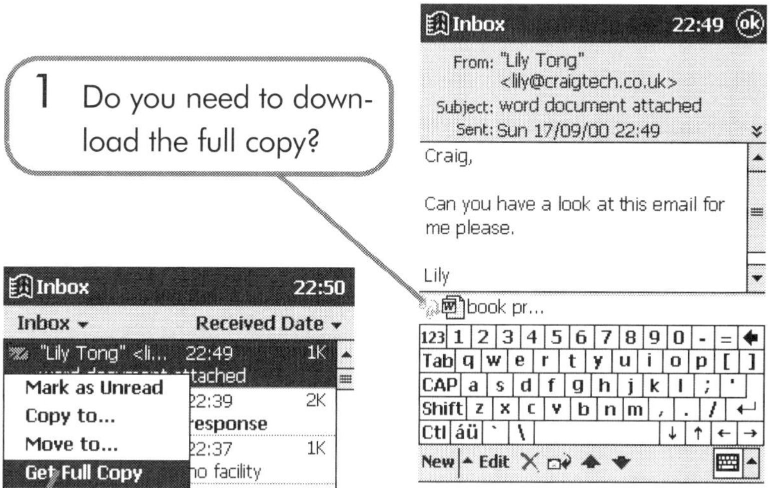

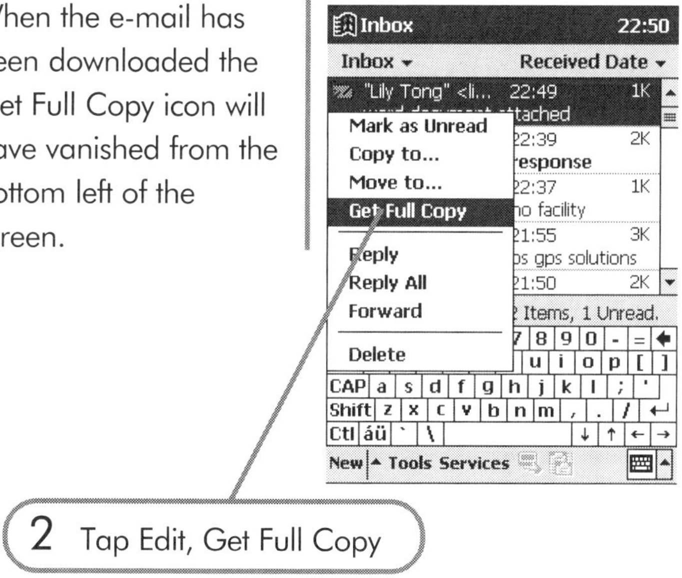

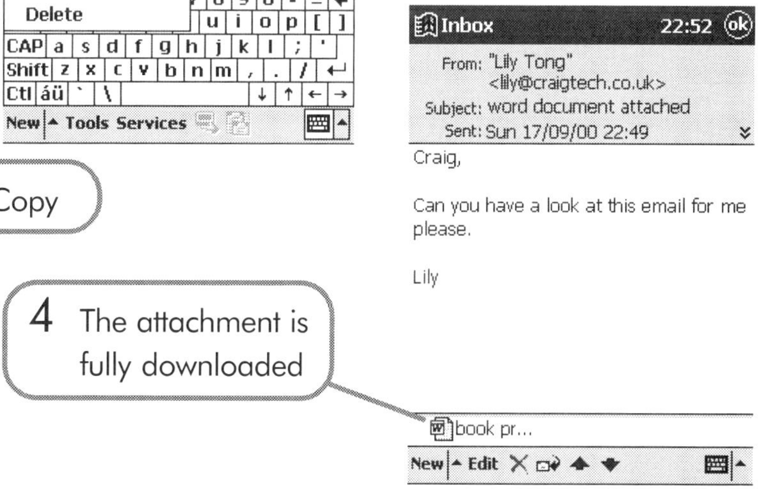

1 Do you need to download the full copy?

2 Tap Edit, Get Full Copy

4 The attachment is fully downloaded

Opening attachments

To open an attachment you just have to click on it, then the application (in this case Pocket Word) will open up the document for you to edit, save or forward on to others.

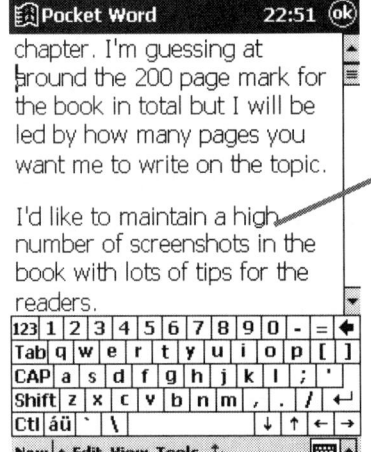

3 Read and action?

1 Tap the icon

Corporate e-mail with XTNDConnect

There are lots of different ways of connecting back to corporate networks so that users of Pocket PCs can remotely access their e-mail, calendar and task information. One of the most popular applications is from a company called Extended Systems. Their XTNDConnect program allows remote users to dial into their office server and get access to e-mail, etc.

In this example, the corporate e-mail server is a Lotus Notes server, which is not natively supported out the box. XTNDConnect allows me to get my Lotus Notes e-mails and calendar wherever I am as well as perform other functions such as remote backup/restore. This solution is made up of both client and server applications.

Basic steps

1 Tap New.

2 In the To: field, enter the e-mail address of the recipient(s).

Or

3 If the person's address is in Contacts, enter the first few letters of the name and tap the Address book icon.

4 Select the recipient(s) from the list and tap ok.

5 Enter a Subject description.

6 Enter your message.

7 Tap the Send icon.

Sending e-mail

When you connect up to your Internet provider, your outbound e-mail is automatically sent and messages waiting for you are transferred to your Pocket PC. If you wish to manually check your e-mail when you are online, simply tap the Send/Receive icon.

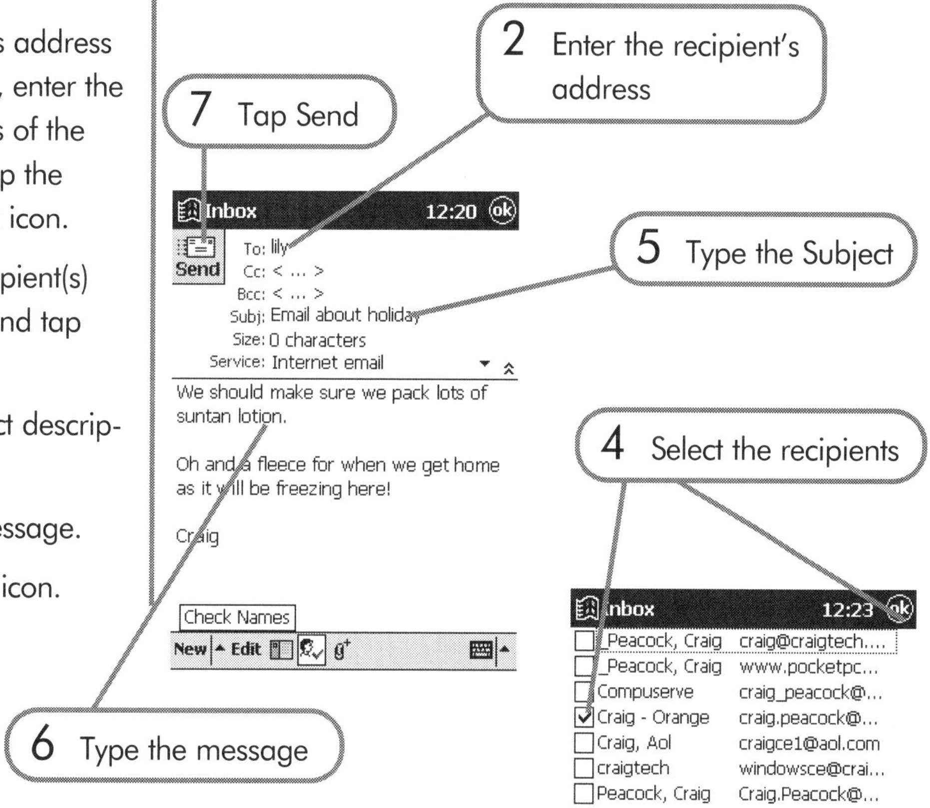

2 Enter the recipient's address

7 Tap Send

5 Type the Subject

Inbox   12:20 (ok)

Send

To: lily
Cc: < ... >
Bcc: < ... >
Subj: Email about holiday
Size: 0 characters
Service: Internet email

We should make sure we pack lots of suntan lotion.

Oh and a fleece for when we get home as it will be freezing here!

Craig

Check Names

New ▲ Edit

4 Select the recipients

Inbox   12:23 (ok)

☐ Peacock, Craig   craig@craigtech....
☐ Peacock, Craig   www.pocketpc...
☐ Compuserve   craig_peacock@...
☑ Craig - Orange   craig.peacock@...
☐ Craig, Aol   craigce1@aol.com
☐ craigtech   windowsce@crai...
☐ Peacock, Craig   Craig.Peacock@...
☐ Peacock1, Craig   craig@pocketpc...

6 Type the message

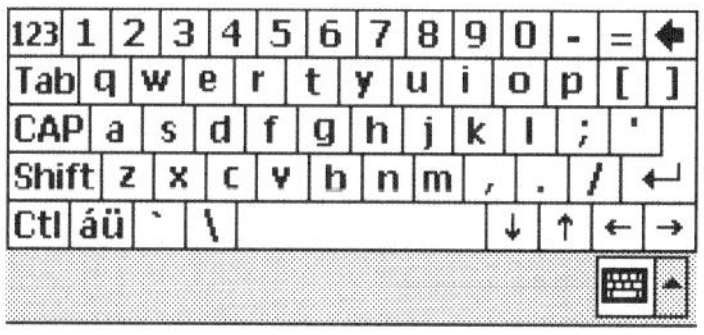

```
123 1 2 3 4 5 6 7 8 9 0 - = ←
Tab q w e r t y u i o p [ ]
CAP a s d f g h j k l ; '
Shift z x c v b n m , . / ↵
Ctl áü ` \              ↓ ↑ ← →
```

Tip

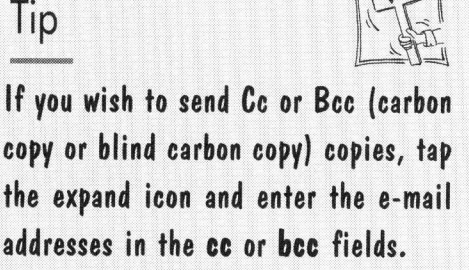

If you wish to send Cc or Bcc (carbon copy or blind carbon copy) copies, tap the expand icon and enter the e-mail addresses in the cc or bcc fields.

Hotmail

One of the many benefits of using a Web-based e-mail account is that you can access it from almost anywhere on the planet. Hotmail has millions of users around the world.

This is how to get access to Hotmail using Pocket Internet Explorer on your Pocket PC – I'm assuming that you already have a Hotmail account, if not head off to www.hotmail.com now and set one up!

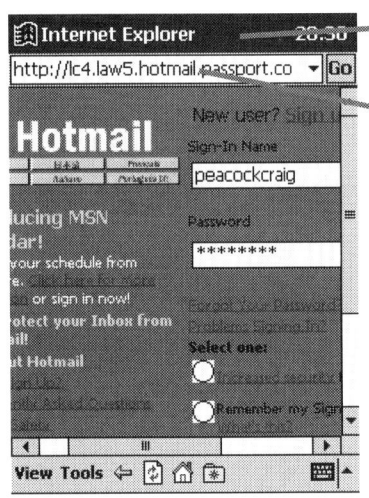

2 Start Internet Explorer

4 Go to Hotmail

When you reach Hotmail, you will be redirected to an available mail server – the address will change

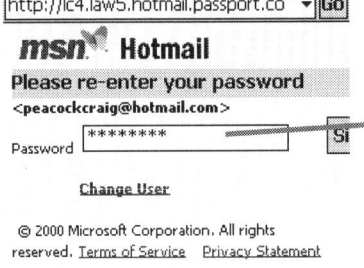

5 Login to the site

6 Tap Yes

Basic steps

1 Connect to your ISP.

2 Open Internet Explorer.

3 If the Address bar isn't showing, tap View, Address Bar.

4 In the address box type in www.hotmail.com

5 Enter your login details.

6 Hotmail checks your details over a secure, encrypted link. You'll see a warning screen when you leave the secure area – tap Yes.

7 Once connected your new messages should appear in the Inbox.

Take note

Internet Explorer stores your user name for sites like Hotmail. For security reasons you will have to re-enter your password.

Basic steps

1 Tap on the name in the From column to open the message to read it.

2 To Reply to or Forward the message, click a link at the top.

3 To delete the message, click Delete at the end or delete several at once by checking them off in the Inbox screen and tapping the Delete Checked box.

4 To compose a new message tap the Compose link on the Inbox screen, enter the recipients, subject and message and send as with normal e-mail.

Dealing with e-mails

Hotmail on your Pocket PC works just like on your desktop PC. All the usual options of reading, replying, forwarding, and sending e-mails are available

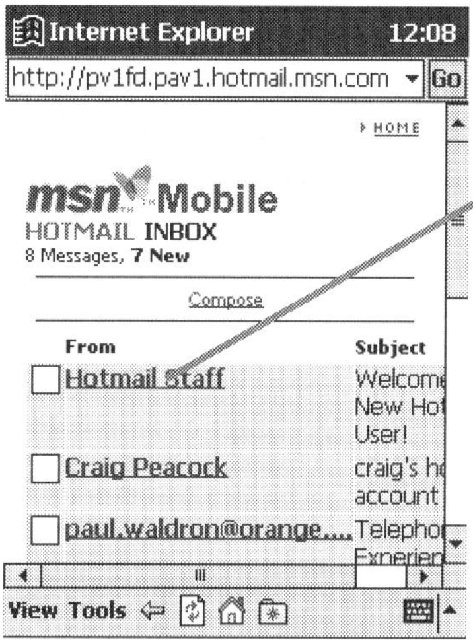

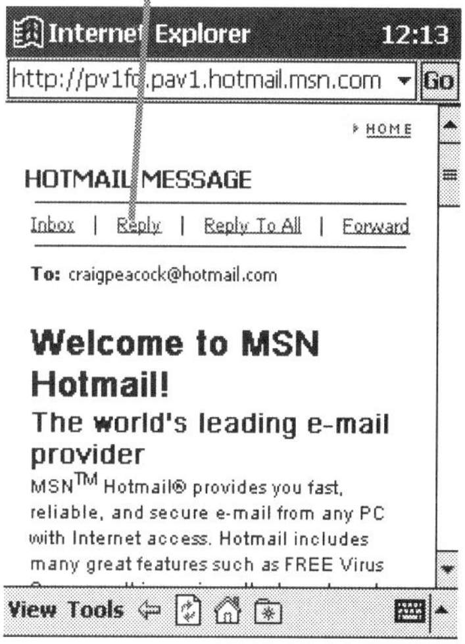

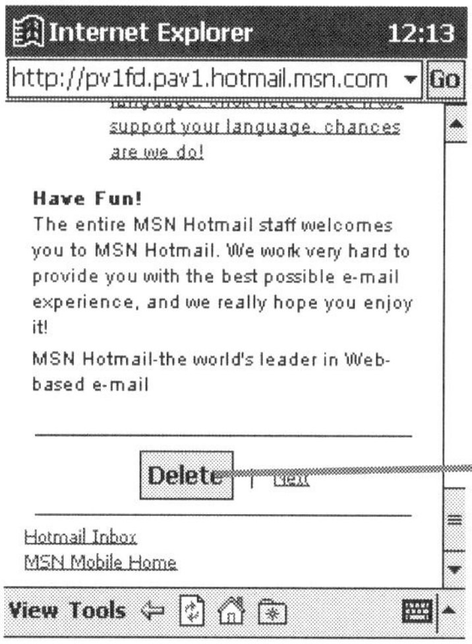

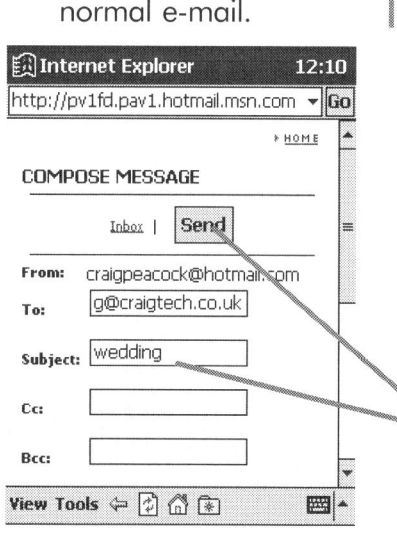

1 Tap to read

2 Respond to the message?

3 Tap to delete

4 Complete and send as normal

Summary

❏ Inbox is the Pocket PC's e-mail software. It extends – but does not replace – the e-mail software on your desktop PC.

❏ You can set up new Inbox folders to provide organized storage for your messages.

❏ Normally, only the first 100 lines of messages are downloaded. If there is an attachment, you may well have to connect up to get the full copy.

❏ When sending a message, you should complete the To, Subject and Message fields. If required, you can also send Cc; or Bcc: copies to other people.

❏ If you access Hotmail through Pocket Internet Explorer, you will have the same range of facilities that you would if you were using your desktop PC.

Take note

The Compaq iPAQ, with its optional jacket, includes an extra battery to help maximize the amount of time you can spend online with a modem on batteries.

8 Pocket Excel

Introducing Excel

You can keep track of your expenses and perform other calculations with Pocket Excel. It has the look and feel of the popular desktop version. Formulas work in the same way and it has the most commonly used features. The financial, date and time, database, and statistical functions are all supported. You can use other features such as AutoFilter, sort colums, hide rows or columns, and even add color to your cells and columns.

We'll start off by creating a simple spreadsheet, in this case one to keep track of golf scores, then I'll show you how to format the text and numbers in selected cells.

The cells to be formatted must be selected first. You can select whole rows or columns, blocks, or single cells.

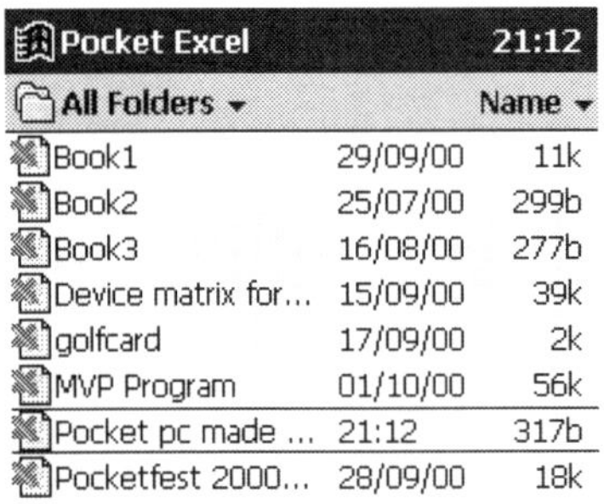

❑ To create a new sheet

1 Tap the New button.

2 Tap into a cell and enter some text or numbers.

❑ Selecting cells

3 Tap a cell to select it.

4 Tap the column heading to select a column.

5 Tap the row heading to select a row.

6 Drag across cells to select a block.

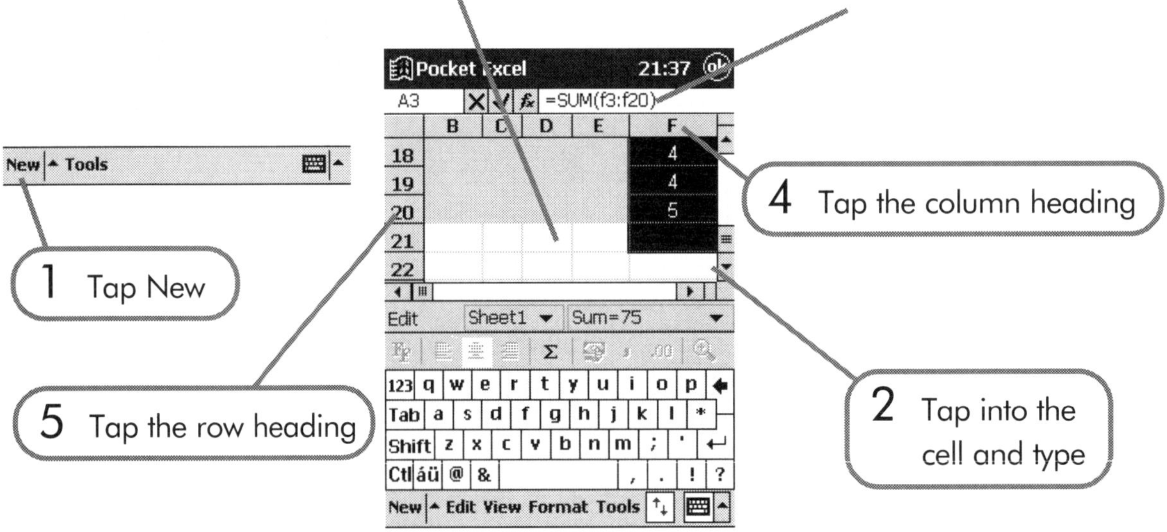

Pocket Excel opens at the list view which shows all Excel files

Pocket Excel		21:12
All Folders ▾		Name ▾
Book1	29/09/00	11k
Book2	25/07/00	299b
Book3	16/08/00	277b
Device matrix for...	15/09/00	39k
golfcard	17/09/00	2k
MVP Program	01/10/00	56k
Pocket pc made ...	21:12	317b
Pocketfest 2000...	28/09/00	18k

The selected cell's data is typed/displayed/edited in the Formula bar

3 Tap a cell to select

New ▲ Tools

1 Tap New

5 Tap the row heading

4 Tap the column heading

2 Tap into the cell and type

Formatting cells

1 Select the cells then tap Format, Cells...

❑ Setting the font

2 Go to the Font tab.

3 Set the Font, Color, Size and Style.

❑ Aligning a column

4 Go to the Align tab.

5 Set the alignment – horizontal *and* vertical.

❑ Highlighting cells

6 Go to the Borders tab.

7 Tap Fills and select an appropriate colour.

8 Tap ok to leave the Format Cells dialog box.

You can make things stand out by using different fonts, style, and sizes, or by adding coloured backgrounds or borders.

You can set the Size, Number format, Alignment, Font, and Border styles from the tabs of the Format Cells dialog.

1 Tap Format, Cells...

3 Define the appearance

8 Tap ok

5 Set the alignment

2 Tap Font

4 Tap Align

6 Tap Borders

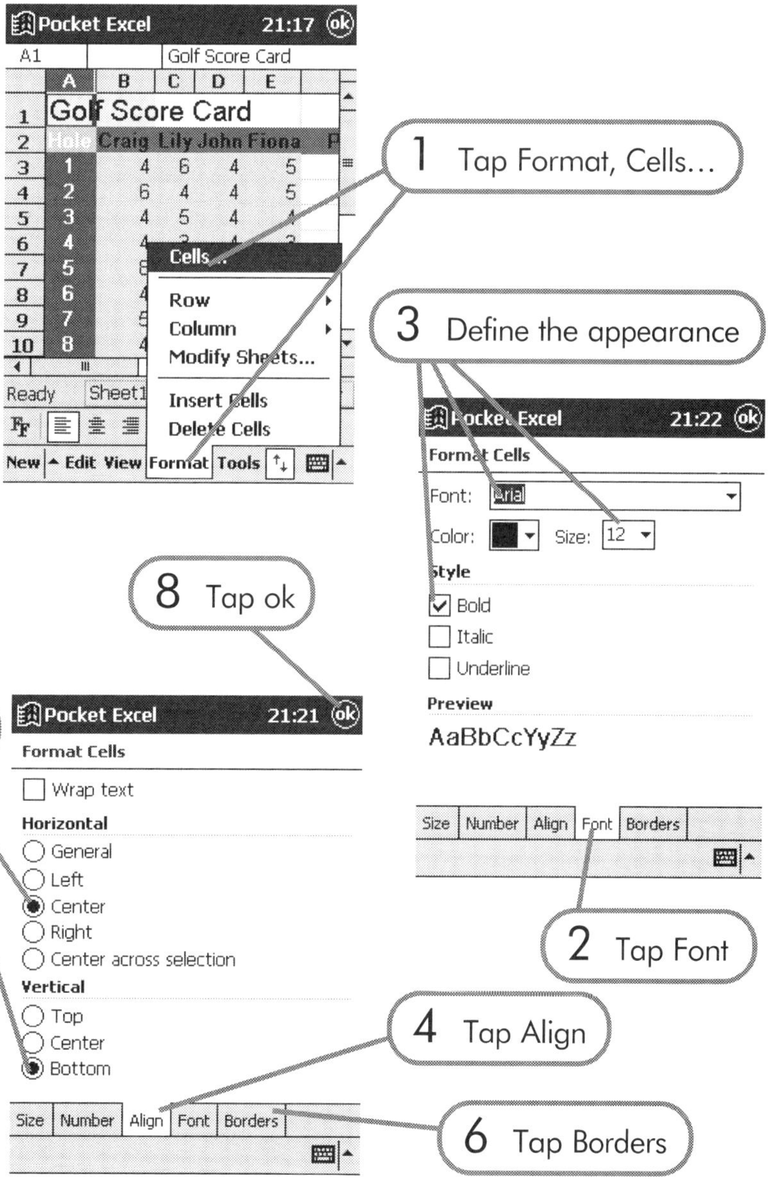

Tip

When setting colors, you can see a sample at the bottom of the screen.

Functions and formulas

Whenever you enter a formula in Excel it always begins with an equal sign =. In the example below, =Sum(F3:F20), we are adding up the values in the cells F3 to F20 and placing the answer in cell F21.

One of the most commonly performed tasks in Excel is to add up numbers. In the example of my golf scores I'm going to add up the par column and then see how well we all did against par.

To add up numbers in a column we can use AutoSum.

To work out how many over or under par we are, I used a simple formula, such as =B21-F21. This takes the player's total (F21) from the par total (B21).

1 Tap on the cell below the last number, where the formula will go.

2 Drag and highlight up to the first cell. The Sum field shows the total of the highlighted cells.

3 Tap the AutoSum icon to enter the formula. Check that it is correct – SUM(F3:F20) in this example.

4 Tap the check on the Formula bar to enter the formula.

5 Repeat to put a Sum below all the columns.

6 Tap the empty cell under the first person's total field.

7 Enter the formula =B21-F21.

8 Enter the appropriate formula for the other fields.

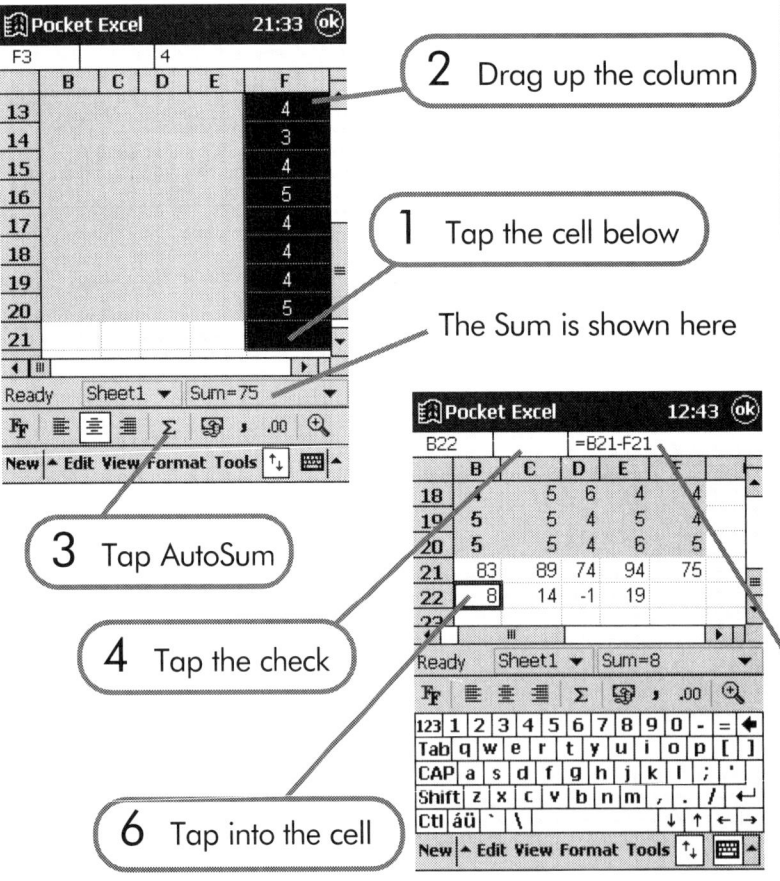

2 Drag up the column

1 Tap the cell below

The Sum is shown here

3 Tap AutoSum

4 Tap the check

6 Tap into the cell

7 Type in the formula

Basic steps

1 Tap on the cell immediately below and to the right of the one you wish to freeze. In my example this is A3.

2 Tap View.

3 Tap Freeze Panes.

4 Scroll around and the titles will remain on display.

Adjusting the view

As screen space is so limited on the Pocket PC compared to the desktop then the ability to 'freeze the panes' is really handy. This fixes the rows above and/or the columns to the left of a selected cell so that they do not move when you scroll the sheet. This keeps the titles of columns or rows in view, wherever you are on the sheet.

Here's how to do it.

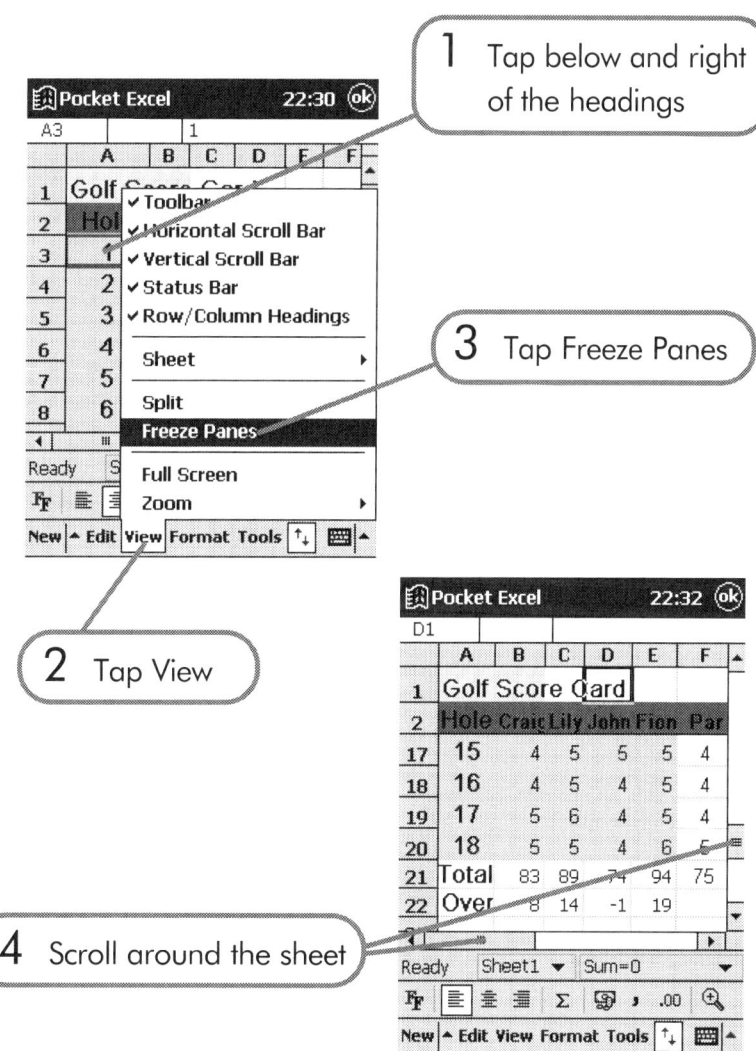

1 Tap below and right of the headings

3 Tap Freeze Panes

2 Tap View

4 Scroll around the sheet

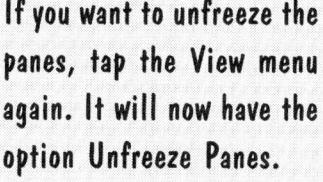

Take note

If you want to unfreeze the panes, tap the View menu again. It will now have the option Unfreeze Panes.

115

Templates and saving

A template is a spreadsheet with all the cells defined but not yet filled in. They are typically used to save you time when entering routine information.

A mileage log template is included with your Pocket PC.

You can also save your own spreadsheets as templates, for later reuse with new data.

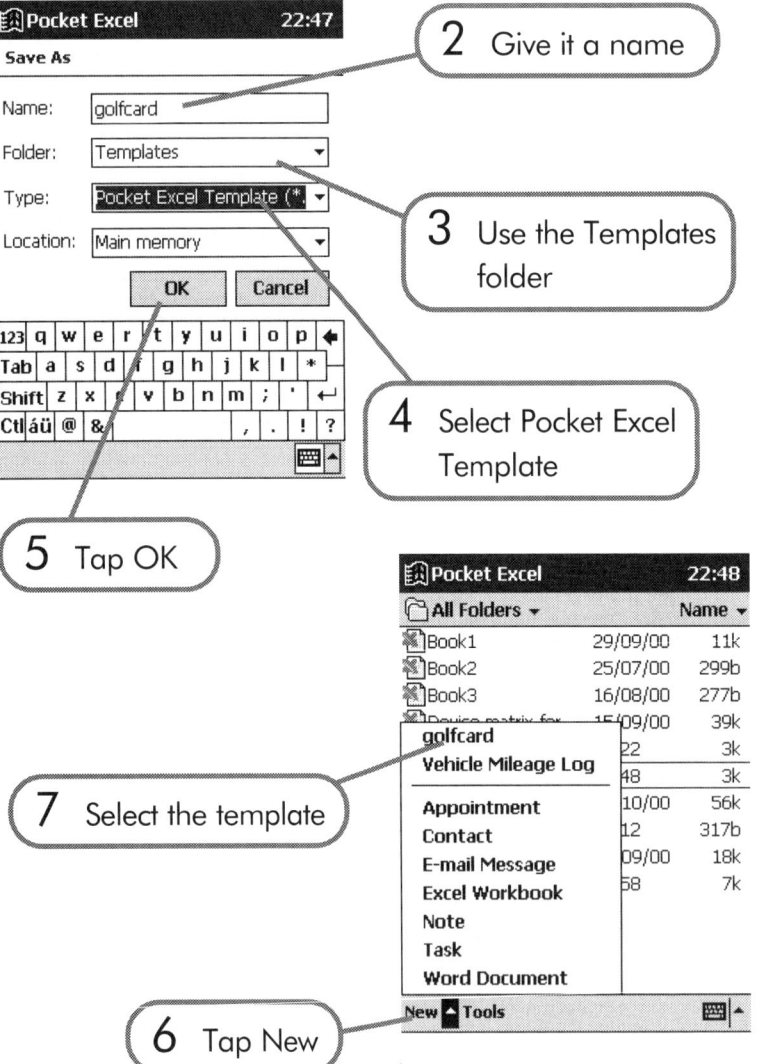

2 Give it a name

3 Use the Templates folder

4 Select Pocket Excel Template

5 Tap OK

7 Select the template

6 Tap New

Basic steps

❏ Creating a template

1 Tap Tools, Save Work-book As.

2 Enter a Name.

3 Select the Templates Folder.

4 Select *Pocket Excel Template* as the Type.

5 Tap OK.

❏ Using a template

6 Tap the New menu icon to see the newly created template.

7 Tap the template name to create a new worksheet based on it.

Take note

To use templates, you must switch on the New menu.

The Save As options

Tip

For a good introduction to Excel check out *Excel Made Simple*.

The Save As routine supports saving Excel sheets in several different formats including Pocket Excel Templates, Excel 95 and Excel 97/2000.

You can also use Save As to save a sheet to a storage card or to a different folder on your Pocket PC.

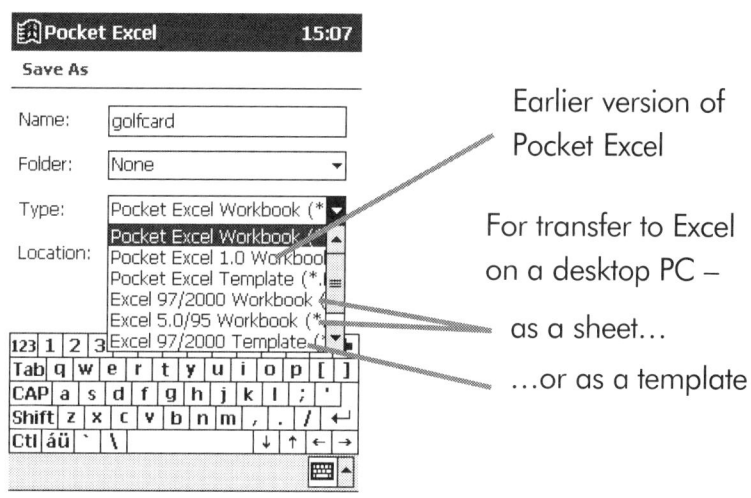

Earlier version of Pocket Excel

For transfer to Excel on a desktop PC –

as a sheet…

…or as a template

Tap New and don't save to abandon the changes you have made

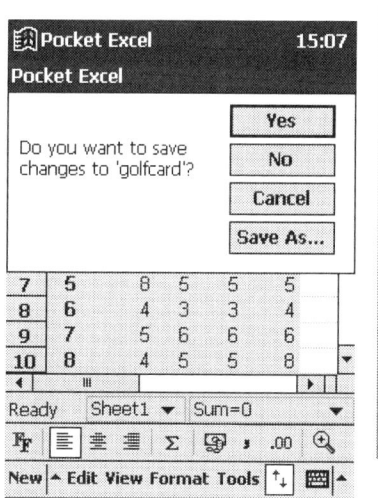

Coping with errors

If you've accidentally made changes to a spreadsheet and don't want to save them, then you have three choices.

- Use the **Revert to saved** option on the **Tools** menu.

- Use the **Save Workbook As** option and give the sheet document a new name so that you can compare the two.

- If you have the new menu enabled, then you can tap New to bring up a dialog box asking if you are sure you want to save changes. If you tap **No** your changes will be lost.

Summary

❏ Pocket Excel has all of the most important features of the desktop version.

❏ The Format options let you set the size, number style, alignment, font, colour and borders of selected cells.

❏ All the important functions are available.

❏ With AutoSum you can quickly produce a formula to find the total of a set of cells.

❏ Formulas should start with '=', and can take values from cell references, functions, or from given values.

❏ The Freeze Panes feature allows you to fix the title columns or rows so that they remain visible wherever you scroll on the sheet.

❏ Files can be saved as templates for later reuse. They can also be saved in formats for use with the earlier version of Pocket Excel format, or Excel 5.0/95 or Excel 97/2000.

9 Multimedia

Microsoft Reader

This e-book reader will allow you to read books on your Pocket PC with a clarity that makes it really easy on the eyes. With features such as the ability to annotate text, look up words, bookmark your favourite pages and even let you listen to audio books, Reader is a powerful and easy-to-use application.

The first screen displayed when you start Microsoft Reader is the **Library screen**, which lists all the titles you have installed on your Pocket PC. Nine titles are displayed per page.

Basic steps

❑ To open Microsoft Reader

1 Tap the Start button.

2 Tap Programs.

3 Tap Reader.

The title screen for Reader – ClearType improves the readability of text on Pocket PC screens

Reader sorting options

List by title, author, last opened, size or date acquired

List those containing certain words

Page Navigator – shown in roman numerals i, ii, iii

Return to Library

Launch Guidebook

Return to previous screen

Navigating in Reader

1 Tap the Page Navigator icon to see the next set of titles.

Or

2 Tap the by arrow and select the display order.

Or

3 Tap Showing all.

4 Tap containing... and enter one or more key words from the desired book – this will search for matching titles and display the results.

If you have lots of titles installed on your device then all the titles won't be displayed on one page, there are several ways to find titles installed on your Pocket PC.

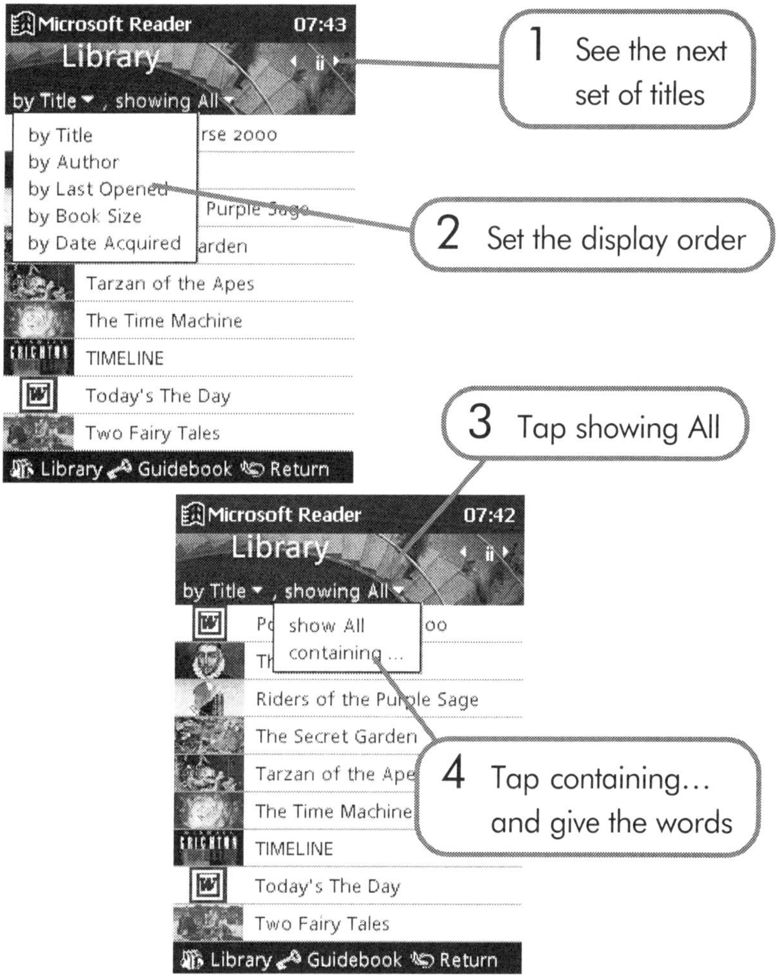

| Microsoft Reader | 07:43 |
| Library | ◀ ii ▶ |

by Title ▼ , showing All ▼

by Title .... rse 2000
by Author
by Last Opened
by Book Size .... Purple Sage
by Date Acquired .... arden

Tarzan of the Apes

The Time Machine

TIMELINE

Today's The Day

Two Fairy Tales

📚 Library 📖 Guidebook 🔖 Return

1 See the next set of titles

2 Set the display order

| Microsoft Reader | 07:42 |
| Library | ◀ ii ▶ |

by Title ▼ , showing All ▼

Po .... oo
    show All
Th containing ...

Riders of the Purple Sage

The Secret Garden

Tarzan of the Ape

The Time Machine

TIMELINE

Today's The Day

Two Fairy Tales

📚 Library 📖 Guidebook 🔖 Return

3 Tap showing All

4 Tap containing... and give the words

Take note

If you think some titles aren't displayed, tap showing All and select show All to display all your titles.

Tip

Tapping on the title picture will take you to the most recently read page in the book.

Reading e-books

To open an e-book and start reading it, you just have to tap on its title or picture. The e-book's cover page will then be displayed, as in the picture below.

Reader showing the cover page of an e-book

The cover page will probably have a contents list – tap on an entry to go to it

Annotations Index   First page
Quick Settings   Most recent
Quick Start   Furthest read
How To
Table of Contents

🏛 Library ✎ Guidebook ↩ Return

(**3**   Previous page)

Microsoft Reader   2:38p

Microsoft Reader Gu... ▼   ◀ 20 ▶

Skipping to a Page

Hold on the page number to se-lect an option from the pop-up menu. Then, tap:

- **Go to**, to specify the page number you want to go to.
- **Go to end**, to go to the end of the book.

Note: If you change the font size of the text (through Quick Set-tings), the book will repaginate to accommodate the size. That is,

(**2**   Next page)

(**4**   Go to a chosen page)

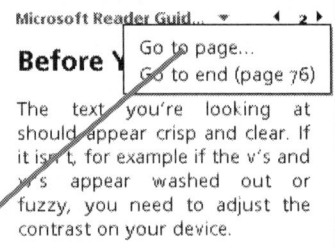

Microsoft Reader   07:36

Microsoft Reader Guid... ▼   ◀ 2 ▶

Before Y   Go to page...
   Go to end (page 76)

The text you're looking at should appear crisp and clear. If it isn't, for example if the v's and w's appear washed out or fuzzy, you need to adjust the contrast on your device.

The text is clearest with a high contrast setting. If your device has a contrast control, try ex-perimenting with the setting to see what contrast level works best for you.

Basic steps

❑ To navigate around a book

1 Use the scroll wheel on the side of your Pocket PC to go forward or back one page at a time.

Or

2 Tap to the right of the page number to go forward a page.

3 Tap to the left of the page number to go back a page

4 Tap the down arrow then Go to page... and enter the number to go to a specific page.

Take note

Cleartype is the technol-ogy that makes the text easier to read on your Pocket PC's display.

Advanced Reader functions

Reader has many functions and features including the ability to bookmark text for quick navigation later on, highlight, annotate text and even draw your own comments regarding a particular title. It's also possible to look up words and copy text.

With most e-books, you can tap and hold on any given word to see a menu appear. The options are shown below.

Take note

Some e-books do not support tap and hold menus.

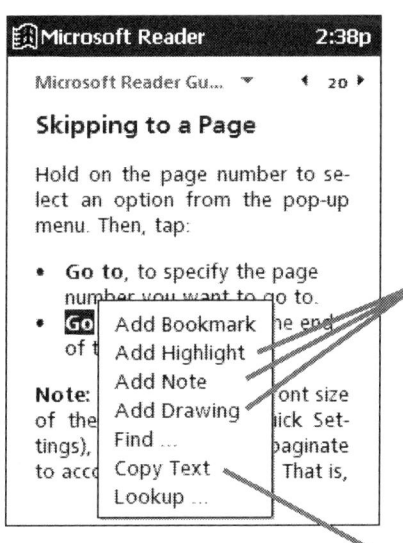

An e-book is a document, and although you can't change its text, you can add your own highlights, notes or sketches – just as you can in the margins of a paper book.

Drag over the text you want before you use the Copy Text option.

Installing books

Installing Microsoft Reader e-books is very easy as the program automatically searches for titles that are copied to *\My Documents* or any folder one level below e.g., *\My Documents\ebooks*.

To install an e-book copy it to the *\My Documents* folder, as shown on page 47, and it will show up in the Library screen when Reader is next started.

Where can I find e-books?

Almost thirty of them are included on the Microsoft ActiveSync CD-ROM that comes with every Pocket PC but there are a great number available from leading online retailers such as Barnes and Noble (**www.bn.com/ebooks**).

Audible books

As well as reading books, Audible (ww.audible.com) has created a way of listening to them on your Pocket PC. Their excellent desktop software very largely automates the process of converting an e-book to an audio file.

Tip

You can find out more details about e-books at www.microsoft.com/ reader.

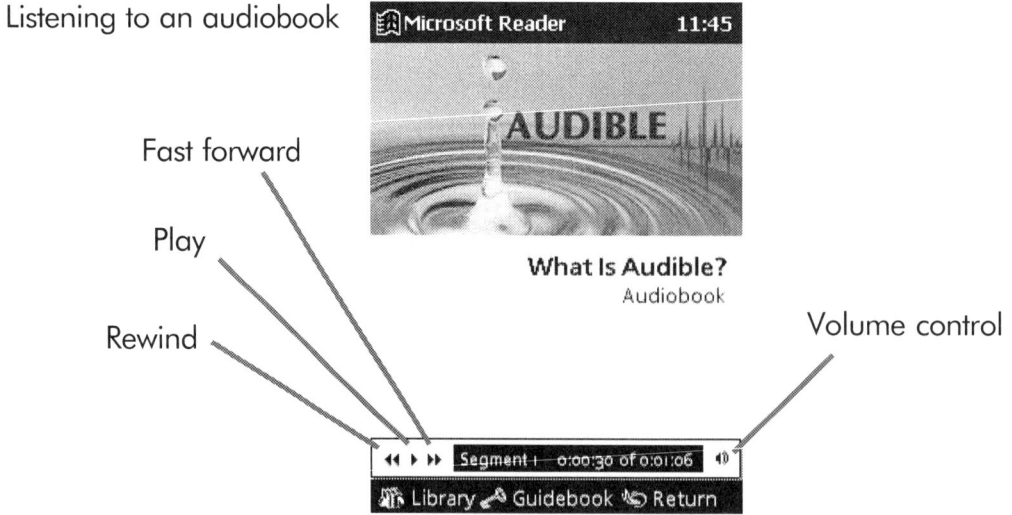

Listening to an audiobook

Fast forward

Play

Rewind

Volume control

Creating e-books

Basic steps

1 On your PC, open a Word document.

2 Click the Reader Icon.

3 Enter the Title, Author and Filename details.

4 Click OK.

❑ Your ebook will be saved in the *\My documents\My Library* folder on your PC. You can then copy it to your Pocket PC for reading.

The Read in Microsoft Reader add-in for Microsoft Word enables you to convert any Word document into a Microsoft Reader format eBook in just a few simple steps.

The software adds another icon to the Word toolbar. When clicked, the Reader icon runs a wizard to step you through the conversion.

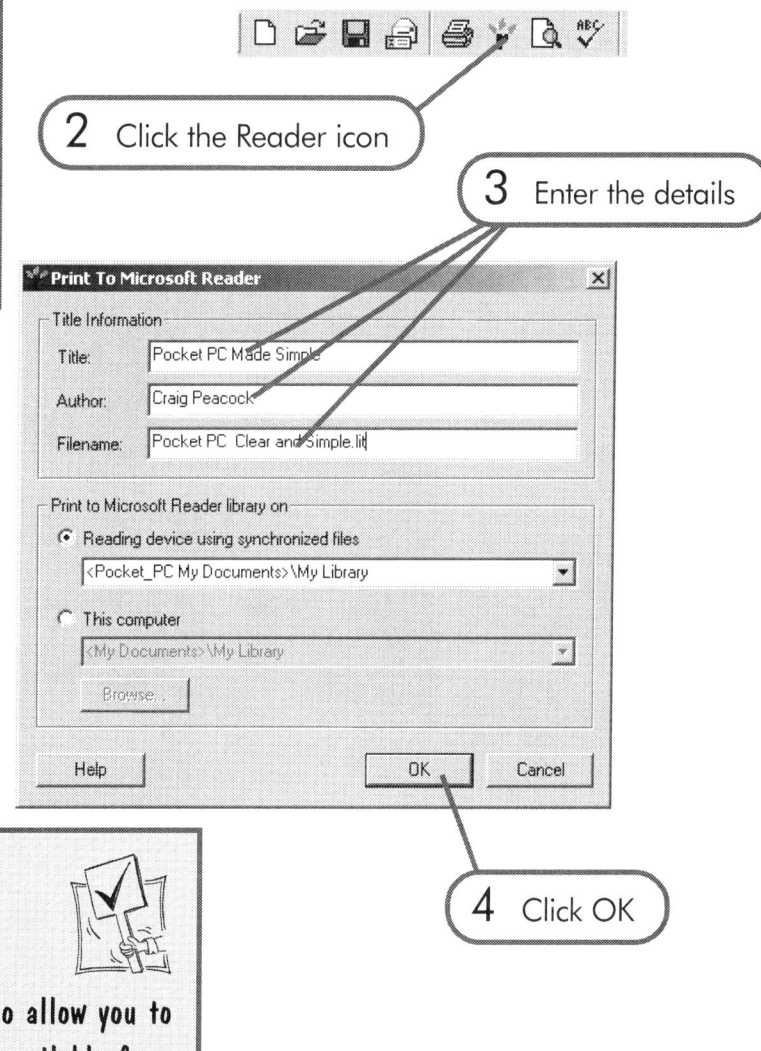

2 Click the Reader icon

3 Enter the details

Print To Microsoft Reader

Title Information

Title: Pocket PC Made Simple

Author: Craig Peacock

Filename: Pocket PC Clear and Simple.lit

Print to Microsoft Reader library on

⦿ Reading device using synchronized files
<Pocket_PC My Documents>\My Library

○ This computer
<My Documents>\My Library

Browse...

Help   OK   Cancel

4 Click OK

Tip

Readerworks software will also allow you to create your own e-books. It's available from http://www.overdrive.com/readerworks/.

Media Player

The Microsoft Media Player on your Pocket PC allows you to play music files such as those recorded in the popular MP3 format or the Microsoft Windows Media Format (WMF).

The application's many features include the facility to let you create your own lists of files and to configure hardware buttons to save you tapping the screen. You can also change the look and feel of Media Player – sometimes known as changing the 'skin.'

Media Player screen

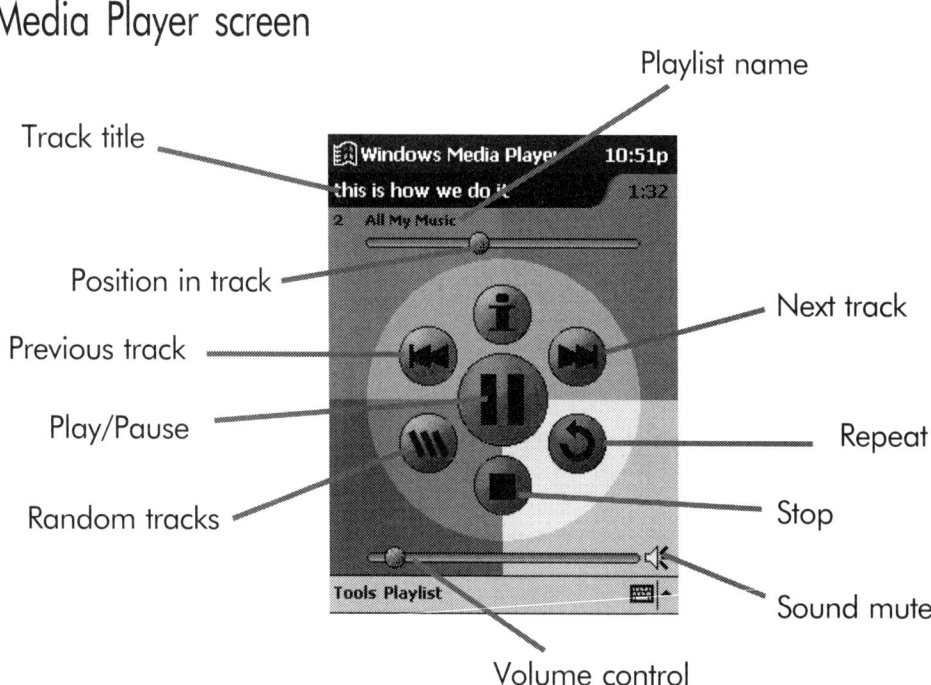

Playlist name

Track title

Position in track

Previous track

Play/Pause

Random tracks

Next track

Repeat

Stop

Sound mute

Volume control

Playing Windows Media Format files

Use Microsoft ActiveSync to copy the files from your PC to your Pocket PC. Once they are in the \My Documents folder, or a folder below it, the files will automatically show up in the Playlist section.

Basic steps

1 Tap All My Music.

2 Tap All Playlists...

3 Tap New.

4 Give the Playlist a name and tap ok.

5 Select the tracks you wish to include and tap ok (see Adding tracks, page 128).

❏ Renaming Playlists

6 Tap the Playlist title, then tap All Playlists...

7 Select the playlist.

8 Tap Rename.

9 Change the name and tap ok.

Playlists

When you copy music files to the \My Documents folder (or folders within it) on your Pocket PC, the system will automatically add the new files to the playlist titled 'All My Music.'

Listening to all the music on your device is the default for the system and for most people it's the only Playlist option they need. For the more adventurous or simply curious here are the options available.

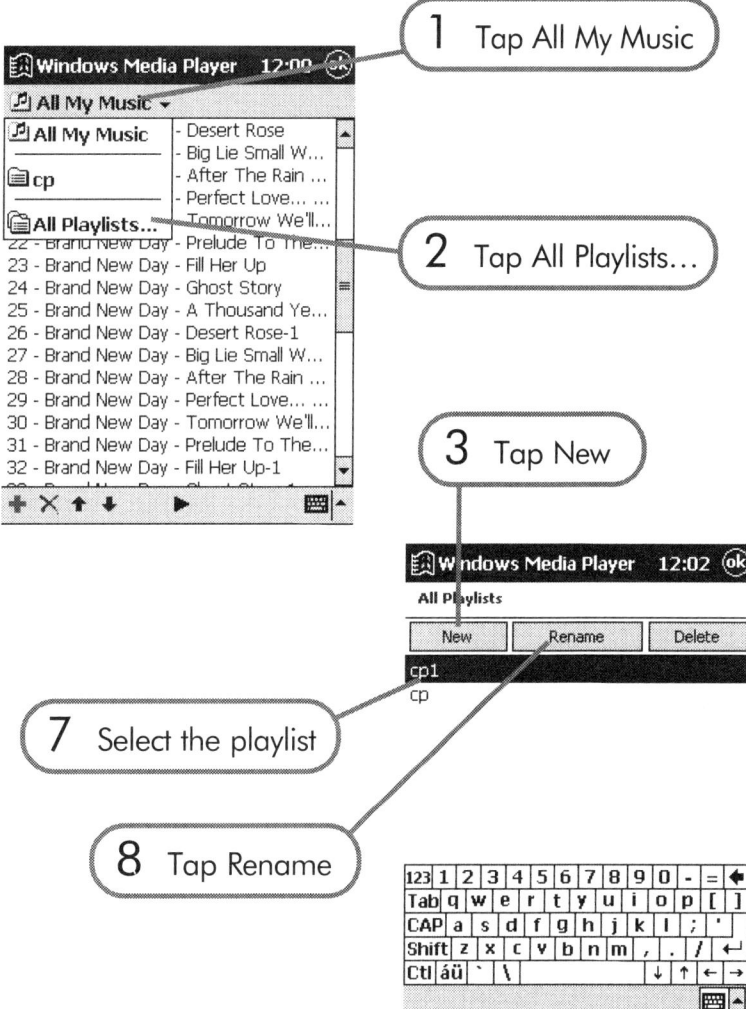

Tip

If you have a storage card that you wish to store music files on, then they must be copied to the \My Documents folder or else they won't appear in the Media Player application.

- Adding tracks
1 Tap Playlist.
2 Tap the plus icon.
3 Check the boxes to select the tracks required.
4 Tap ok.
- Selecting Playlists
5 Tap Select Playlist.
6 Tap the playlist title.
7 Tap the play icon to start playing the music.

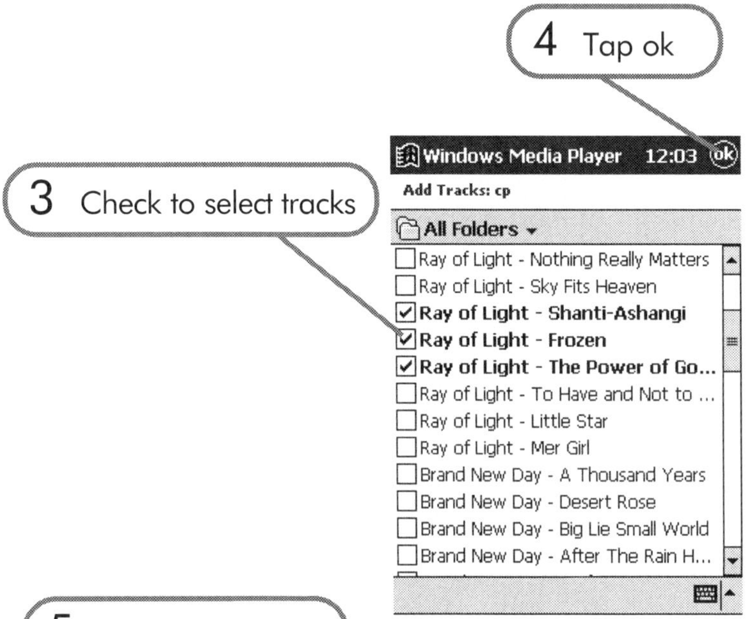

4 Tap ok

3 Check to select tracks

Windows Media Player 12:03 ok

Add Tracks: cp

All Folders ▾

☐ Ray of Light - Nothing Really Matters
☐ Ray of Light - Sky Fits Heaven
☑ **Ray of Light - Shanti-Ashangi**
☑ **Ray of Light - Frozen**
☑ **Ray of Light - The Power of Go...**
☐ Ray of Light - To Have and Not to ...
☐ Ray of Light - Little Star
☐ Ray of Light - Mer Girl
☐ Brand New Day - A Thousand Years
☐ Brand New Day - Desert Rose
☐ Brand New Day - Big Lie Small World
☐ Brand New Day - After The Rain H...

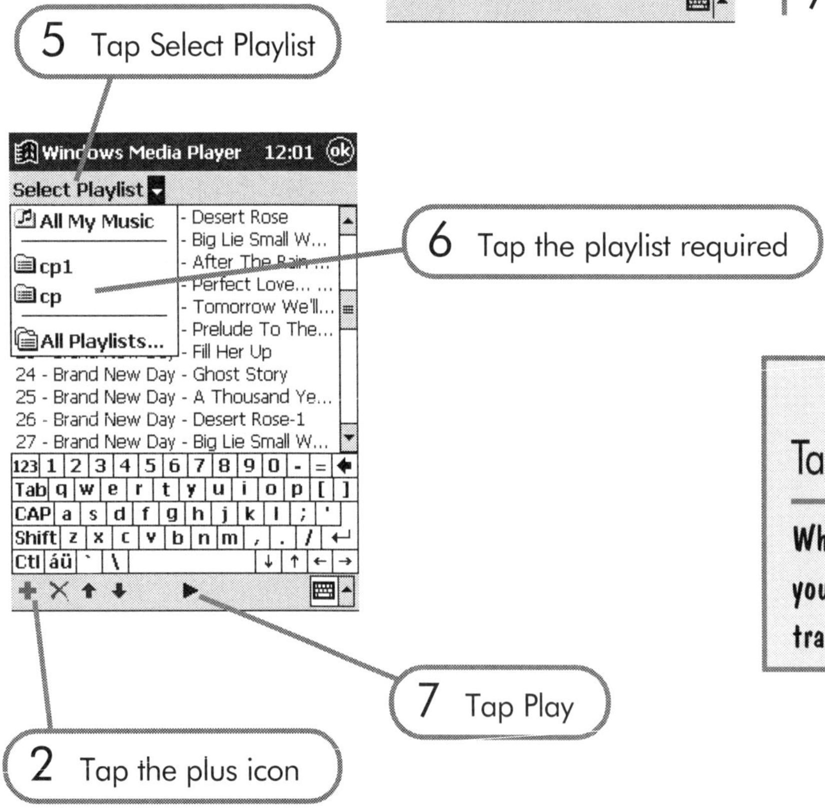

5 Tap Select Playlist

Windows Media Player 12:01 ok

Select Playlist ▾

♫ All My Music
🗎 cp1
🗎 cp
All Playlists...

- Desert Rose
- Big Lie Small W...
- After The Rain ...
- Perfect Love... ...
- Tomorrow We'll...
- Prelude To The...
- Fill Her Up
24 - Brand New Day - Ghost Story
25 - Brand New Day - A Thousand Ye...
26 - Brand New Day - Desert Rose-1
27 - Brand New Day - Big Lie Small W...

123 1 2 3 4 5 6 7 8 9 0 - = ◆
Tab q w e r t y u i o p [ ]
CAP a s d f g h j k l ; '
Shift z x c v b n m , . / ↵
Ctl áü ` \ ↓ ↑ ← →
＋ ✕ ↑ ↓ ▶ ▦

6 Tap the playlist required

7 Tap Play

2 Tap the plus icon

Take note

When you create a new playlist, you are taken to the Add tracks screen automatically.

Media Player skins

❑ To create your own skin

1 Download the Skin Chooser into your desktop PC.

2 Open up ActiveSync and click Explore.

3 Double-click on *My Pocket PC*, then on *Windows*.

4 On your PC, open the folder where you saved the Skin Chooser.

5 Drag and drop the Skin Chooser onto the Start Menu folder.

continued...

If you like to customize the look of your application then there is a free download available for the Media Player application that allows you to do this quickly and easily. It's called the Media Player Skin Chooser.

The Skin Chooser can be downloaded from:

http://www.microsoft.com/windows/windowsmedia/en/software/players/Skins.asp

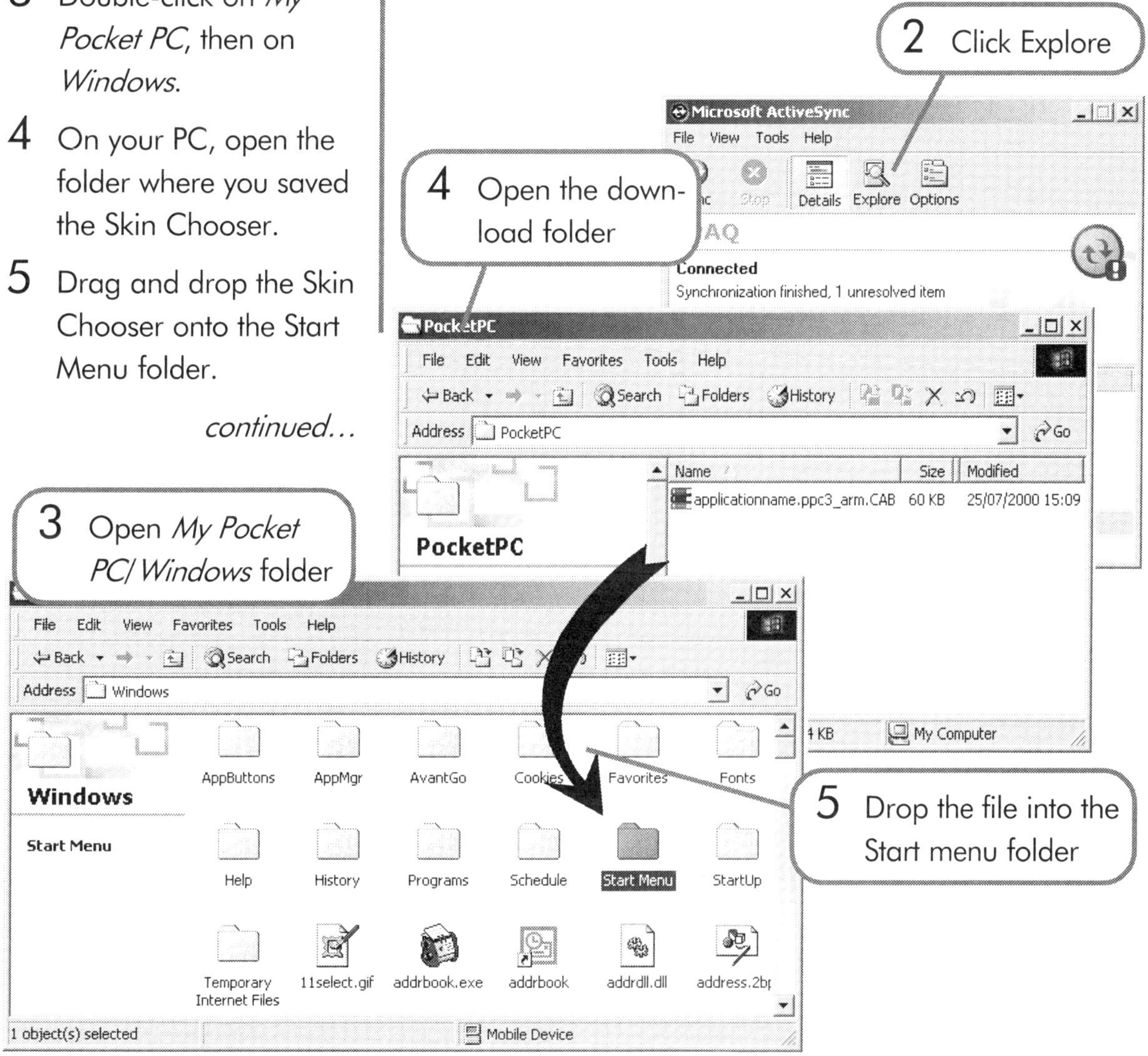

> 2 Click Explore

> 4 Open the download folder

Microsoft ActiveSync

File   View   Tools   Help

Details   Explore   Options

AQ

Connected
Synchronization finished, 1 unresolved item

PocketPC

File   Edit   View   Favorites   Tools   Help

Back ▾ → ▾ 🔄   🔍Search   🗂Folders   🕘History | 🗐 🗐 ✕ ∽   🖩▾

Address 🗋 PocketPC   ▾ ∂Go

Name	Size	Modified
📄applicationname.ppc3_arm.CAB	60 KB	25/07/2000 15:09

PocketPC

> 3 Open *My Pocket PC/ Windows* folder

File   Edit   View   Favorites   Tools   Help

Back ▾ → ▾ 🔄   🔍Search   🗂Folders   🕘History | 🗐 🗐 ✕ ∽   🖩▾

Address 🗋 Windows   ▾ ∂Go

Windows

AppButtons   AppMgr   AvantGo   Cookies   Favorites   Fonts

Start Menu

Help   History   Programs   Schedule   Start Menu   StartUp

Temporary Internet Files   11select.gif   addrbook.exe   addrbook   addrdll.dll   address.2bp

1 object(s) selected   🖳 Mobile Device

4 KB   🖳 My Computer

> 5 Drop the file into the Start menu folder

📖 File Explorer		12:45
Show ▾		Name ▾

My Device 4/09/00 63.8K
  My Documents 4/09/00 208B
   • OuterSpace 4/09/00 2.04K

📄 pushed	14/09/00	5.82K
📄 region	14/09/00	8.49K
📄 seekthumb	14/09/00	80B
📄 super	14/09/00	348B
📄 volumethumb	14/09/00	832B

Edit   ⌨ ▴

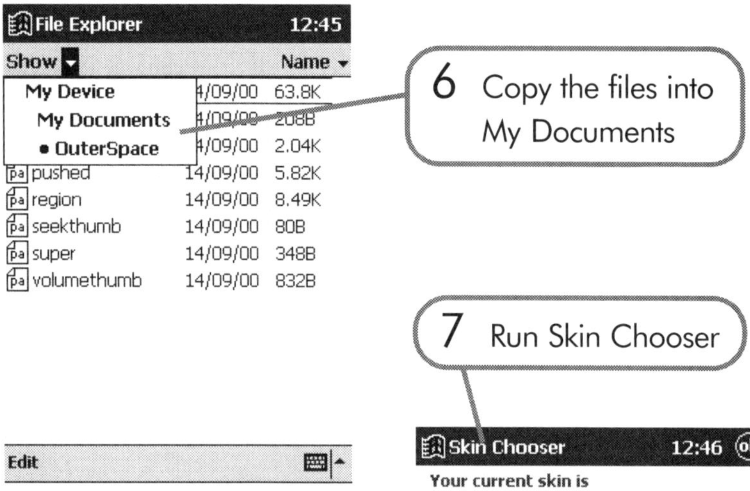

This screen shot from File Explorer (see page 134) shows the skin file in the My Documents folder

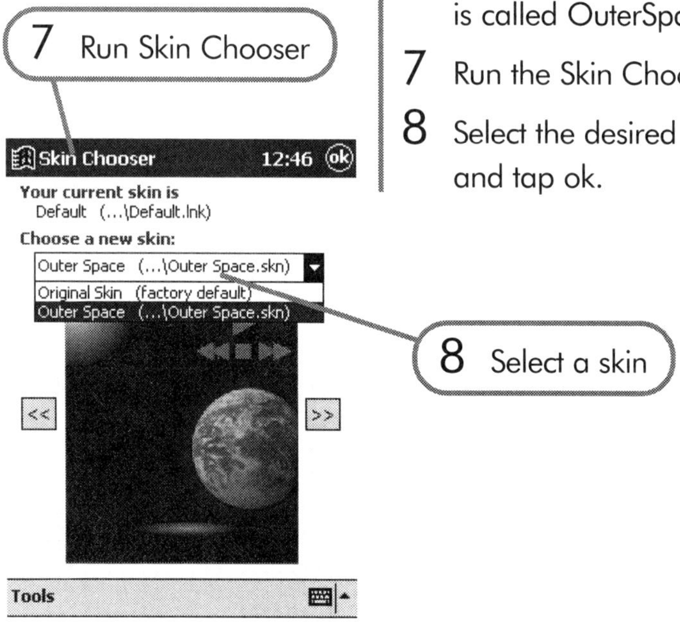

6   Copy the files into My Documents

7   Run Skin Chooser

📖 Skin Chooser	12:46 (ok)

Your current skin is
Default (...\Default.lnk)
Choose a new skin:

Outer Space (...\Outer Space.skn) ▾
Original Skin (factory default)
Outer Space (...\Outer Space.skn)

◄◄ ■ ►►

<<   >>

Tools   ⌨ ▴

8   Select a skin

continued...

6   Copy the files for the skin you've created to your Pocket PC into the \My Documents folder. In the example the skin is called OuterSpace.

7   Run the Skin Chooser.

8   Select the desired skin and tap ok.

📖 Windows Media Player	12:47

Media Player with its new skin!

Tip

On your PC, visit **www.pocketpchelp.com.** It includes links to free downloads for your Pocket PC.

Tools Playlist   ⌨ ▴

Video

Several third-party vendors have written applications that allow you to watch video clips on your Pocket PC. The video clips can be either locally stored on your Pocket PC or reached via an Internet server.

Pocket TV

Pocket TV plays files in the standard MPEG format and with a little technical knowledge you can take feeds from video cameras and with the appropriate hardware and software have the video clips shown on your Pocket PC. Showing how to record your own clips is outside the scope of this book but playback is straightforward.

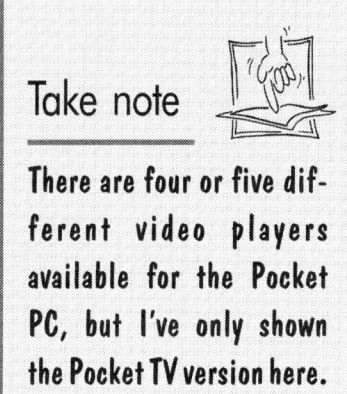

Take note

There are four or five different video players available for the Pocket PC, but I've only shown the Pocket TV version here.

Tap the file on the main screen to run the clip

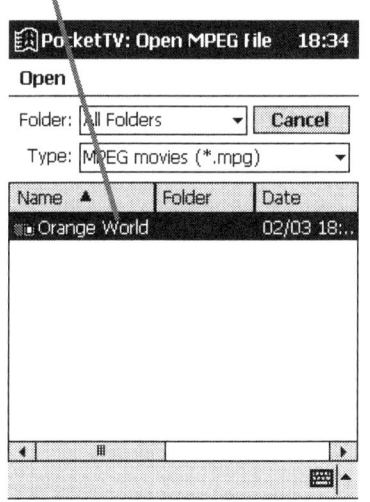

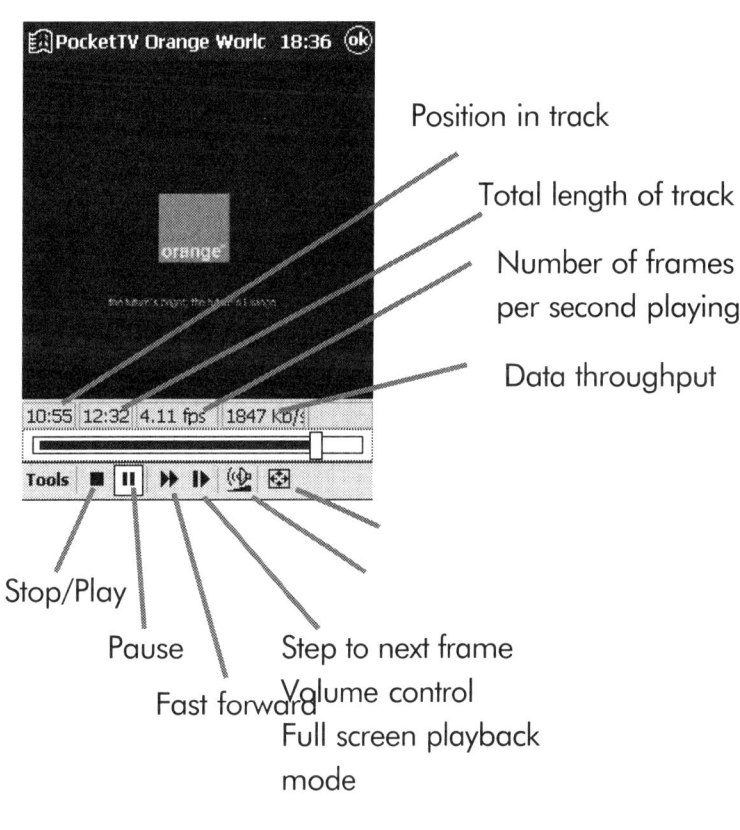

Position in track

Total length of track

Number of frames per second playing

Data throughput

Stop/Play

Pause

Fast forward

Step to next frame

Volume control

Full screen playback mode

Tip

Pocket TV can be downloaded from **www.pockettv.com**.

Summary

❑ Microsoft Reader doesn't just display e-books, it also manages your e-library!

❑ You can navigate around Reader with the hardware buttons or with the page icons.

❑ When reading e-books, you can easily flip back and forwards, or go to specific pages.

❑ Bookmarks, notes, and highlighting can be added to an e-book, although you cannot change its text in Reader.

❑ You can create your own e-books with the Reader add-on for the desktop version of Word.

❑ Media Player can play audio files in the MP3 and WMF formats.

❑ You can set up your own playlists, and add new tracks to them at any time.

❑ If you get the Skin Chooser software, you can give Media Player a new skin.

❑ Video clips can be played with suitable software, such as Pocket TV.

10 Other applications

File Explorer

Using File Explorer you can move files around on your Pocket PC and also create folders to organize your documents and notes more efficiently. It can also be used to move files between the My Documents folder and the \My Documents folder on a storage card, as you can see in this example.

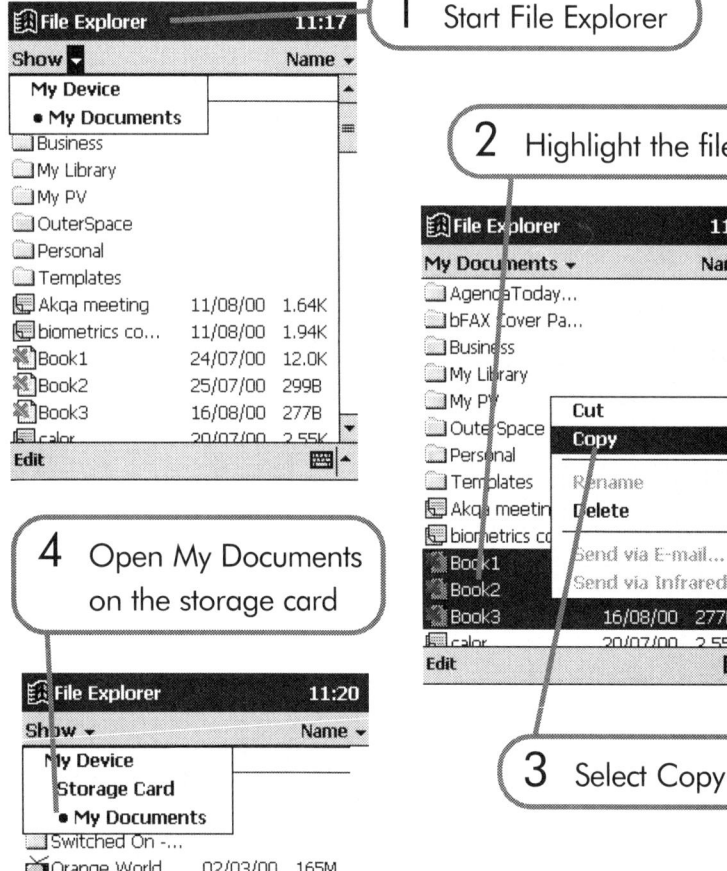

1 Start File Explorer

2 Highlight the files

4 Open My Documents on the storage card

3 Select Copy

5 Tap Edit, Paste

Basic steps

❑ To copy files

1 Tap Start, Programs, File Explorer. It will open in the *\My Documents* Folder.

2 Select the files you want to copy by dragging over their names.

3 Tap and hold on the highlighted file(s) and select Copy from the pop-up menu.

4 Tap the My Documents label, then My Device, Storage Card and My Documents.

5 Tap Edit and select Paste.

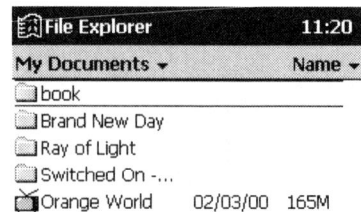

Basic steps

1 If you want to create the folder within another one, navigate to that folder first.

2 Tap Edit.

3 Tap New Folder.

4 Replace '*New Folder*' with a more meaningful name.

Creating a new folder

In the Edit menu in File Explorer is the New Folder option. This lets you create folders on your Pocket PC so that you can have more organized file storage.

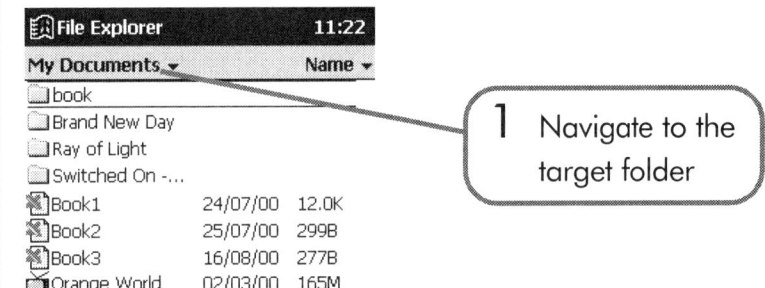

1 Navigate to the target folder

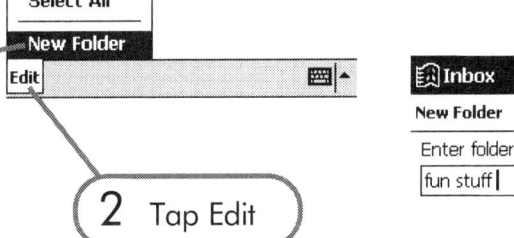

3 Tap New Folder

2 Tap Edit

 Tip

If you want to move files from My Documents to your newly created folder — or between any two folders — follow the steps for copying, but at step 3 select Cut instead of Copy from the pop-up menu.

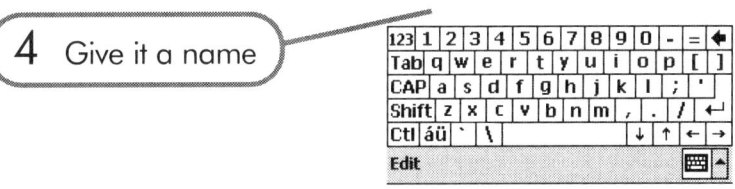

4 Give it a name

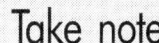

 Take note

Only files and folders in \My Documents or below will show up in the built-in applications like Pocket Word and Excel.

135

Pocket Money

Pocket Money is another one of the applications included on your Pocket PC which really shows it to the full potential when you synchronize it with your desktop version of Money.

Pocket Money is designed to allow you to perform the most common tasks quickly and easily. These include viewing and entering transactions as well as checking account balances. You can also check the value of a stock portfolio by connecting up to MSN MoneyCentral.

Account Manager screen

The Account Manager screen gives an at-a-glance view of all your accounts. A total balance of all the accounts will be shown at the bottom of the screen.

Tip

The type-ahead feature in Pocket Money remembers if you've previously made a transaction and enters the same details again.

Type of account navigator

Various accounts

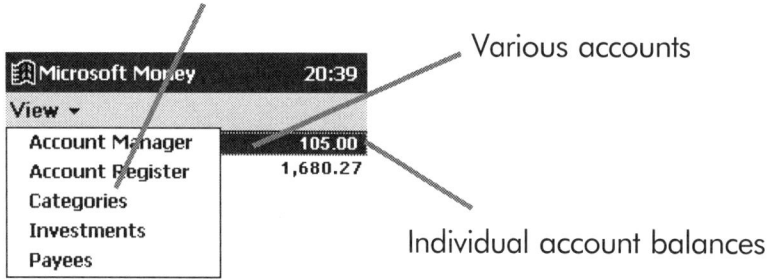

Individual account balances

Total balances

Take note

The version of Money shipped on your Pocket PC is compatible with Microsoft Money 2000, but can only synchronize with USA versions of the desktop software Microsoft Money.

Basic steps

1 Double-tap on the account on the Account Manager screen.

2 Tap New.

3 Set the Type – the default is *Withdrawal*, i.e., a payment.

4 Enter Payee details.

5 Enter the Date – these are in the US format.

6 Enter the Amount.

7 Tap the ok button.

❑ Deleting a transaction

8 Tap and hold on the transaction.

9 Tap the Delete Transaction prompt, then tap Yes to confirm.

Take note

If you delete a Transaction or account there is NO Undo or Undelete function.

Entering and deleting transaction

When entering a transaction, it's easiest to enter the appropriate account first. In this example I've shown a payment from my Business account.

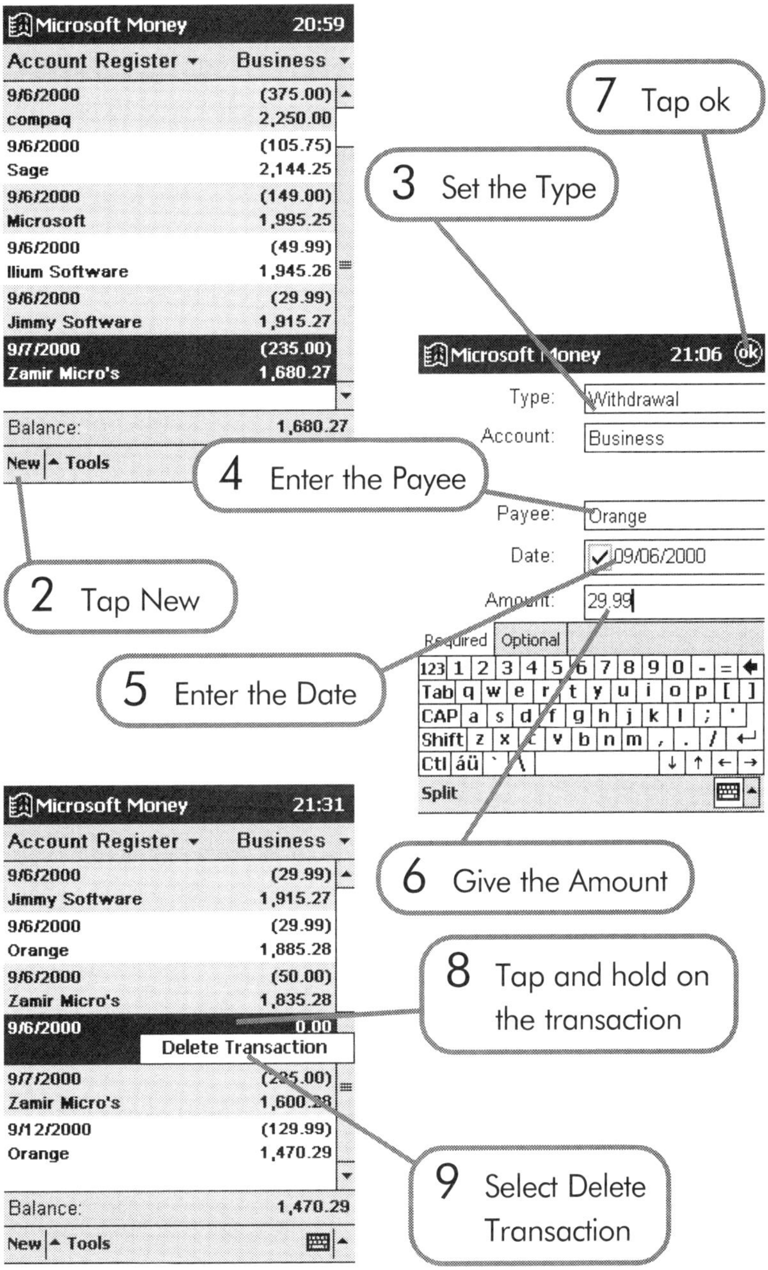

Microsoft Money   20:59

Account Register ▾	Business ▾
9/6/2000	(375.00)
compaq	2,250.00
9/6/2000	(105.75)
Sage	2,144.25
9/6/2000	(149.00)
Microsoft	1,995.25
9/6/2000	(49.99)
Ilium Software	1,945.26
9/6/2000	(29.99)
Jimmy Software	1,915.27
9/7/2000	(235.00)
Zamir Micro's	1,680.27

Balance: 1,680.27

New | ▲ Tools

7 Tap ok

3 Set the Type

Microsoft Money   21:06 ⊛

Type: Withdrawal
Account: Business

4 Enter the Payee

Payee: Orange
Date: ✓ 09/06/2000
Amount: 29.99|

Required | Optional

123	1	2	3	4	5	6	7	8	9	0	-	=	←
Tab	q	w	e	r	t	y	u	i	o	p	[	]
CAP	a	s	d	f	g	h	j	k	l	;	'
Shift	z	x	c	v	b	n	m	,	.	/	↵
Ctl	áü	`	\			↓	↑	←	→

Split

2 Tap New

5 Enter the Date

Microsoft Money   21:31

Account Register ▾	Business ▾
9/6/2000	(29.99)
Jimmy Software	1,915.27
9/6/2000	(29.99)
Orange	1,885.28
9/6/2000	(50.00)
Zamir Micro's	1,835.28
9/6/2000	0.00
	Delete Transaction
9/7/2000	(235.00)
Zamir Micro's	1,600.28
9/12/2000	(129.99)
Orange	1,470.29

Balance: 1,470.29

New | ▲ Tools

6 Give the Amount

8 Tap and hold on the transaction

9 Select Delete Transaction

Find

The Find utility in your Pocket PC is one of its most powerful and useful functions and it's incredibly quick. It's one of those applications that reminds me of a duck gently gliding along the water, but it's actually working really hard.

I rarely have to change the default option of searching All data when using the find application on my Pocket PC. Even with over 1,000 contacts and numerous e-mails, documents, and notes on my Pocket PC it takes less than 2 seconds to search through all this and display the results.

Basic steps

1 Tap Start.

2 Tap Find.

3 Enter one or more key words to identify the information you seek.

4 Tap Go.

5 Tap the result you are looking for.

Narrowing your search

6 Tap the drop-down arrow at the end of the Type area.

7 Select the appropriate criteria from the list.

8 Tap Go.

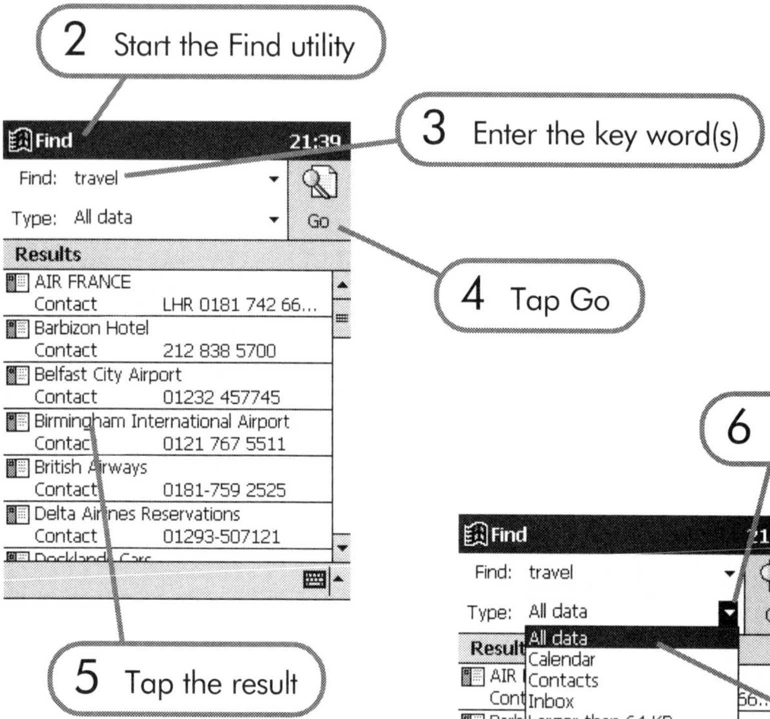

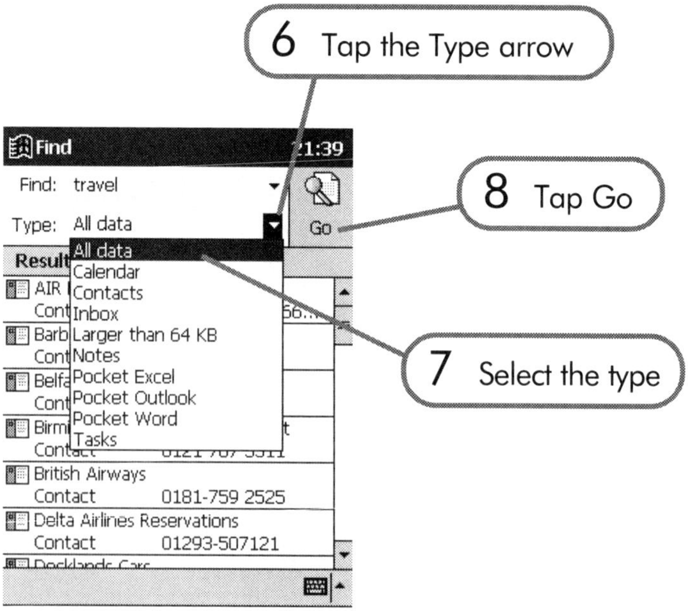

2 Start the Find utility

Find   21:39

Find: travel

Type: All data   Go

Results

AIR FRANCE
Contact   LHR 0181 742 66...

Barbizon Hotel
Contact   212 838 5700

Belfast City Airport
Contact   01232 457745

Birmingham International Airport
Contact   0121 767 5511

British Airways
Contact   0181-759 2525

Delta Airlines Reservations
Contact   01293-507121

Docklands Cars

3 Enter the key word(s)

4 Tap Go

5 Tap the result

6 Tap the Type arrow

Find   21:39

Find: travel

Type: All data   Go

Result

All data
Calendar
Contacts
Inbox
Larger than 64 KB
Notes
Pocket Excel
Pocket Outlook
Pocket Word
Tasks

AIR
Cont

Barb
Cont

Belfa
Cont

Birmi
Contact

British Airways
Contact   0181-759 2525

Delta Airlines Reservations
Contact   01293-507121

Docklands Cars

8 Tap Go

7 Select the type

Basic steps

1 Tap Start.

2 Tap Help.

3 Tap on an underlined link to go to its Help page – pages will carry links to others.

Start Help from within the Today screen to get Help on all your applications

Help

The built-in help provided on the Pocket PC is both comprehensive and easy to use.

The Help system on the Pocket PC is context sensitive. Regardless of which application or function you are in the Help system is accessed the same way. Here I've shown accessing Help from the Media Player application.

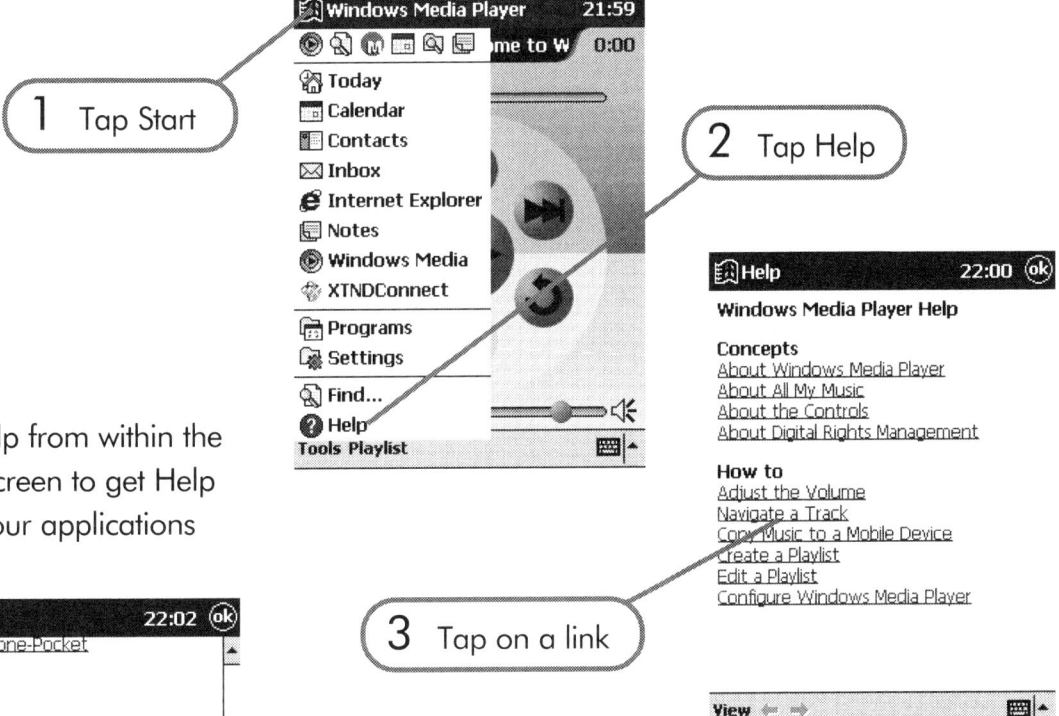

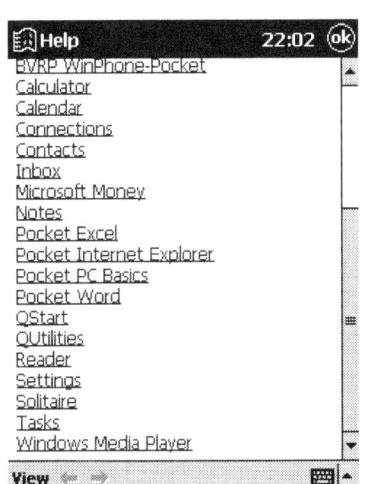

Accessing Help for all applications

You can access the Help files for all the applications on your Pocket PC through the Today screen. Just tap Start, Help there, and select the application from the list.

Games

Solitaire

The old favourite solitaire has been shipping with versions of Windows since as long as I can remember, but with the version on your Pocket PC it's possible to cheat!

Follow the steps and you'll have a perfect hand of solitaire every time – the cards will all be in sequence so tap the deck until the aces show up. When you've unloaded all the cards in the deck proceed with the ones on the main part of the screen.

Other games

At the time of writing there almost 100 games available for the Pocket PC, from companies like **www.jimmysoftware.com**. Their games include some which have really high level of graphic details.

TankZone 2000

Stellarmetrics' TankZone 2000 is 'charityware.' If you download it and enjoy playing it, the authors ask that you make a donation to the charity of your choice. The object of the game is to survive the relentless barrage of attack.

Get your copy from:

http://www.stellarmetrics.com/

Basic steps

1 Start Solitaire.

2 Bring up the software keyboard.

3 Tap Ctrl.

4 Tap Shift.

5 Tap New.

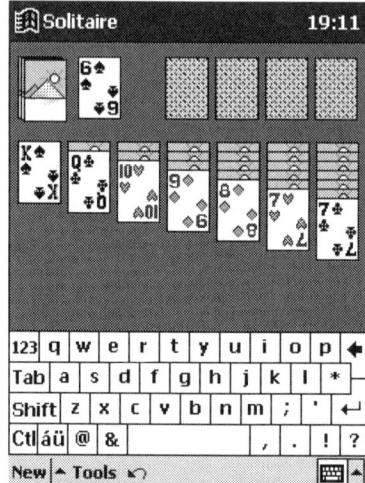

You can cheat at solitaire on the Pocket PC

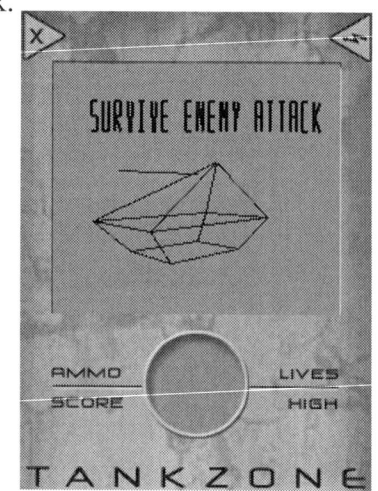

Tankzone is an exciting game of survival

Pocket PC newsgroups

<h1 style="text-align:right">Web sites</h1>

If you have a newsreader application such as Outlook Express on your PC, then the Pocket PC newsgroups are the best place to ask for help – you'll find me hanging out there quite a lot, so ask away if you have any questions.

microsoft.public.pocketpc – questions and answers on Pocket PCs

microsoft.public.pocketpc. developer – where the Pocket PC programmers hang out

My Pocket PC Web sites – www.craigtech.co.uk, www.pocketpchelp.com
Microsoft Pocket Pc – www.pocketpc.com
Anyware Consulting – hometown.aol.com/anyware
Audible – www.audible.com
AvantGo – www.avantgo.com
Barnes and Noble – www.bn.com/ebooks
Bsquare – www.bsquare.com
Conduits Technologies Inc. – www.conduits.com
DeveloperOne – www.developerone.com
GrundleSoftware – www.grundlesoft.com
Hotmail – www.hotmail.com
Ilium Software – www.iliumsoft.com
Jimmy Software – www.jimmysoftware.com
Microsoft e-books – www.microsoft.com/reader
Pocket TV – www.pockettv.com
Pocket Video – www.pv.com
Readerworks software – www.overdrive.com/readerworks/
Syware – www.syware.com
Stellarmetrics – www.stellarmetrics.com

The hardware vendors
Compaq – www.compaq.com/products/handhelds
HP – www.hp.com/jornada
Casio – www.casio.com/personalpcs
Symbol – www.symbol.com
Orange – www.orange.co.uk

Summary

❑ Use File Explorer to organize your files – you will probably need to start by creating some new folders.

❑ Pocket Money can help you to manage your money. It can be synchronized with the (US-only) desktop versions of Money.

❑ If you can't remember where you stored something, the Find utility will help you to track it down.

❑ There is plenty of Help available in all applications.

❑ There are currently over 100 games available for the Pocket PC.

Index

W

X

Y